Robert G. Lee's

SOURCEBOOK OF 500 ILLUSTRATIONS

Robert G. Lee's

SOURCEBOOK OF 500 ILLUSTRATIONS

FOR: PUBLIC SPEAKERS
MINISTERS
SUNDAY SCHOOL TEACHERS

ZONDERVAN PUBLISHING HOUSE
OF THE ZONDERVAN CORPORATION | GRAND RAPIDS, MICHIGAN 49506

ROBERT G. LEE'S SOURCEBOOK OF 500 ILLUSTRATIONS

Seventeenth printing 1981

Library of Congress Catalog Card No. 63-1904
ISBN 0-310-27471-0

Printed in the United States of America

CONTENTS

ADVICE

Ten Ways for a Long Life

1. Eat a good diet, low in calories, but generous in proteins, vitamins, minerals and liquids.
2. Keep the body and mind free of waste.
3. Get adequate rest.
4. Have daily periods of freedom from regular routine and avoid accumulated fatigue.
5. Avoid the consuming fires of anger, jealousy, hatred and fear. They raise the blood pressure, strain the heart and impair the mind.
6. Preserve a sense of pride in your job and remember that it is a privilege to work. Maintain physical fitness.
7. Cultivate a sense of humor. It relaxes tension, diminishes anxiety, promotes friendship and imparts joy to lessen the load of the day.
8. Maintain companionship with your friends and community. Isolation is one of the great curses of old age leading to depression.
9. Increase your participation in community affairs.
10. Keep growing mentally with added years. Keep the proper incentive: The will to live.

Roasted Chickens

RECENTLY in Montgomery, Alabama, about sixteen thousand, five hundred chickens were roasted when flames engulfed a barn. Firemen said the building and the chickens were a "complete loss." The blaze occurred about 4 A.M. and was caused by wiring in the wooden chicken barn.

Thus we see that fire which is a good servant when it cooks chicken for human consumption can be a cruel and bad master when it is uncontrolled.

Many Matches

IF all the matches produced in France last year were laid end to end they would stretch eight times the distance between the earth and the moon. This is the report of the state-controlled match industry. During 1963 seventy million matches were manufactured, bringing in 132 million francs (about $26 million).

What power for illumination to dispense with darkness is one little match – when properly used. And what power for destruction when carelessly used is one little match – as witness conflagrations that have destroyed whole forests and cities.

A Recipe for Arrested Growth

A SOUTHERN BAPTIST editor wrote: "Sometimes it is profitable to analyze a question negatively as well as positively. The positive may be the better, but the contrast with the negative is frequently helpful. Consider the matter of the growth of Southern Baptists. Usually the subject is approached from the positive point of view. 'How shall we grow?'

"View the subject from the other direction – 'How shall Southern Baptists not grow?' What are some of the courses which may lead to mediocrity if not to oblivion? Several suggestions may be listed.

1. Practice open church membership — this will devaluate our Baptist position.

2. Disregard the Scriptural meaning of, and invitation to, the Lord's Supper — this will cheapen baptism.

3. Play down the importance of baptism — this will stifle our testimony.

4. Emphasize ecumenicity — this will erase our distinctives.

5. Be apologetic regarding the use of the name 'Baptist'—this will weaken our prestige.

6. Deny direct kinship with the New Testament Christians — this will tap the root of Biblical and doctrinal strength.

7. Minimize the importance of training — this will close the churches on Sunday evenings.

8. Take the side track of fanatical conservatism or radical liberalism — this will produce a series of splinter groups.

9. Solicit financial support from non-Baptists — this will make beggars of the churches.

"There are other roads which might open the way to denominational nothingness,' but this combination would probably make others unnecessary.

Remarkable Remarks

ADMIRAL George W. Anderson, chief of naval operations, in accepting the University of Notre Dame's Laetare Medal at South Bend, Indiana, said: "Today, with planes streaking across the sky with twice the speed of sound, with missiles constantly set to hurtle thousands of miles a few seconds after an order is given, time for reflection, for cautious deliberation may be denied us. Now, as never before, we need to hear God's voice."

Opening an eight-day crusade in Paris, Evangelist Billy Graham told an audience of six thousand that people the world over are shouting for freedom. He added: "In Birmingham, Ala.—in my own country—people are shouting for freedom. In the United States there is social revolution going on. There are people who want to be free."

Representative Emanuel Celler (Dem., N.Y.) chairman of the House Judiciary Committee, demanded on a television program that federal antilottery laws be enforced against the New Hampshire state lottery. He asserted: "It will take a miracle to have any kind of honest administration of a lottery because the opportunities for crookedness are so pervasive."

Dr. Harry Ransom, chancellor of the University of Texas, told the spring meeting in Dallas of the Association of Governing Boards of State Universities and Allied Institutions that a college or university is confronted by this fact: Its resources are limited, no matter what its resources are. Said he: "It cannot do everything. Being all things to all men means only one thing for an educational institution: Being a failure."

Astronaut Gordon Cooper, who was scheduled to make a 22-orbit space flight is not a regular churchgoer. But he regards religion as important. He said at Cape Canaveral: "Religion is important in all the things we do, but I don't think a man needs to fall back on his faith any more or less in this space project than in any other undertaking."

"The size of a dog in a fight is not as significant as the size of the fight in the dog" (Rains County Leader).

"L. D. Archibald of Fallon community, who has only one arm, has won forty-four trophies in drag racing, his favorite sport. His wife, the former Nell Williams, has also won two trophies" (Mexia Daily News).

"The twister that hit Cannon dumped three and a half inches of rain in the gauge of Perry Hunter within twenty minutes and uprooted pecan trees that were a hundred years old" (Van Alstyne Leader).

"A large crowd helped W. O. Ketner celebrate his 89th birthday in Quinan" (Tawakoni News).

"Dr. John Turner said Wednesday that Everett Higginbotham was scheduled for surgery in Tyler, but no certain date was set because he 'didn't know when he could get Higginbotham down there'" (Canton Herald).

"Chaplain James Baker, before removal of a growth on his tongue, had to wash the area ten minutes. His first assignment after the operation was to address the troops on 'Clean Speech'" (Farmersville Times).

"We need not wait until the day of judgment to behold the fulfillment of the law of sowing and reaping. Look at our own country. Today, America is sowing the flesh as she has never sown before" (Leonard Graphic).

"An elderly woman walked in and said, 'Doctor, you probably don't remember me. But ten years ago you told me to go home, go to bed and stay there till you called back. But you never called.' And the doctor replied, 'Didn't I? Well, what're you doing out of bed?'" (Celina Record).

Currency in Cans

R. S. Altman, of Troy, Ohio, died at seventy-six years of age, July 28th, 1963, at Mayo Clinic, Rochester, Minnesota.

A few hours before he died he told his son, George I. Altman of Erwin, Penn. and his daughter, Mrs. Mary Jane Ward of Troy, he had buried all his money under the mill.

"We knew it was quite possible that old Mr. Altman was delirious and there was no real expectation of finding anything buried there, money or otherwise," said William Sutton, who represents the family. "We decided to dig anyway. We couldn't lose anything."

So, an estimated $350,000 in currency, buried by this elderly mill owner who often told relatives he didn't trust banks, has been recovered.

Attorney Sutton of Pittsburgh, who announced the find, said the recovery of the money "was a tremendous surprise to everyone." The money, undamaged, although in two unsealed ten-gallon milk cans, was buried under the Altman Mills feed plant on Ohio 25A four miles north of Troy.

Currency hoarded in cans is as useless as grains of wheat in a mummy's hand.

Bones Brought Back

I am sure that the great editor of *The Watchman-Examiner* will not object to the author of this volume using what he wrote about the bones of an emperor:

"The golden, jeweled coffin containing the bones of Charlemagne was returned to Aachen in a United States Army truck after having been removed from the Aachen Cathedral in 1939 for safekeeping. It was almost nightfall when the telephone rang in the office of the Aachen military government. Major Jack Bradford of Minneapolis, Minnesota, said to be governor of Aachen, heard the voice at the other end say: 'I've got the bones with me. Where will I put them?' That is how the remains of Europe's most famous 'displaced person' arrived back home. The casket had been moved to almost a score of places during the war as the Allied bombings reached deeper into Germany. Its last resting place was in Siegen, east of Cologne. Charlemagne (Charles the Great) lived A.D. 742-814. He was Roman emperor and king of the Franks. By virtue of military prowess and diplomatic manipulations, he came to be the head of the Holy Roman Empire. Innumerable legends have gathered round the memory of the great emperor. He rode from battlefield victories to a wide dominion over many peoples. He won the favor of Pope Adrian and Pope Leo III, who crowned him emperor and Augustus amid the acclamations of the crowd in St. Peter's, Rome. He died in 814 on January 28th, and on the same day his body was buried in the Church of St. Mary at Aix (Aachen). The story that in the year one thousand Emperor Otto III found the body sitting upright upon a throne with a golden crown on the head and holding a golden scepter in the hand is generally regarded as legendary. The tomb was again opened by Emperor Frederick I in 1165, when the remains were removed from a marble sarcophagus and placed in a wooden coffin. Fifty years later, they were transferred by order of the Emperor Frederick II to a splendid shrine. It was from this shrine that the relics were taken by the Nazis. They came back home, bouncing on the floor of a U. S. Army truck, a solemn warning to the earthly great

The boast of heraldry, the pomp of pow'r,
And all that beauty, all that wealth e'er gave,
Await alike the inevitable hour;
The paths of glory lead but to the grave.

Instant Photos

SOME time ago, the Army announced the development of a "rapid" new camera shutter that takes photographs in one five billionth of a second. The shutter was designed for scientific research studies of high-speed shock waves, explosions and certain types of nuclear reactions. The secret of this camera's quick work is a hermetically-sealed chemical-type shutter triggered electronically.

Just recently a photographic invention now gives instant pictures through a little electricity and heat. A film carrying electrostatic charges takes the picture. Just a little heat develops it in one-tenth to one-hundredth of a second.

But one thousand times more interesting and of more value are the truths set forth in these words:

"Separate yourselves from among this congregation, that I may consume them in a moment. And they fell upon their faces, and said, O God, the God of the spirits of all flesh, shall one man sin, and wilt thou be wroth with all the congregation?" (Numbers 16:21, 22).

"What is man, that thou shouldest magnify him? and that thou shouldest set thine heart upon him? And that thou shouldest visit him every morning, and try him every moment?" (Job 7:17, 18).

"They spend their days in wealth, and in a moment go down to the grave" (Job 21:13).

"For his anger endureth but a moment; in his favour is life: weeping may endure for a night, but joy cometh in the morning" (Psalm 30:5).

"I the Lord do keep it; I will water it every moment: lest any hurt it, I will keep it night and day" (Isaiah 27:3).

"Behold, I shew you a mystery; We shall not all sleep, but we shall all be changed, in a moment, in the twinkling of an eye, at the last trump: for the trumpet shall sound, and the dead shall be raised incorruptible, and we shall be changed" (I Corinthians 15:51, 52).

"For our light affliction, which is but for a moment, worketh for us a far more exceeding and eternal weight of glory" (II Corinthians 4:17).

Wedding on Wavy Hair

COLUMNIST Ann Landers gives us this:

"Dear Ann: I'm twenty-two years old and have never been so head-over-heels in love in my life. I'm walking on air. The man is thirty, has beautiful wavy hair and a perfect build. I want to marry him and he is begging me to say yes, but I am not quite ready to make the leap because of three things. (1) He drinks a little too much and sometimes forgets where I live, where he parked the car, where he put his wallet, etc. (2) He likes to job-hop. He has no trouble getting a job, but after a few months he becomes bored and quits. (3) He teases me a lot which is very cute — says things that aren't true just to get my reaction. Later, he tells me he was only fooling. I am willing to overlook his faults because I know nobody is perfect. He is the most exciting man who ever lived. He says marriage will change him. Will it? IVORY.

Dear Ivory: Congratulations — an offer of marriage from a job-hopping lush with a faulty memory. Marriage won't change *him,* but it will *you.* You won't find him so thrilling when he forgets to bring home the pay check. The teasing and spells of unemployment won't be so cute when you have children to feed and doctor bills to pay. If you want a thoroughly messed up life, go ahead and marry a guy because his hair is wavy."

Honey Crop High

"IF you have an empty purse, keep honey in your mouth." That's what shrewd Spaniards used to tell their captured victims to keep them in line.

Honey has played an important role as a friend maker for a long time. Conquered peoples used to pay tribute in honey to Egyptians. The Egyptians, in turn, paid their taxes with honey and even fed it to "sacred" animals to appease their gods. Highly valued honey also served widely as a cure for body ailments.

"Honeyed" talk is still an accepted human relations tool, whether your purse is full or empty. It's still being used to win and keep friends by salving their taste buds with distinctive honey-flavored foods from the family kitchen. It works every time.

There'll be plenty of honey again this year, for any use we want to put it. The United States Department of Agriculture estimated the 1963 crop at almost two hundred and seventy-five million pounds — slightly more than the previous record and twelve per cent above average.

Most of this honey will be used in the home. Its flavor will enhance sauces, sandwiches, salad dressings, hot breads and baked goods of all kinds, meat and vegetable dishes and numerous desserts. Commercial bakeries also use a lot of honey, since cakes and cookies stay moist longer when made with honey. An increasing amount is being used in honey-coated cereals. Smaller quantities are used in making confections, ice creams, jams, jellies and in canning some hams. Some honey also is used in honey facials and in medicines like cough syrup.

The Bible speaks of honey in these words: "carry . . . the man a little bit of honey" (Genesis 43:11). "And all they of the land came to a wood; and there was honey upon the ground" (I Samuel 14:25). "The judgments of the Lord . . . are sweeter than honey" (Psalm 19:10).

"My son, eat thou honey, because it is good; and the honeycomb which is sweet to thy taste" (Proverbs 24: 13).

"Hast thou found honey? eat so much as is sufficient for thee, lest thou be filled therewith, and vomit it" (Proverbs 25:16).

"The full soul loatheth an honeycomb; but to the hungry soul every bitter thing is sweet" (Proverbs 27:7).

"Butter and honey shall he eat, that he may know to refuse the evil, and choose the good" (Isaiah 7:15).

"Thy lips, O my spouse, drop as the honeycomb: honey and milk are under thy tongue; and the smell of thy garments is like the smell of Lebanon" (Song of Solomon 4:11).

". . . for ye shall burn no leaven, nor any honey, in any offering of the Lord made by fire" (Leviticus 2:11).

Problems and Prevailing Pessimism

WHAT problems? The problems of old age.

What pessimism? The pessimism of old age – so prevalent.

The greatest foe of old age is pessimism, a University of Louisville psychiatrist told Duke University's 16th annual medical symposium.

"Too often the aged accept their aches and pains as normal for that age. They are not normal. They are pathological, and being pathological, we can do something about it.

"So, let the old people complain, let them gripe on all the problems that affect them. That is the only way we are going to make progress in the treatment and prevention of these problems."

This was the message of Dr. Spafford Ackerly, chairman of the Psychiatry Department at the University of Louisville.

But David gave better advice by praying:

"Cast me not off in the time of old age; forsake me not when my strength faileth" (Psalm 71:9).

But David gave better counsel when he made this declaration:

"Those that he planted in the house of the Lord shall flourish in the courts of our God. They shall still bring forth fruit in old age; they shall be fat and flourishing; to shew that the Lord is upright" (Psalm 92:13, 14).

And Israel was strengthened by God's comforting words through the prophet Isaiah:

"Even to your old age I am he; and even to hoar hairs will I carry you; I have made, and I will bear; even I will carry, and will deliver you" (Isaiah 46:4).

Surely, too, Paul gave the aged better counsel when he urged the aged men "to be sober, grave, temperate, sound in faith, in charity, in patience" and when he urged the aged women "that they be in behaviour as becometh holiness – not false accusers, not given to much wine, teachers of good things" (Titus 2).

Nothing

MAYBE some of my readers are ready to label what I am writing "Nothing." But here is something about "nothing" – unless you call the something of others nothing.

"Nothing comes amiss to a hungry man."

"Nothing comes fairer to light than what has been long hidden."

"Nothing costs so much as what is given us."

"Nothing down, nothing up."

"Nothing for nothing – and very little for a half-penny."

"Nothing in haste but catching flies."

"Nothing is certain but uncertainty."

"Nothing is easy to the negligent."

"Nothing is fine but what is fit."

"Nothing is new."

"Nothing is ours but time."

"Nothing is safe from fault finders."

"Nothing sharpens sight like envy."

"Nothing stands in need of lying but a lie."

"Nothing that is violent is permanent."

"Nothing ventured, nothing have."

Walking as God Wants

MAZZINI says: "The times that have ceased to believe in God may continue illogically to speak of progress and duty, but they have denied the first of its basis and robbed the second of its sanction."

And somebody, making comment on these words, taught us that when we become materialistic and "bow down to a mud god" and live by the ethics of pleasure, not duty, then justice will forsake the laws our fathers left us, and liberty will fade from our institutions, glory depart from library and chapel, and peace pass from the American home.

Time—Bank of Life

IF you had a bank that credited your account each morning with $86,400, that carried no balance from day to day, allowed you to keep no cash in your account, and finally every evening cancelled whatever part of the amount you had failed to use during the day, what would you do? Draw out every cent – of course!

Well, you have such a bank and its name is "Time." Every morning it credits you with 86,400 seconds. Every night it rules off – as lost – whatever of this you have failed to invest to good purpose. It carries no balances. It allows no balances. It allows no overdrafts. Each day the bank named "Time" opens a new account with *you*. Each night it burns the records of the day. If you fail to use the day's deposits the loss is yours. There is no going back. There is no drawing against tomorrow. You must live in the present – on today's deposits. Invest it so as to get from it the utmost in health, happiness and success!

Keeping Christmas

DR. HENRY VAN DYKE speaks:

"There is a better thing than the observance of Christmas Day, and that is keeping Christmas. Are you willing to forget what you have done for other people and to remember what other people have done for you? To ignore what the world owes you, and to think what you owe the world? To own that the only good reason for your existence is not what you are going to get out of life, but what you are going to give it? Are you willing to stoop down and consider the needs and the desires of little children? To remember the weakness and loneliness of people who are growing old? To stop asking how much your friends like you, and ask yourself whether you love them enough? To try to understand what those who live in the same house with you really want, without waiting for them to tell you? To trim your lamp so it will give more light and less smoke, and to carry it in front so that your shadow will fall behind you? To make a grave for your ugly thoughts and a garden for your kindly feelings, with the gate open? Are you willing to believe that love is the strongest thing in the world –

stronger than hate, stronger than evil, stronger than death – and that the blessed Life which began in Bethlehem nineteen hundred years ago is the image and brightness of Eternal Love? Then you can keep Christmas. And if you keep it for a day, why not always? But you can never keep it alone."

How tragic is the ruling out of religious Christmas carolling in eight of the schools in a California school district! I think that is defying the Constitution. It is stated in the Constitution that we have freedom of speech and freedom of religion. Not being able to sing religious Christmas songs is going against the Constitution. Also it is taking away the freedoms our forefathers fought to gain for us. If we don't stop this before it gets a good start in America, we will be a Communist nation as Russia is.

Taking the Long Look

I WAS reading Spurgeon's autobiography today and ran across this little story that aptly illustrates the importance of taking the long look.

"During one of my many holidays at Stambourne, I had a varied experience which I am not likely to forget. My dear grandfather was very fond of Dr. Watts' hymns, and my grandmother, wishing to get me to learn them, promised me a penny for each one that I should say to her perfectly. I found it an easy and pleasant method of earning money, and learned them so fast that grandmother said she must reduce the price to a halfpenny each, and afterwards to a farthing, if she did not mean to be quite ruined by her extravagance. There is no telling how low the amount per hymn might have sunk, but grandfather said that he was getting overrun with rats, and offered me a shilling a dozen for all I could kill. I found, at the time, that the occupation of rat-catching paid me better than learning hymns, but I know which employment has been more permanently profitable to me. No matter on what topic I am preaching, I can, even now, in the middle of my sermon, quote some verse of a hymn in harmony with the subject; the hymns have remained with me, while those old rats for years have passed away, and the shillings I earned by killing them have been spent long ago.

Sermon Hearers

DR. LOFTON HUDSON suggests some types of hearers which most preachers face every Sunday:

1. Umbrella Hearers. They put up their umbrellas when he is preaching and let the rain drop on their neighbors.
2. Prize-Fight Hearers. They are never satisfied unless the pastor is fighting something and hands a boisterous knockout.
3. Spy Hearers. This hostile group sit with poker faces watching for some evidence which may be led to condemnation.
4. Grasshopper Hearers. These hear a little here and a little there with a long hop in between.
5. Cattle Show Hearers. These can tell you the exact dimensions of a good sermon. Like some cattle judges, they forget the steaks and roasts.
6. Flat Tire Hearers. The progress of their spiritual journey is completely arrested because of some distracting trouble.
7. Well Bucket Hearers. This kind go right down into the water of life and sink until they are filled. Bless their hearts! They are worth hundreds of "gospel hardened sinners"

and "truth hardened saints."

We need to be *doers,* not just hearers of the Word.

Strange Names

WHAT'S the Name? George Pappavlahodimtrakopoulous retained the distinction of having the longest name in the Lansing, Michigan, telephone directory. Pappavlahodimtrakopoulous, a restaurant owner, has a standing offer of a free meal for anyone who can pronounce his name correctly the first time. Few win!

The Sports page had this announcement: "Righthander Arnold Portocarrero was placed on the disabled list by Manager Lou Boudreau after a medical examination showed the Kansas City Athletics pitcher has a sore and inflamed tendon in his shoulder."

Not to be silly, we would read this in the *Missouri Ruralist:* A DeKalb county (Missouri) man says that he was traveling in Arkansas and stopped over night at a cabin. The family consisted of a man and his wife and six children, three girls and three boys. The old wife smoked a cob pipe but told the DeKalb county man that she had made up her mind right from the start that she was a goin' to do the best she could for the children and give them the best names she could find so that when they went away from home, if they ever did, they wouldn't be ashamed to compare names with anybody. Whenever she heard a big word she recollected it and gave it to one of the children. She said she didn't pretend to know just what the names meant, but she knowed that they sounded almighty high-toned and that the children need never to be a mite ashamed of them.

The DeKalb man asked what the names of the children were and the mother proudly said that the name of the oldest girl was Telepathy, the second was named Phrenology, and the third Tuberculosis. The three boys were Theodolite, Doxology and Epluribusunum. She said that she didn't want to brag none, but she had always thought Epluribusunum was the most high-sounding name for a boy that she had ever heard. The man told her that he fully agreed with her.

But there are some unusual names in the Bible, namely: Buz—meaning "contempt," Huz (Genesis 22:21). Bur-lahai-roi, Bethdiblathaim, Bethlehemephratah, Chepharhaamonai, Elonbethhanon, Habazamiah, Hazzenontamar, Jashubilehem, Jegarshadadutha, Maherohalalhashbaz.

Anyway, no matter whether one's name be long or short, spellable or unspellable, 'tis forever true: "A good name is rather to be chosen than great riches, and loving favour rather than silver and gold" (Proverbs 22:1). "A good name is better than precious ointment . . ." (Ecclesiastes 7:1).

A Failure Out of Life

DR. PERRY F. WEBB, former pastor of the First Baptist Church, San Antonio, Texas, tells how to make a failure out of life:

Follow the line of least resistance. Be neutral on moral, spiritual and righteous issues. Straddle the fence.

Alienate yourself from the church membership. Go to church when you "feel" like it and when it is most convenient. Disregard the mid-week prayer meeting.

Indulge your carnal appetites. Take it easy on Sunday; it is a rest day. Be lazy, be selfish. Accept the pleasures offered by the world.

Look at the inconsistencies and sins of others. Pick flaws, find fault and criticize. Ignore your own faults.

Unite with worldly organizations. Join some good lodge; be a member of some club or fraternity. They do lots of good and you don't have to be narrow either.

Run around with carnal believers and worldlings. Don't bring religion into your social life.

Make intimate friendship with people of character, regardless of their attitude toward the Christ.

Eclipse your salvation with business interests. You have a living to make and a home to keep. Work overtime and Sundays because it will make you more money. Get dollars. Business first.

Along with these wise words, we read that God tells how to be a success:

"This book of the law shall not depart out of thy mouth; but thou shalt meditate therein day and night, that thou mayest observe to do according to all that is written therein: for then thou shalt make thy way prosperous, and then thou shalt have good success" (Joshua 1:8).

"For the Lord God is a sun and shield: the Lord will give grace and glory: no good thing will he withhold from them that walk uprightly" (Psalm 84:11).

"If any man serve me, let him follow me; and where I am, there shall also my servant be: if any man serve me, him will my Father honor" (John 12:26).

These Things I Know

B. C. FORBES writes these words under the above title:

"We may have less to live *on*, but we have just as much as ever to live *for*. We may own less – but no man is rich because he owns something. Only those men are truly rich who have become something!

"Our cash income may be less – but the happiness that comes from sharing and serving is just as deeply satisfying as it ever was!

"We may have more pressing business problems to solve than at other times – but business is the process of learning to live usefully and triumphantly – that it is not a mere dollar chase!

"We may find it necessary to change habits and methods – but we are glad that character is still more important than possessions and right motives still have more effect on our progress than selfish desires!

"We may have need for more courage and more faith – but the loyalty of our associates and kindliness of our friends warms the heart more than it ever did!

"We may be tempted to be discouraged or tired – but little by little we are learning that a sportsman finds fun in the playing of the game – not merely in the winning!

"We may be disappointed at times by the results which we accomplish – but we are encouraged by the certainty that now and always good workmanship brings better results than poor workmanship.

"We may become impatient for financial rewards – but we have only to turn our thoughts away from our seeming needs to see the bounteous blessings which fill our lives!

"We may even admit thoughts of fear and worry – but these flee from us when we remember that the real values of life are unshaken!

"It may seem that for us victory is long delayed – but intelligence reminds us that victory does not merely happen – it is made up of many little victories – and each time we win a victory over laziness, selfishness, fear or discouragement we are adding to the score that will show in the final tally!"

More wonderful and helpful are the "know" assertions in the Bible:

"Ye *know* that your labour is not in vain in the Lord" (I Corinthians 15:58).

"For we *know* that if our earthly house of this tabernacle were dissolved, we have a building of God, an house not made with hands, eternal in the heavens" (II Corinthians 5:1).

"For ye *know* the grace of our Lord Jesus Christ, that, though he was rich, yet for your sakes he became poor, that ye through his poverty might be rich" (II Corinthians 8:9).

"For yourselves *know* perfectly that the day of the Lord so cometh as a thief in the night" (I Thessalonians 5:2).

". . . nevertheless I am not ashamed: for I *know* whom I have believed, and am persuaded that he is able to keep that which I have committed unto him against that day" (II Timothy 1:12).

"Forasmuch as ye *know* that ye were not redeemed with corruptible things, as silver and gold, from your vain conversation received by tradition from your fathers; but with the precious blood of Christ, as of a lamb without blemish and without spot" (I Peter 1:18, 19).

Waiting Minutes Utilized

Ruth Millett gives good counsel about what to do while we have to wait. In this age of hurry, hurry, hurry, most people have odd minutes – twenty here, thirty there – that add up to hours each week.

"Waiting in the dentist's outer office, waiting at home for a friend to pay a promised call, waiting for a husband to get home for dinner, for a service man to come to look at the washing machine. We hurry, hurry, hurry – and then we wait and wait and wait.

"Do you simply pace the floor or sit and tap your foot nervously or watch a clock while all those waiting minutes tick by? Or have you learned the productive art of making use of waiting minutes? What can you do with an unexpected ten or fifteen minutes – besides pace the floor and fume because so-and-so is late, as usual? People who get a lot done and who stay calm through periods of waiting put those stray minutes to use.

" 'I'm writing this letter under the hair drier,' or 'on the bus' or 'in the doctor's waiting room.' Obviously she keeps pen and writing paper in her purse to make use of such brief periods of time.

"Still others use such extra minutes for really noticing the world about them, watching storm clouds gather in the sky, listening to a bird's song, watching children play – or studying the people who pass by.

"People who say they love a railroad station because it is so interesting to watch people know how to use their waiting moments. They are always full of stories about the amusing and curious and touching things they see while they happened to be waiting for a train or standing in line at a ticket window.

"So don't be a clock watcher, a pacer, or a foot tapper next time you have to wait. Instead, put your wait ing minutes to work for you. You'll be surprised at how interesting, entertaining and productive those waiting minutes can become."

I have put Ruth Millett's words into practice – having written several sermons and articles while waiting for planes, for trains and for people exasperatingly late for appointments.

Achievements in the Cattle World

I HAVE a friend in Senatobia, Mississippi, – Mr. M. C. "Hot" Moore. He is the owner of the Circle M Ranch at Senatobia. He sold fifty four head of Polled Hereford cattle for $400,225 and set a new all time world's record sale average of $7,965.

The former world's record sale average of $7,230 was also established by CMR in 1953. Moore sold a one-fourth interest in the top herd bull for $50,000 to top the fifty four head sale. Sales were made to thirty-seven buyers in fifteen states. Two of the top bulls and one of the top cows went to other Mississippi herds.

Mr. Moore has earned the enviable reputation of being the nation's most successful breeder of Polled Hereford cattle. In addition to his big lead in cattle sales, his entries have won more blue ribbons and cash prizes in the nation's show rings than any other herd in the USA.

Mr. Moore deserves the commendation of all Mississippians for his achievements in the cattle world. He has demonstrated the possibilities in Mississippi in cattle production when science is combined with production skill, good management and marketing ability. Our cattlemen should know that superior type, quality and finish, are the hallmarks of CMR cattle. Most of our cattlemen need to improve the breeding of their animals and do a better job of growing feed and providing pasturage. There is no substitute for proper feeding.

From Newark, New Jersey, comes this news: A one-ton black Angus bull reportedly worth more than $100,000 was unloaded as his new owners looked on. The bull was shipped from New Zealand to the United States after being purchased by Edward Marcus of Lewisville, Texas, and Robert Goodyear of Aiken, S. C. Marcus said he hoped to use the bull for breeding purposes for about eight years. "Elegance" has been siring prize-winning calves in Scotland and New Zealand. His new owners are billing him as the "first round the world bull."

Thinking of our children, we can say that just as cattle men need to improve the breeding of their animals so we as parents and preachers and teachers should do a better job of training our young people and providing them better examples in Christian living.

The Deciding Vote

A REVERED old Negro preacher once told his congregation: "Folks, when something hard to handle hits you, the Lord votes for you, the devil votes against you and you cast the deciding vote."

That deciding vote often determines the well-being not only of an individual but often of an entire community. It is eloquently expressive of the man or woman who feels his or her direct responsibility for the good of others. We elect our city officials and give them the authority to administer our civic affairs. But we can not delegate to them our responsibility as citizens. Authority can be committed to others but not responsibility. Delegation of authority is useless unless supported by the responsibility of those who do the delegating. The elected must have the backing of the electing.

A public school teacher remarked that her work would be much more rewarding if the parents recognized their responsibility at home for the conduct and the work of the children at school. She said that she always got a better response from a child when there was sympathetic response from the home. If there should arise conditions in a community to encourage juvenile delinquency, the source of the trouble may actually be in our indifference and neglect. We may have failed to cast the deciding vote for surroundings that are reasonably conducive to good conduct.

In the church, we may find at times the same situation. There are members who leave all the work to be done by the pastor and chosen officials. Too many in the pew cast no deciding vote by the service of their own hands and hearts. The British financier, Lord Josiah Stamp, once made this statement: "It is easy to dodge our responsibility but we can not dodge the consequences of dodging our responsibilities."

A Voice of Authority

SUCCINCTLY and cogently, a Negro leader has annotated the real steps members of his race should take in their determined climb toward racial equality. Dr. J. H. Jackson, of Chicago, president of the national organization of Baptist churches, said there is too much talk of "racial integration" and not enough about "racial elevation." The Negro leader suggested that no government or social group lifts a people. "They must climb themselves – and it takes patience and courage" . . . Of the so-called kneel-ins, Dr. Jackson said: "If you have religion in your church, use it. Don't go kneeling in somebody else's church." . . . Of sit-ins: "You can't get anywhere by sitting down. Even if you do put a store out of business, what have you gained?"

What Dr. Jackson offers by way of advice to members of his race, he has been saying for a long time. Dr. Jackson, as a Negro speaking to members of his own race, speaks more authoritatively, and should be listened to by all races.

Marrying a Goat

A YOUNG Indian girl married a goat at a village near Calcutta, India, to prevent the stigma of early widowhood. The marriage conformed with the Indian practice that if a woman marries an animal or a plant, evil spirits will mistake the animal or plant for her real husband and kill it. Thus no curse remains to prevent the woman from living with a real husband if she desires to subsequently.

Anyway, I suppose some women who are married to drunkards and liars might think that widowhood is desirable.

I think of Abigail who was married to churlish Nabal.

"Now the name of the man was Nabal; and the name of his wife Abigail: and she was a woman of good understanding, and of a beautiful countenance: but the man was churlish and evil in his doings; and he was of the house of Caleb" (I Samuel 25:3).

"Nabal was very drunken." "His heart died within him, and he became as a stone." Better be unmarried, better be a widow, than to have a husband like Nabal.

Darning Needle Title

THIS is Leeds, England: A contest hailed as the world darning needle threading championship was decided there. It was won by a man. No women had entered. Roy Norton, 21-year-old engineering student, was acclaimed champion after threading 1,067 pieces of No. 40 mercerized thread through the eye of a No. 13

darning needle inside a two-hour limit. Norton attributed his victory to Providence.

Thinking of this needle title, we would be helped to remember the words of Jesus in relation to the rich young ruler "who was very sorrowful, for he was very rich:

"And when Jesus saw that he was very sorrowful, he said, How hardly shall they that have riches enter into the kingdom of God! For it is easier for a camel to go through a needle's eye, than for a rich man to enter into the kingdom of God" (Luke 18:24, 25).

And we might get some profit in remembering a historic needle;

In May, 1959, Able and Baker became the world's most famous monkeys when they took a fifteen-hundred-mile ride through space in the nose cone of an Army Jupiter missile. But there's one item connected with the historic event which the Smithsonian will never see. That is a two-inch curved strip of aluminum with a hole in one end. It is the needle which was used to stitch the nylon mesh material of monkey Able's space suit just before she went on her famous trip. The needle is now worn on a silver necklace chain by a woman who worked with the Able-Baker experiment. The woman who has the needle is Mrs. June Reeve, of Huntsville, Alabama.

Within hours after recovery of the nose cone and the monkeys, Able and Baker became the center of attraction. They were probably the only monkeys who ever held a press conference. On the night of the firing, Capt. Edward S. Wilbarger, Jr., member of the Army's Medical Corps, used two needles to sew Able and Baker into their nose cone to keep them from sliding down into a sitting position.

Back in Huntsville, Mrs. Reeve and many others with hands in the historic event, watched huge television screens for the first orange sign of a blast-off. After it was history, Captain Wilbarger gave Mrs. Reeve her needle for the diligence and efficiency she showed in the project. It was completely his idea and came to her as a surprise. The other needle was given to Mrs. Wilbarger.

Mrs. Reeve's pride in the project, represented by the needle, is such that she once turned down a hundred dollar offer for the sliver of aluminum. "When I first put the needle on my neck chain," she said, "it was almost as a joke. But now I wouldn't part with it."

Her Smile Worth Ten Thousand Dollars

How much is a smile worth? Judge Harold Canavan in Municipal Court in Boston has awarded $10,000 to Mary Shafter, age 6, for an injury that impaired her ability to smile. The child's father, suing for his daughter, said she was injured when struck by an automobile in July, 1961.

It makes us to remember that a laugh is worth a hundred groans in any market. The smile gives evidence of a merry heart. And the Bible says: "A merry heart maketh a cheerful countenance" (Proverbs 15:13). "A merry heart doeth good like a medicine" (Proverbs 17:22).

The Gospel in the City

Dr. Wm. B. Riley wrote this:

"There was never an hour when the opportunities of the church were what they are at this moment. There never was a moment since Calvary when the city cried for the help of Christians as it is crying now. The heart of the modern metropolis has been largely abandoned by the modern churches and the new theologians; and these great centers – threatening to become the black holes of our cities – have been flung at our feet as our special charges. Evangelical ministers and evangelistic churches will either shine there or darkness will reign; we will either be the salt to the city, or corruption and decay are its destiny. If we put Christ upon the throne of our affections, if we make His church the medium of our endeavors, if we tithe our time and tithe our income we will conquer. Thousands will yet throng the courts of the Lord, the walls of His church will be compelled to widen by their incoming, and into every dark spot of the city we will send our young men and maidens, carrying the torchlight of life, and our mission stations will become the lighthouses for the storm-tossed of every region, and hospitals for those suffering from moral hurts, yea, homes into which Christ shall walk, and with his voice raise the dead."

If

If you are not saved – you are lost.

If you do not pray – you have no power.

If you are not meek – you are haughty.

If you are not humble – you are proud.

If you have no peace – you have no rest.

If you have no rest – you have worries.

If you have no joy – you get despondent.

If you have no hope – you are discouraged.

If you are not honest – you are deceitful.

If you lose your temper – you commit sin.

If you are not merciful – you are hard-hearted.

If you have no forbearance – you lack patience.

If you are discourteous – you are inconsiderate.

If you use profanity – Satan uses your tongue.

If you have hate in your heart – you are a murderer.

If you do not love the brethren – you do not love God.

Yes! And:

"If we say that we have no sin, we deceive ourselves, and the truth is not in us. If we confess our sins, he is faithful and just to forgive us our sins, and to cleanse us from all unrighteousness" (I John 1:8, 9).

"And this is the confidence that we have in him, that, if we ask any thing according to his will, he heareth us" (I John 5:14).

"Love not the world, neither the things that are in the world. If any man love the world, the love of the Father is not in him (I John 2:15).

Success Tips

From the electric bell: "Never knock."

From the knife: "Be sharp and bright."

From the barrel: "Keep your head."

From the hen: "Go out and scratch."

From the train window: "Stick."

From the ice: "Always keep cool."

From the crow bar: "Open up."

From the blackjack: "Relax."

From the mat: "Step on it."

From the lawn mower: "Push."

From the hammer: "Drive."

From the yeast: "Work."

From the pick: "Dig."

And we read this: "Seest thou a man diligent in his business? he shall stand before kings; he shall not stand before mean men" (Proverbs 22:29).

And: "He that diligently seeketh good procureth favor" (Proverbs 11: 27).

And here is another "tip" to success:

"Only be thou strong and very courageous, that thou mayest observe to do according to all the law, which Moses my servant commanded thee: turn not from it to the right hand or to the left, that thou mayest prosper withersoever thou goest. This book of the law shall not depart out of thy mouth; but thou shalt meditate therein day and night, that thou mayest observe to do according to all that is written therein: for then thou shalt make thy way prosperous, and then thou shalt have good success. Have not I commanded thee? Be strong and of a good courage; be not afraid, neither be thou dismayed: for the Lord thy God is with thee withersoever thou goest" (Joshua 1:7-9).

Profit of Paddling

FROM Washington, D.C., March 14, 1963, comes the news that an educator named Hansen, defends paddling of school children – believes that an "open hand, foot ruler, lightweight paddle" is the answer to unruly students. Corporal punishment applied to the "hand or buttocks of a pupil under justified circumstances" would go far toward bringing order in the public schools.

"I just can't figure out how some parents can trust teachers with their children's heads but can't trust them with their children's bottoms. If I couldn't trust teachers to spank my children, I certainly wouldn't trust them with their education. A sore bottom is better than a 'sorehead.'"

It seems to be a fad now for some parents to take teachers to court for spanking their children. But it is impossible for a parent to win a victory over her child's teacher – through court or otherwise – because whatever the outcome of a parent-teacher clash, the child will lose every time. The child suffers tremendously when his parent makes a big fuss over him. Teachers who have to work with thirty to thirty-five youngsters each day would much rather not be bothered with a child whose parent is doting and cantankerous.

Mr. Hansen told Congress in testimony on a corporal punishment bill for district schools that these measures would be used only when a teacher believes "this action may result in improved behavior on the part of the pupils."

They are needed, he said, to deal with the "insolent pupil who says 'you don't dare touch me.'" Without such authority, teachers are hampered in keeping the peace and quiet in the classroom, Hansen noted. "A disordered classroom has never produced an orderly and disciplined mind."

Hansen's proposal of corporal punishment stems from a report on Washington's public school problems made after a riot occurred following a Thanksgiving Day high school football game. The investigation was made by a special citizens committee which reported that a surprising lack of discipline and disregard of teachers' instructions contributed to the cause of the riot.

Hansen, acting on the report, recently recommended the lifting of a ban on corporal punishment as one means to improve public school discipline.

God's Bible teaches that we should not only be defenders but advocates of paddling – of corporal punishment.

"He that spareth his rod hateth his son: but he that loveth him chasteneth him betimes" (Proverbs 13:24).

"Chasten thy son while there is hope, and let not thy soul spare for his crying" (Proverbs 19:18).

"Foolishness is bound up in the heart of a child; but the rod of correction shall drive it far from him" (Proverbs 22:15).

"Withhold not correction from the child: for if thou beatest him with a rod, he shall not die. Thou shalt beat him with the rod, and shalt deliver his soul from hell" (Proverbs 23:13, 14).

"The rod and reproof give wisdom: but a child left to himself bringeth his mother to shame" (Proverbs 29:15).

"Correct thy son, and he shall give thee rest; yea, he shall give delight unto thy soul" (Proverbs 29:17).

Yes, while the legislators debate capital punishment and school principals ponder corporal punishment, many students remain recalcitrant – with insolence. We are inclined to remember when progressive education was calculated by the acceleration with which a mutinous scholar was propelled to the woodshed. We are inclined to agree with the fellow who blames the inventor of the safety razor for the rise in juvenile delinquency. Application of the razor strap at home would considerably lessen the problem of crime and punishment in today's schools.

Pat's Praise of Pat

In Fort Mill, South Carolina, an interesting advertisement pointed praisefully to Pat Rogers' dyeing, cleaning and pressing business.

Pat was an Irishman who lived there about thirty years. He died about twenty years ago. His place of business and living quarters were in the brick structure on Tom Hall street. Pat quite evidently was Pat's greatest admirer. His ad read in part:

"I have been in Fort Mill for seven years and not a single complaint has been heard or said about my work. I don't make my living like a mosquito bite.

"I believe I can take a pinetop, a bucket of molasses, a bucket of tar, a gallon of varnish and a bushel of clay, mix well together, and working by moonlight can do better dyeing than anything that has hit Fort Mill in the last seven years. I dye to live, Patrick Rogers."

Pat was certainly, as Solomon would express it, letting his own works praise him in the town. Perhaps such praise is permissible in business. But Solomon said, "Let another man praise thee, and not thine own mouth; a stranger, and not thine own lips" (Proverbs 27:2).

Nailing Up the Hole

Harold Booker, whose pen pricks me with delight writes: "When you get a politician backed up against the wall, he always tries to do or say something that will get the minds of the people off of the main issue. Well, the people ought to be like the little boy whose father took him on his knee and told him the story of the lost sheep; how it found a hole in the fence and crawled through; how glad it was to get away; how it wandered so far that it could not find its way back home. And then he told him of the wolf that chased the sheep, and how, finally, the shepherd came and rescued it and carried it back to the fold. The little boy was greatly interested, and when the story was over, he asked: 'Did they nail up the hole in the fence?'"

Many nails would be needed today to nail up all the holes in our educational walls and many other prohibitive walls through which people stray into our Satan-devised wilderness, where no spiritual water is, and the Satan-sown fields barren of spiritual fruit.

Mousy Papas and Midget Mamas

FROM Cincinnati comes the condemnatory comment that misguided parents are blamed by Traffic Court Judge Frank M. Gusweiler for many traffic violations by teen-agers.

"Rather than deny children's demands for the family car, these weak-kneed parents permit them to tear over our highways," he said. "The old-fashioned father who told his children what they could do has been succeeded by yes-men bearing a distinct resemblance to a mouse."

So many parents have reckless children of disobedience because they heed not this truth from God's holy Word: "Train up a child in the way he should go: and when he is old, he will not depart from it" (Proverbs 22:6). "Foolishness is bound in the heart of a child; but the rod of correction shall drive it far from him" (Proverbs 22:15).

I fear sometimes, when it comes to the use of automobiles, some teen-agers are like this bit of news: Raymond Heingartner, Jr., who is almost 5, was riding with his uncle when they passed a cemetery. The uncle explained that the dead were buried there. "Am I going to die some day?" asked Raymond. His uncle said he would, and, in answer to another question, said he, too, would die.

"Good," said Raymond. "Then we can have your car."

For What Do You Listen?

A NATURALIST walking with his friend through the busy streets of a great city, stopped suddenly, and asked: "Do you hear a cricket?"

"Of course not," laughed his friend. "You could never hear a cricket with all this roar of traffic."

"But I hear a cricket," persisted the naturalist, and, turning over a stone, he uncovered the insect.

"Did you actually hear that cricket chirping above the noise of the street?" asked his friend in astonishment.

"Certainly," said the naturalist. "I spend my time listening to nature, whether I am in the forest, the field, or the town. Everyone hears that for which he is listening."

Taking a coin from his pocket, he dropped it on the pavement, and each passer-by put his hand in his pocket to see if he was the one who had dropped it.

For what are you listening? Gold or God? Your ears are tuned to listen for something, even as the receiving set is tuned to receive the program from a distant radio station. God's ears are tuned to hear our prayers. Are ours tuned to hear His commands?

Too Much Baggage

SPEAKING of Frederick the Great, the historian said: "Frederick the Great won Rossbach by his miraculous marching on the lightest possible equipment."

Another historian, speaking of General Grant, said: "When Grant started out to capture Vicksburg, he took nothing with him but a gun coat and a toothpick."

What are the historians saying? That we must not give too much attention to baggage. Think of the baggage many young people are trying to carry today. And the reason why young people fail, and become disappointed old people is that they have given too much attention to excess baggage.

Keeping What You Give Away

Dr. E. M. Poteat, one-time president of Furman University, blessed my life immeasurably. One day, in the classroom, he gave the following words to his students, most of whom sat somewhat awed at the brilliance of his mind.

Carve your name high o'er shifting sand
  Where the steadfast rocks defy decay;
All you can hold in your cold, dead hand
  Is what you have given away.

Build your pyramids skyward and stand,
  Gazed at by millions, cultured they say;
But all you can hold in your cold, dead hand
  Is what you have given away.

Count your wide conquests by sea and land,
  Heap the gold, hoard as you may;
All you can hold in your cold, dead hand
  Is what you have given away.

Honor and fame and gold are so grand
  Kings of the salon mart, a day;
All you can hold in your cold, dead hand
  Is what you have given away.

Christianity a Need for Politics

In Athens, Texas, one day in 1953, Attorney General John Ben Shepperd told some 150 delegates attending the third annual state-wide Christian Men's fellowship that he is not so much worried about getting Communists out of government as he is about getting Christians into it.

Shepperd spoke at the Christian Youth Foundation there as one of the leading speakers for the three-day retreat. Delegates were present from all over the state. Shepperd said he had heard many a Christian say politics is too dirty a business to get mixed up in.

"How long will freedom tarry in the hands of people who stand in the church door and cast horrified glances at the sinners in the city hall? It is time to recognize that government belongs to God, to stop looking down on it or away from it, and start looking into it," he said.

Shepperd reproved Christians who are "guilty of Pontius Pilate politics" – who stand washing their hands of all responsibility while democratic government is led away to be crucified on a cross of public apathy.

"Let no man feel that in attending Caesar he is robbing God. The Psalmist said, 'Let us go into the house of the Lord.' How much happier God must be to be invited out of the chapel and into the city hall."

Describing current fear of Communism and Socialism, the Attorney General called on Christians to forget their "obsession with the left and the right and give more attention to the above and below."

Horsefly Pet Wins

In Shelton, Connecticut, in October, 1953, Dickie Munson, 14, won first prize for the most unusual entry in a pet show. He displayed a horsefly in a cage carved out of a cork.

More unusual would be some of our habits put in a cage so they could hurt not nor handicap any more.

Six Imperishable Words

What are they? "Evening, that brings all things home." This is a line of Greek verse written by Sappho. These six words are all that remain of the poem. But what vitality that fragment of the poem has! It has survived the changes of 2500 years!

What a thought of simple, universal beauty! No wonder these words have survived the centuries! What they picture to us – "Evening, that brings all things home" – makes them to live and to be loved by peer and peasant.

Of these six immortal words you cannot say, in the words of Pope:

Words are like leaves; and where they most abound,
Much fruit of sense is seldom found.

Nor concerning them can you say: "And ten low words oft creep in one dull line."

Nor what Richard Barnfield said: "Words are but wind, and wind is all in vain."

And maybe Sappho, could she be "made flesh to live and write again," would rejoice in what Rev. John Ray, who departed this life in 1705, said: "He that uses many words to explain any subject doth, like the cuttle fish, hide himself for the most part in his own ink."

One Happy Hoover

MELVIN HOOVER spent most of his more than fifty years as a butler serving the Louis Mendelssohn family. In Evelyn Mendelssohn's will, he was bequeathed $100,000 – with the tax already taken out.

Hoover, who lived one hundred miles east of Toronto, Ont., came to Detroit because his uncle, then a gardener for the Mendelssohns, had found a job here for him. Instead, Hoover began working in the family's garden and stayed with them when they moved to a three-story mansion on Lake St. Clair.

"She said she'd take care of me, and she did," the five-foot-five Hoover said.

Treasure on earth is this for this happy Hoover. We hope he has treasure in heaven, too, where "moth and rust can not corrupt and where thieves can not break through and steal."

Ant Wins Award

AT RICHFIELD SPRINGS, New York, August 5, 1953, there was held a children's pet show. There was a prize for the smallest entry in the children's pet show, so Ralph "Skippy" Wilkinson displayed an ant. He won, feet down.

Amusing this news item. I would that all the children and those with them at the pet show would treasure the Bible's words:

"Go to the ant, thou sluggard; consider her ways, and be wise: which having no guide, overseer, or ruler, provideth her meat in the summer, and gathereth her food in the harvest" (Proverbs 6:6-8).

"There be four things which are little upon the earth, but they are exceeding wise: the ants are a people not strong, yet they prepare their meat in the summer; the conies are but a feeble folk, yet make they their houses in the rocks; the locusts have no king, yet go they forth all of them by bands; the spider taketh hold with her hands, and is in king's palaces" (Proverbs 30:24-28).

Cato's Three Laments

PLUTARCH says that Cato himself declared that in his whole life he most repented of three things:

That he had trusted a secret to a woman.

That he went by water when he might have gone by land.

That he had remained one whole day without doing any business of importance.

If there is a lesson for us in this, let us learn it.

Liberty to Speak

WHEN Jean Jacques Rousseau was hunted and hounded from one place to another on account of his opinions, Voltaire heard of it and although Voltaire did not share Rousseau's views, he invited him to come and live in his home. And when Rousseau finally arrived, Voltaire embraced him and said: "I do not agree with a word you say, but I will fight to the death for your right to say it."

Forgetting

ONE day the landlord of a block of flats called on one of his tenants, a young artist.

"The rent of your rooms is six months behind," he commenced; "but times being what they are, I don't want to be hard on you. I'll tell you what I propose to do. I'll meet you halfway — forget half the debt. How about that?"

The tenant smiled gratefully. "That's fine!" he said, "and I'll forget the other half."

Both halves forgotten! Any two halves make a whole. And the whole of what some people owe me has been forgotten. And what I say, others can say, too.

Cursed

JOHN WITHERSPOON, first president of Princeton, says:

"Cursed be all learning that is contrary to the cross of Christ.

"Cursed be all learning that is not coincident with the cross of Christ.

"Cursed be all learning that is not subservient to the cross of Christ."

In this we concur. And when we think that this is not advocated by many educators today, we remember that a poet said:

Voice . . . . .
That rings across the sea whence no man
steers,
Like joy-bells crossed with death-bells in
our ears.

"Bear Down"

THE University of Arizona has a beautiful campus, gymnasium, and stadium. On both sides of the standing room of the gymnasium in tremendous letters is printed: "BEAR-DOWN." These were the last words of Captain Button of the 1926 Arizona team just before he died in an auto accident before Arizona's final game.

Yes, *Bear Down.*

Not bad advice for the Lord's work!

Peter's Sword

"THEN, Simon Peter having a sword, drew it, and smote the high priest's servant, and cut off his right ear!"

Peter learned that there is a time when it is too late to draw a sword. And is there not a time when it is too late to offer apologies, too late to frame words of sympathy, too late to bring flowers, too late to shed tears, too late to whisper words of endearment? Who of us wants tears or dears or flowers after we are dead? Who wants folks to draw swords for us — after awhile?

Strange Swimming

PENGUINS are strange birds. They use their wings for swimming instead of flying. So, in a way more ridiculous than the penguins which use their wings for swimming, do some use talents meant to be used for God's glory, in service to the devil.

Addison said: "A man of great talents, but void of discretion, is like Polyphemus in the fable, strong and blind, endowed with an irresistible force, which for want of sight is of no use to him." Just as penguins use their wings for swimming instead of flying, so many use their talents so in reverse from God's purpose – making steam shovel abilities do teaspoon work.

Deserter and Refugee

"An old Negro accused of deserting his wife was brought before the judge. After the judge had lectured him severely on the sin and trifling character of desertion, he asked the old Negro: "What have you to say?"

"Jedge," solemnly answered the old Negro; "you done git me wrong, I ain't no deserter, I is a refugee."

Thinking of his answer, one thinks the old Negro would have some solace in what Heine wrote: "Every man who marries is like the Doge who weds the Adriatic sea; he knows not what he may find therein – treasures, pearls, monsters, unknown storms." Or in what Epicharmus said, he might have found some comfort: "Marriage is like casting dice. If chance bring you a good and virtuous wife, your lot is happy. If you gain instead a gadding, gossiping, and thriftless queen, no wife is yours, but everlasting plague in woman's garb; the habitable globe holds not so dire a torment anywhere." Maybe, too, he would agree with him who said: "Better be half-hanged than ill-wed." Maybe, too, he would have nodded approval of the statement: "He is dreadfully married." Maybe this black refugee would agree with what Montaigne said: "A good marriage would be between a blind bride and a deaf husband."

An Ill-Adjusted Life

Martha Banning Thomas writes of the ill-adjusted life in these striking words:

Here lies the fretful heart of one
Who had not patience with the sun;
Who yanked the window curtains down
To save the carpet's patterned brown;
Here lies the stark and still remains
Of her who cried against the rains,
And would not suffer flakes of snow
Upon her doorstep!

May these words save some reader from an ill-adjusted life. And may we remember that some live a life that is lifeless– as "lifeless as a string of dead fish"; as "lifeless and lumpish as the bagpipe's drowsy drone"; as "lifeless as an icy morn." The Apostle Paul knew that, for he wrote by the Holy Spirit: "She that liveth in pleasure is dead while she liveth" (I Timothy 5:6).

Maybe many live ill-adjusted lives because they have poor conceptions of life – like James G. Huneker, who wrote: "Life is like an onion – you peel off layer after layer and then you find there is nothing to it." Maybe they are ill-adjusted because they see despairingly, as did Mme. de Stael: "Life often seems like a long shipwreck, of which the debris are friendship, glory, and love."

How different from the conceptions and words of the Apostle Paul: "For me to live is Christ, and to die is gain" (Philippians 1:21).

Forgetting Crossings

Railroads announce that folks should cross crossings cautiously. And because people are guilty of such oversight, they come to the tragedy here mentioned.

There was a prudent man who brushed his teeth twice a day, wore rubbers in wet weather, did his daily dozen, slept with windows open, was careful with his diet, had a medical examination twice a year, never smoked, drank or indulged in any kind of excess. He was set to live to be one hundred years old.

The funeral was held last Wednesday. He is survived by eighteen specialists, four health institutes, six gymnasiums and numerous manufacturers of health foods and antiseptics.

He forgot to look out for a train at a grade crossing.

Reliability

SOME young people asked me what I considered one of the greatest things about a loyal church member. I said, "RELIABILITY." Yes, and our confidence in things is their reliability. Imagine trying to live in a world of irregularity – a hit-and-miss world, a world of caprice, of chance. Suppose we lived in a world where fire sometimes furnished heat and sometimes furnished cold. Suppose we lived in a world where sugar is sometimes sweet and sometimes bitter. Suppose the sun warmed everything in the morning and froze everything in the evening. Suppose one child in a family was born with two hands, two feet, two eyes, two ears, but the second child might be born with one hand, three feet and four eyes and five ears. In a capricious world of that kind we would simply be in despair. So also we are sometimes, as preachers, "tasting of despair" because of the lack of reliability of our church members.

Christ at Elbow

WHEN David Hume, the infidel, was charged with inconsistency in going to listen to John Brown, the godly Scotch minister of Haddington, he replied: "I don't believe all that he says, but *he* does, and once a week I like to hear a man who believes what he says. Why, whatever I think, the man preaches as though he thought the Lord Jesus Christ was at his elbow."

Do our young people, especially the skeptical, enjoy hearing us preachers in the pulpit and our church officers and our teachers for the reason given by Hume? Does it abide in their minds that those of us who are in places of spiritual leadership preach, teach, talk as though Christ were at the elbow? If they were made a jury, would they find us *not guilty* of preaching the truth and teaching the truth as though it were fiction? Some questions these, which all of us may well ponder.

AMAZING TRUTHS

Longest Fence

THIS is a story of perhaps the longest fence in the world. It's around Kruger National Park in South Africa, set up to prevent spread of hoof-and-mouth disease. It is five hundred and ninety miles of fence, at a cost of $520,000. It's effective, too. Animals outside the fence no longer get the disease. In Mexico one summer, there was the slaughter of thousands of cattle – and a few government men picked off by rifles of ranchers losing their herds. 'Twas a horrible sight.

Job had no thoughts of horror when he said: "Thou hast fenced me with bones and sinews" (Job 10: 11).

Perhaps he had some unpleasant thoughts when he said: "He hath fenced up my way that I can not pass, and he hath set darkness in my paths. He hath stripped me of my glory, and taken the crown from my head. He hath destroyed me on every side, and I am gone: and mine hope hath he removed like a tree. He hath also kindled his wrath against me, and he counteth me unto him as one of his enemies" (Job 19:8-11).

A Long Time

IT TOOK years to build the Taj Mahal, the greatest mausoleum on earth. Twenty thousand men worked on it.

It took seven and one-half years to build Solomon's Temple. And one hundred and eighty-three thousand six hundred men worked on it.

It took seventy-six years to build the great Pyramid of Egypt.

It took many years to build Verdun into a fortress. This city-fortress the Crown Prince strove in vain to carry by storm during the World War. He marched his men in solid mass, shoulder to shoulder – eight hundred thousand died. But the fortress-city was never taken. And that without the inner circle of guns ever being fired.

There are things we can build, even though it may take a long time, which the tooth of time can never gnaw.

Conscience

LUCRETIUS said: "Though the dungeon, the scourge, and the executioner be absent, the guilty mind can apply the goad and scorch with blows."

Things About Bugs

ON A SINGLE antenna of an ordinary June beetle, there are as many as twenty thousand olfactory pits.

The bombardier beetle employed gas against his enemy centuries before the Oriental invented a stinkpot or man resorted to gas warfare.

The dragon flies have eyes with as many as thirty thousand facets, to furnish the intense vision required in capturing darting, fast-flying prey.

The adult May flies of some species have done away with mouths and stomachs because their mature lives are too short to need them.

The plant lice have eliminated males from all but one of their many annual generations, and under laboratory tests have produced ninety-four generations without the interposition or birth of a single male.

Carpet beetles have lived two years in a corked bottle with nothing whatever to eat save the cast-off skins of their own transformations.

Hornets and wasps were the world's first manufacturers of paper. The manner in which they enlarge a little nest smaller than a hen egg into one as large as a half bushel measure without disturbing its symmetry or opening up its interior, is a masterpiece in building.

The katydid and crickets hear with their front legs, in which are located the ears that catch the music of their sweetheart's songs.

Among short-horned grasshoppers, their ears are in their abdomen, immediately back of and above the point where the hind legs emerge from their bodies.

All of this gives evidence of design and an omniscient Designer, of law and an omniscient Lawmaker.

Comparisons

PROF. SHOWWALTER gives us some interesting comparisons. If you measure man's strength and achievements in engineering by the standards set by the insects, man's success is overshadowed entirely in some ways.

In the Olympics it is a standard jump that clears the bar at six feet six inches. Yet the comon flea is capable of jumping one hundred times as high as his own head. Were champion Olympic jumpers to do as well proportionately they would jump clear over the Washington Monument at one bound with some eighty feet to spare.

If the modern baggage man could carry loads as heavy in proportion to size as an ant, he could lift a half-ton trunk to the top of Washington Monument without apparent fatigue.

If a man could dig in a few days out of hard clay or sand, with no other tools than his nails and teeth, five or six caverns twenty feet deep and four or five feet square, it would not be any more comparatively than that which the wild bee does when it digs a hole in a hard bank of earth six inches deep, six times its own size.

But as wonderful as are all these accomplishments in the insect world, more wonderful it is that "they that wait upon the Lord shall renew their strength, they shall mount up with wings as eagles, they shall run and not be weary." And in view of what God does for those who "wait on him," how sad to see evidence of strengthlessness among people and to know people whom Francis Thompson describes in these words:

Strengthless as a noon-belated moon,
Or as the glazing eyes of watery heaven,
When the sick night sinks into deadly
swoon.

Sad it is that people with giant abilities do pigmy work. We meet with those who are "weak as a lamb that can't stand the weight of its wool" – "weak as unfledged nestling in the falcon's grip" – "weak as the puny rillets of the hill" – "weak as young corn withered, whereof no man may gather and make bread" – "weak as a poor straw upon a torrent's breast." "Ye shall receive power, after that the Holy Ghost is come upon you" (Acts 1:8).

Giving and Living

Get Guiterman's wisdom:

Though right it is to *give* thanks,
True gratitude will *live* thanks!

Palm-Tree Virtues

Of all the trees on all continents, the palm-tree is most useful. The encyclopedia tells us that there are eight hundred different uses for the palm-tree. Yet sometimes there are eight hundred "good-for-nothing" people in churches. What fruit into God's kingdom basket would fall – if each of the eight hundred were good for eight hundred uses!

Mother of Twenty-Six Children

From St. David de Falardeau (wherever it is) comes this announcement: Mrs. Lucian Savard, 47, has given birth to her 26th child. She thinks she may have more. Christened Lucie, the latest baby "is as beautiful and as adorable as the first," Mrs. Savard said, adding, "It's always new."

Seventeen of her children are living, three of them married. The other fourteen live in the eight-room Savard home in a community, 120 miles north of Quebec City.

Lucie, who weighed 9 pounds, 4 ounces at birth, was born November 24th. Mrs. Savard was tending her home within a week and thinking about further additions to her family. "The doctor told me I could have another, too," she said.

Her husband is a forest ranger,

earning $160.00 a month and receiving $70.00 a month in family allowances. On the few occasions the family travels a bus is rented.

What a wonderful service to mankind all these children will render if they are brought up "in the nurture and admonition of the Lord" (Ephesians 6:4).

Toscanini Talks

I READ somewhere (just where I do not now remember) that Toscanini, the world-famous conductor, who was very exacting and almost tyrannical in rehearsals, once practiced the Ninth Symphony of Beethoven with an orchestra. First, it was practiced piecemeal – each group of instruments alone, and then, together, at full concert strength. At last rehearsals were over, and master and orchestra were ready for the concert performance. When the performance was over, the first violinist said to the second violinist: "If he scolds us after that, I will jump up and push him off his platform." But Toscanini did not scold. He stood silent – his arms still outstretched, his deep eyes burning with an inner fire, the light of a great rapture upon his face, and a spirit of utter contentment enfolding him. After a long silence he spoke: "Who am I? Who is Toscanini? Who are you? I am nobody. You are nobody. . . ." The crowded hall was hushed. The master stood with arms still extended. The multitude waited in awed silence. Then with the light upon his face of one who had seen a vision, he added: "Beethoven is everything – everything!"

This meant that God does matter. No one else matters. God is *everything*. If you can only remember one thing amidst thousands – yea, tens of thousands of other things, remember that outside God there is nothing but death.

Bee Business

MARVELOUS the structure and the intricacy of the mysterious operations of bees. Each bee has three pairs of legs. The bee's nose has two to three thousand tiny sense plates. The wings of the bee in flight beat 190 times a second, or 11,400 times a minute. The wax manufactured by a hive of bees floats on water and is strongly resistant to heat – enduring a temperature of 140° Fahrenheit before melting. No other wax has such a high melting point.

A red clover blossom contains less than one-eighth of a grain of sugar. Seven thousand grains are required to make a pound of honey. A bee, flitting here and there for sweetness, must visit 56,000 clover heads for a pound of honey; and there are about 60 flower heads to each clover head. When a bee performs that operation $60 \times 56{,}000$, or 3,360,000 times, it secures sweetness enough for only one pound of honey. Amazingly interesting! But more amazing – and certainly more comforting – is what the Psalmist said about Israel's deliverance from the nations which, with purpose to destroy encompassed Israel about.

"They compassed me about like bees; they are quenched as the fire of thorns: for in the name of the Lord I will destroy them. Thou hast thrust sore at me that I might fall: but the Lord helped me" (Psalm 118: 12, 13).

God shows, too, how small creatures as are bees can, working together put human beings to flight.

"And the Amorites, which dwelt in that mountain, came out against you, and chased you, as bees do, and destroyed you in Seir, even unto Hormah" (Deuteronomy 1:44).

Two-Year Coma

IN ROCK HILL, South Carolina, August 27, 1953, Mrs. Rosa Kate Turner McFadden, 74, died after being in a coma for two years – after injury in an automobile accident.

But I know some church members who are still alive who have lived a coma life for years. They seem not to know that "he that sleepeth in harvest is a son that causeth shame" (Proverbs 10:5). And they seem to have deaf ears to the words of God: "Wherefore he saith, Awake thou that sleepest, and arise from the dead, and Christ shall give thee light" (Ephesians 5:14).

So perpetually do men – in a coma spiritually – seem to be ignorant of these words: "For this cause many are weak and sickly among you, and many sleep" (I Corinthians 11:30).

So many there are who act as though they had never known the warnings of these words: "How long wilt thou sleep, O sluggard? when wilt thou arise out of thy sleep? Yet a little sleep, a little slumber, a little folding of the hands to sleep: so shall thy poverty come as one that travelleth, and thy want as an armed man" (Proverbs 6:9-11).

What sober words are these: "But while men slept, his enemy came and sowed tares among the wheat, and went his way" (Matthew 13:25).

Atmosphere Operates Clock

A SPECIAL to the Courier-Journal, Louisville, Kentucky, mentions the so-called atmospheric clock. This clock never has to be "wound," for it gets the energy required for its operation from changing atmospheric pressure.

A closed and collapsible box like that in an aneroid barometer is used in the clock. As the air pressure increases, the box is collapsed; as the pressure goes down, the box expands.

The alternate contraction and expansion of the box drives a series of gears, through a rachet mechanism, thus winding the spring that actually drives the clock.

But no matter how many marvels we have as to showing the time, man can get nothing that can recall time – nothing in the atmosphere or the earth or in the heavens above the earth or in the waters beneath the earth. Not one minute of all the hours and centuries that men's clocks have recorded can be unlived or relived.

Ancient Advertisement

MISS ALINE BARBER, who lives in Fort Mill, South Carolina, ran across a clipping from an ancient newspaper that told how want ads were worded in the year 1796. Here it is:

> Wanted for a sober family, a man of light weight, who fears the Lord and can drive a pair of horses. He must occasionally wait at table, join in household prayer, look after horses and read a chapter in the Bible. He must, God willing, rise at 7 in the morning, and obey his master and mistress in all lawful commands; if he can dress hair, sing psalms and play cribbage, the more agreeable. N.B. He must not be familiar with the maid servants, lest the flesh should rebel against the spirit and he should be induced to walk in the thorny paths of the wicked. Wages 15 guineas a year (about $7 a month).

I make no comment on this. Maybe you have some thoughts you would like to put into words.

Mother Refuses to Bury Hero's Ashes in Winter

IN FARMINGTON, Maine, after World War II, a soldier was brought home for burial. In a sealed casket, the body of Pvt. Earl E. Sawyer was kept in his mother's parlor from November 15th until the coming of spring. The mother said she could not bear to think of her son's body in a cold vault during Maine's harsh winter.

"My feelings on this may seem unusual to a majority of people," Mrs. Rita Brown declared, "but the fact that my son is home again brings me a great deal of comfort."

Sawyer was killed in the Battle of the Bulge. His body was buried when the warm weather came.

Sometimes now we find not a dead and unburied body in the home, but a dead love and a dead home wrapped about with the grave clothes of the impious forgetfulness of God. Homes do die sometimes in houses.

Truths About Hummingbirds

THE smallest known bird is the hummingbird. It is found only in the New World, of which it is a native. It ranges from the Strait of Magellan, at the southern tip of South America, to Alaska. There are 488 different kinds of these birds, but only sixteen kinds are found north of Mexico. There is only one kind found east of the Mississippi River and north of Florida. This is the common ruby-throated hummingbird which is familiar throughout the eastern half of the United States and Canada.

This interesting little bird received its name from the humming sound of its fast-moving wings. The ruby-throat is so-named because of the bright red spot on the throats of the males.

The size of the hummingbird seems very diminutive when compared with the world's largest bird, the ostrich. The smallest hummingbird is found in Cuba, and its body is about one and one-fourth inches long, while the ostrich may be eight feet in height and weigh as much as 300 pounds. The beautiful colors of the hummingbirds are due to refractions of sunlight from the feathers. Many iridescent hues are produced, and color varies according to the angle of the light. This is why the colors seem to change as the birds change their position. So beautiful are the colors that Audubon, the great bird authority, has called these birds "glittering fragments of the rainbow." Others have called them "feathered gems."

Hummingbirds have very ugly tempers. There is scarcely anything that can exceed their fierceness when they are disturbed during the mating season. They attack intruders with bewildering courage for such tiny creatures, and they seem to be absolutely fearless. Many are the times we watched with amazement as one of them would put to flight a large crow or hawk.

Perhaps Nature, thinking that the beautiful colors of the hummingbirds were sufficient adornments for them, saved the song abilities for the birds less brilliantly clothed.

A Wonderful Synthesis

FORMALDEHYDE! Carbolic acid! Ninety per cent of all the pipe stems, imitation woods, beads, and gaily colored automatic pencils are made of a synthesis of formaldehyde and carbolic acid. Some poor foolish ones say they cannot believe that, in Cana Jesus changed water into wine!

Copper Output

MONTANA's copper mines have yielded more than seven billion pounds of ore representing about 47 per cent of the total output in the United States since about 1845.

Sometimes I wonder if the output of service in our churches doesn't come from 47 per cent of our members. Do we not do God's work in our churches on less than 50 per cent of our ability? Please answer. Then weep.

Greatness of Glass

LOOK at the properties of glass. Glass is one of the most versatile materials in the world. Chemically, glass is the most stable of all materials excepting the noble metals. It will not rot, oxidize, or disintegrate. Dimensionally, glass is very, very stable, too. It keeps its shape. The coefficient of expansion is lower than practically any other material. The surface of glass is among the hardest in the world. It is non-porous; will not absorb odors or moisture. It is more acid-resistant than any structural material. It offers unusual resistance to abrasion.

It can be coated, polished, or etched. In large sheets, it can be made smoother than any other material. Its weathering qualities are unequaled. Glass is strong. Make no mistake on that point. A square foot, quarter-inch sheet, the way we temper it, will withstand a pressure of 60 pounds per square inch. Double the thickness and you quadruple the strength. Our tempered glass has a modulus of rupture of 30,000 pounds per square inch, and it will withstand a thermal shock of 400 degrees Fahrenheit. Actually, tempered glass is stronger than many metals.

Glass is stable. The Bible speaks of the whole world being stable. "Fear before him, all the earth: the world also shall be stable, that it be not moved" (I Chronicles 16:30).

Glass will not rot. God speaks of a tree that will not rot. "He that is so impoverished that he hath no oblation chooseth a tree that will not rot" (Isaiah 40:20).

But that is not true of the names of the wicked. "The memory of the just is blessed: but the name of the wicked shall rot" (Proverbs 10:7).

Glass can be made very smooth. But better for humanity the truth: "Every valley shall be filled, and every mountain and hill shall be brought low; and the crooked shall be made straight, and the rough ways shall be made smooth" (Luke 3:5).

Glass can be polished and made beautiful. How much more glorious the statement: "That our sons may be as plants grown up in their youth: that our daughters may be as cornerstones, polished after the similitude of a palace" (Psalm 144:12).

Glass is strong. How much more to be desired for men is their obedience to these words: "Watch ye, stand fast in the faith, quit you like men, be strong" (I Corinthians 16:13). "Say to them that are of a fearful heart, Be strong, fear not: behold, your God will come with vengeance, even God with a recompence; he will come and save you" (Isaiah 35:4). "Finally, my brethren, be strong in the Lord, and in the power of his might" (Ephesians 6:10).

Glass is often very clear, having a clearness that is beautiful. How much more beautiful the realities pictured by these words in Revelation: "And before the throne there was a sea of glass like unto crystal: and in the midst of the throne, and round about the throne, were four beasts" (Revelation 4:6). "And the building of the wall of it was of jasper: and the city was pure gold, like unto clear glass . . . And the twelve gates were twelve pearls; every several gate was of one pearl: and the street of the city was pure gold, as it were transparent glass" (Revelation 21:18, 21).

Youth Must Be Won

THE honorable and wise J. Edgar Hoover, diligent director of the F.B.I., speaks sober truth in these words: "Godless forces of totalitarianism attempt to lure our boys and girls into the fear, the injustice and misery of slavery under dictatorship. . . . Where-ever they go they contaminate because of the indifference and apathy of our citizens. As a result our America is at the crossroads." This teaches that youth must be won for the cause of righteousness.

Dr. Wilbur Chapman once tested a meeting where 4,500 were present. The result showed: 400 became Christians before ten years of age; 600 between sixteen and twenty; 25 became Christians after thirty years of age. 1,875 were unsaved.

This teaches that youth must be won.

Nineteen out of every twenty who become Christians do so before they reach the age of twenty-five.

After twenty-five, only one in 10,000

After thirty-five, only one in 50,000

After forty-five, only one in 200,000

After fifty-five, only one in 300,000

After sixty-five, only one in 500,000

After seventy-five, only one in 700,000.

This teaches that youth must be won for God.

Lord Byron once weepingly said:

Untrained in youth my heart to tame,
My springs of life were poisoned.

This wail warns that youth must be won to disciplinary devotion to right living while, like Rehoboam of old (II Chronicles 13:7), they are young and tender.

We must win our youth to "fear the Lord from their youth," to trust God from their youth (Psalm 71:5), to remember their Creator in the days of their youth (Ecclesiastes 12:1), to observe God's commandments from their youth (Matthew 19:20), to flee youthful lusts (II Timothy 2:22), to let no man despise their youth (I Timothy 4:12).

Tungsten Metal

THE most common form of artificial light is the ordinary incandescent bulb with the tungsten filament. These vary in size from the tiny "grain of wheat" lamps to the thirty thousand-watt lamp, the size of a football. The "grain of wheat" lamp is just the size and shape of a grain of wheat. It is used in the instruments with which surgeons explore the interior of the human body.

Tungsten metal is the best filament material because it withstands the necessary heat better than any other substance. It is produced from an ore called wolframite. This is mined in Colorado, California, China and Africa, as well as in some of the European countries. Most of that used in this country comes from China, and the crude ore is reduced to tungsten in America.

At the time the crude ore is worth forty dollars a ton. After it has been reduced to bars of tungsten in the electric furnace it is worth four thousand dollars a ton, and after it has been drawn into filament wire, which is stronger than steel and not much larger than a human hair, it is worth seventy dollars a pound, or one hundred and forty thousand dollars a ton.

From forty dollars a ton to one hundred and forty thousand dollars a ton is quite an increase in value. But a more wonderful increase in value and power does Isaiah, the prophet, speak of in these words:

"Fear not, thou worm Jacob, and ye men of Israel; I will help thee, saith the Lord, and thy redeemer, the Holy One of Israel. Behold, I will make thee a new sharp threshing instrument having teeth: thou shalt thresh the mountains, and beat them small, and shalt make the hills as chaff" (Isaiah 41:14, 15).

From a soft and weak little worm to a strong threshing instrument. Increase in human values. How great!

Work — Don't Worry

Mrs. Matilda ("Aunt Sis") Rogers of Waynesville, N. C., when she reached her 111th birthday, said her recipe for longevity is: "Plenty of hard work and no worry. I used to go into the clearings and chop, grub, pile and burn – just like a man," she recalls, "And, oh, the days I've plowed in the corn and worked in the tobacco – all such as that – the young girls of this day wouldn't know anything about it."

At 111, "Aunt Sis" read without glasses – and her mind was alert.

Since she reached the age of 100, Aunt Sis received yearly birthday messages from the President of the United States, two from President Truman and eight from President Eisenhower.

Mrs. Rogers, the matriarch of a clan of 284 living descendants, had five sons, four daughters, 65 grandchildren, 79 great-grandchildren, 125 great-great-grandchildren, and to top it all, six new great-great-great-grandchildren born since she turned 110 years. Her oldest child is a son, 92.

As to old age, we have in the Bible many precious promises:

"Thou shalt come to thy grave in a full age, like as a shock of corn cometh in in his season. Lo this, we have searched it, so it is; hear it, and know thou it for thy good" (Job 5:26, 27).

"And thine age shall be clearer than the noonday; thou shalt shine forth, thou shalt be as the morning" (Job 11:17).

"Those that be planted in the house of the Lord shall flourish in the courts of our God. They shall still bring forth fruit in old age" (Psalm 92:13, 14).

"Even to your old age I am he, and even to hoar hairs will I carry you. I have made and I will bear; Even I will carry, and will deliver you" (Isaiah 46:4).

To the aged, Paul gives this counsel:

"But speak thou the things which become sound doctrine: that the aged men be sober, grave, temperate, sound in faith, in charity, in patience. The aged women likewise, that they be in behaviour as becometh holiness, not false accusers, not given to much wine, teachers of good things" (Titus 2:1-3).

Help for a Hemophiliac

Twenty-six-year-old Donald Horton of Taylor, S. C., had two teeth extracted. That in itself is not unusual. But Mr. Horton is a hemophiliac – one who tends to bleed profusely – and in the post-extraction period he had to be administered forty-nine pints of blood plasma. The dental work and treatment took place during July at the University of North Carolina Memorial Hospital at Chapel Hill, where extensive research on hemophilia is being carried out. He is again at home and at work.

There still remains, however, the necessity for replacing the forty-nine pints of blood, a physical impossibility for his family. They have now come to the point of asking for volunteer donors as a help toward replacing the blood used for Mr. Horton. Mr. Horton, native of Newberry, has been plagued with the danger of hemophilia all his life, as has his twin brother, Ronald. Hemophilia is a tendency, usually hereditary, to profuse bleeding, even from slight wounds. It is transmitted by the female, but only the male is affected.

All these statements about blood make us to think of some Bible words:

"For it is the life of all flesh; the blood of it is for the life thereof: therefore I said unto the children of Israel, Ye shall eat the blood of no manner of flesh: for the life of all flesh is the blood thereof: whosoever eateth it shall be cut off" (Leviticus 17:14).

"Only be sure that thou eat not the blood: for the blood is the life; and thou mayest not eat the life with the flesh" (Deuteronomy 12:23).

Thirty Thousand Dollars for Pony

THAT price set a new record. Sam Taylor's Horseshoe Pony Farm at Germantown has set a second record in pony prices, with a thirty thousand dollar sale. Mr. and Mrs. Ray Ward and sons of Ninety Six, S. C., paid that amount for Taylor's two-year-old colt, "Little Masterpiece II." The colt is the son of Taylor's "Little Masterpiece" (the first) which he sold in 1954 for twenty-five thousand dollars which was a record. Not so high was the price Solomon paid for a horse:

"And they fetched up, and brought forth out of Egypt a chariot for six hundred shekels of silver, and an horse for an hundred and fifty: and so brought they out horses for all the kings of the Hittites, and for the kings of Syria, by their means" (II Chronicles 1:17).

But David said: "A horse is a vain thing for safety" (Psalm 33:17).

Bleak Descriptions

Two men paint bleak pictures of Twentieth Century Christianity and life. Dr. Hugo Kleiner gave this description: "The church has lost her spiritual sensitivity. Her image has been tarnished and corroded. It is a day of dire spiritual poverty; never before in her history has the church been beset with more ruthless enemies. The bloody persecution of early Christians was terrible. But in comparison, the full-bodied perversions and atrocities in modern Communism make their tyrannies look rather anemic. No matter how oppressive those ancient Caesars set out to be, men could still live their own thoughts and submerge themselves in any one of numerous activities that did not directly touch the life of the state. Most distressing is the languor in the realm of the spirit. Intellectualism and humanism and pragmatism and materialism are having a heydey. God is being shoved around and kept at arm's length."

Ray W. Carroll, Baytown, says: "Our highly-touted 'American Way of Life' is mockery. We have more murders, divorces, robberies, adult and juvenile delinquents, sick, lazy and crazy people, crooks, traitors, sex maniacs, etc., per square mile, than any nation on earth, even though we have more churches than we ever had. Our nation is divided and our moral fiber is at low ebb. We are being governed by Harvard theorists and immature derelicts. Minority groups are being pampered and given special privileges."

Collapse of Time

SOME people say: "It is later than you think." Dr. Earl Waldrop speaks of it as "The Collapse of Time."

"If you want to be shocked awake to the fact of just how much time has collapsed on us in the moral and spiritual field consider some relative time explosions. Take for instance the collapse of time in the tempo of life, as it relates to speed. In the time of Nero, man could travel only as fast as a horse could run. This remained static for many centuries, in fact until 1830. It was then that man invented an iron horse which could run faster than a horse. Now the tempo begins to step up a bit. In 1910, the first military aircraft traveled at top speed of forty-two miles per hour. In 1918, at the end of World War I, man could travel at the speed of one hundred fifty miles per hour. By 1939, the beginning of World War II, speeds of more than two hundred miles per hour were attained. By 1945, the end of the war, he could travel four hundred and seventy miles per hour. In 1948, man broke the sound barrier. In 1956 man attained a speed of one thousand, six hundred miles per hour, and then in 1960, a man traveled at the unheard-of speed of eighteen thousand miles per hour.

"I hope you can see by all this that today if in any area of life we are thirty or less months behind, we are further behind than our fathers were if they were twenty or thirty years behind. Now let me pose the question as to how we have kept up this pace in the moral and spiritual fields. Any one can see we are far behind in this area. We are trying to run a space age on a horse and buggy moral and spiritual condition. This will not suffice. Time has collapsed on us. How much longer do we have? It depends on how much religion we have to control the use of our technology. Technology has no morals; it must depend on man to furnish this. Technology doesn't care if it is used for good or evil. It can eliminate people or it can eliminate disease. It can destroy city or produce enormous power for good. Here is the question I pose: will our technical progress create a hell on earth or a paradise? It will depend on how you and I respond to the Love of God."

Cat Makes Two-Thousand Mile Journey

A CAT, Skunky by name, after traveling two thousand miles in one and one-half years, turned up at his old home in Minneapolis -- all the way from Alhambra, California. Ralph Morie, who came to Alhambra three years ago with his wife and three children, tells the story:

"We left Skunky – a black cat with a white stripe – with my sister-in-law, Mrs. Joyce Johnston, in Columbia Heights near Minneapolis. The kids put up a fuss so we had him shipped out to us by air. A year and a half ago Skunky disappeared. Now we get a letter from my sister-in-law saying the cat is there – skinny and starved and footsore – but alive.

"I don't know how he did it – he came out by air so he couldn't have seen any landmarks to travel by."

Is Morie going to send for the cat again?

"I think we'll leave him where he wants to be," Morie said, "he's earned it."

Facts of Fingerprints

AT THE start of the current fiscal year, the Federal Bureau of Investigation had 167,523,012 sets of fingerprints in its files. However, the FBI explained that many of the fingerprints in the files are duplications, since the files include both criminal and civil files. A man with a criminal record who has seen military service, worked for a defense contractor and traveled abroad, might have his fingerprints in the files four times.

The FBI receives about 22,000 sets of fingerprints daily. And remember – with amazement – all fingerprints are different.

One Thousand Megaton

A UNITED States Air Force adviser says Soviet scientists probably are working on a gigantic nuclear warhead of one thousand megatons – equivalent to one billion tons of TNT. Presently, the Russians claim a warhead of one hundred megatons, and have tested one of fifty megatons. The largest American warheads are in the twenty-forty megaton range. The bombs that were dropped on Hiroshima and Nagasaki were twenty kiloton – twenty thousand tons of TNT.

Concerning this power, Arnold Toynbee, British historian, wrote:

"If we know the past we can predict the future. And, being that the human race is armed with weapons of tremendous destruction, predicting the future is not a luxury but a matter of life and death."

Plenty O' Pigs

A sow owned by farmer Aksel Egedee, has given birth to thirty-four piglets, which Danish veterinary experts in Copenhagen believe is a world record. The sow produced fifteen piglets one day and another nineteen early the next day.

Rare Tigers

THE Bristol, England, zoo has received from India two of the rarest animals in captivity – blue-eyed, blackstriped blonde tigers named Champos and Chemeli. Purchase and transport costs came to nearly twenty-eight thousand dollars.

America's First Quints

JAMES and the four Marys born to Andrew James and Mary Ann Fischer at Aberdeen, S. D., two months prematurely, have a good chance of becoming the first quintuplets born in this country to ever survive.

Even before they came, their parents had difficulty rearing their first five children with the father's take-home pay of seventy-six dollars a week as a wholesale grocery shipping clerk. They kept two cows, a money saver in feeding five youngsters, calves, chickens and two pet dogs, on a rented farm with a drafty nine-room house.

The quints have changed all that. The nation's response has been spontaneous. The Aberdeen Chamber of Commerce has become a clearing house for the gifts that cascaded from neighbors, friends and strangers across the land. They will have substantial savings accounts from banks, baby food by the case, a new sizable house to be built by volunteers and equipped with modern appliances, and clothing, toys, medicines, drugs, to carry them far into the future.

For the thirty-year-old red-headed tomboy and her thirty-eight-year-old husband who first met at a bowling alley, the event has changed their lives. She is a business school graduate; he has been working since the age of eleven and could only finish the eighth grade. But they found common interests in home and church and the outdoors. Now they are the nation's most famous parents.

Generous Americans will not let them forget their new distinction. Already, the quints and their brother and four sisters promise to be well provided for to their maturity and beyond. After all, there is only one quintuplet birth in forty-two million and these are the first in the history of the nation who survived birth.

Mummy and Her Fifth

In Sidney, Australia, a husband said: "Mummy has done it again." John Struthers said this to two of his daughters after his wife gave birth to her fifth set of twins. A Sidney gynecologist said the odds against that many twins in one family are about three billion to one. The boy and girl, each weighing five pounds, brought the Struthers brood to fourteen children. Four arrived singly.

Wool-Classing Machine

Ninety dollar machine may save millions. An Australian grazier (rancher) has invented a wool-classing machine which he believes could save the world's wool industry millions of dollars a year. Today, wool is classed by highly trained experts on the feel and sight of the newly shorn fleeces.

The inventor of the new machine is Clive Wawn, World War II Spitfire pilot, who lives at Dunkeld, near Hamilton in western Victoria. Wawn's machine projects a magnified image of a wool sample on to a revolving screen. The screen carries a graduated scale which measures the distance between the kinks (or crimps) in the wool fiber. The scale is accurate to within 1-600th part of an inch, Wawn says. He claims the machine would enable more accurate classing of wool and could increase the value of the clip by about a penny a pound. He estimates the machine can be produced for ninety dollars. Its saving to the Australian industry alone would be about six million pounds ($13,440,000).

Aged Wood Pipes

Wood water pipes, one hundred and fifty-three years old, were recently dug up from under Washington D.C.'s Pennsylvania Avenue by the construction crew of a utility company.

The National Lumber Manufacturers Association said the pipes were well-preserved, fifteen-inch diameter logs of ten feet in length with a neatly bored hole through the core. The logs were joined with cast-iron nipples that formed water-tight joints by the swelling action of the wood.

In the first little mountain pastorate God gave me – Lima Baptist Church – the C. C. Goodwin family brought water from a mountain spring two hundred yards from the home by means of several dozen logs through the cores of which holes had been bored. These logs served as water carriers for fifty years.

England's Hardest Hitting Tanks

Racing out of a ditch, the British Army's latest battle tank – the fifty-ton Chieftan – was put through its paces at a testing ground at Chertsey, England. The tank is claimed by the army to be the hardest hitting tank in the world and five years ahead of any other tank available to NATO forces. Its main armament is a newly-developed 120-millimeter gun. It has a top speed of twenty-five miles per hour and can run on all types of fuel.

America's "Starlifter"

THE C141 Starlifter, a giant jet military transport plane, made its debut in rollout ceremonies at the Lockheed Aircraft plant. President Kennedy pressed a gold key at the White House which rolled back the hangar doors. The huge four-engine jet can fly any ocean non-stop with one hundred fifty-four troops and a seventy thousand pound cargo. It is the world's fastest plane of its type.

Massive Elevator Constructed

MANY a kernel of grain can be accommodated in the massive elevator being built about a mile north of Plainview, Texas, by Producers Grain Corporation. Job superintendent Bill Walraven of Albuquerque, N. M., said the elevator would be over a fifth of a mile long when finished. The tower is two hundred and twenty-eight feet tall. Capacity of the elevator will be nearly five million bushels.

Echo I — Going Strong

ECHO I, the balloon-satellite that has been America's silvery star in the sky, marked its third birthday in space – on August 12, 1963. The rugged little plastic balloon has demonstrated an endurance that amazes scientists.

When Echo I was launched from Cape Canaveral on August 12, 1960, experts predicted it would remain inflated for about two weeks and that after it collapsed it might orbit for a year or two. But Echo I has kept sailing right along. By its third birthday, it had racked up a total of thirteen thousand, five hundred orbits around the earth and traveled nearly four hundred and twenty-five million miles in space. And though it is wrinkled and battered and only about half its original hundred-foot diameter in size, Echo I is still capable of bouncing radio signals.

History was made on August 13, 1960, when Collins Radio Company space tracking antennas located at Cedar Rapids, Iowa, and at Richardson, Texas, locked on Echo I for the first two-way voice radio transmission via a man-made satellite.

A week later, Collins engineers and Associated Press personnel, utilizing AP wirephoto equipment, "bounced" a picture of President Eisenhower off the surface of Echo I for the first facsimile transmission in space. Since then Collins engineers have continued to use Echo I for radio and teletype transmissions. In keeping a constant check on the satellite they may have found the reason for its unexpected long life.

When Echo I was put into orbit, it had an apogee of one thousand and thirty-six miles and a perigee of nine hundred and fifty-eight miles. As was to be expected, Echo I started settling toward the earth. But when its perigee – the lowest point in its orbit – reached five hundred, fifteen miles, Echo I surprised the scientists by starting to climb again. Since then, its apogee – the highest point of its orbit – has reached thirteen hundred miles. Now it is sailing along with an apogee of eleven hundred, fifty two miles and a perigee of six hundred, sixty four miles.

Echo I's up-and-down traveling appears to have a regular cycle with about one year required to complete that cycle.

"The best explanation we have for Echo I's long life is that the sun apparently gives it life," Richard Kaiser, Collins' senior staff engineer and manager of its space communications research station at Richardson, says. "But because of its comparatively large surface in relation to its weight of only a hundred and thirty-six pounds, it appears to be able to utilize solar energy and what is called 'a solar wind' helps push Echo I around."

Statistics on Telstar

TELSTAR is a 34½ inch sphere; it weighs one hundred seventy pounds and has fifteen thousand parts. The planned orbit: Apogee, 5,705, Perigee, 3,450 miles. Orbit period: one hundred fifty-six minutes. It has an expected life of two years. Sponsors: Bell Telephone Laboratories and American Telephone and Telegraph Co., in co-operation with National Aeronautics and Space Administration. The purpose: Test broadband microwave communications in space; study effects of radiation and micrometeorites on satellite. Cost: About fifty million dollars.

It is considered to be one of the greatest scientific advances in the history of mankind. Research engineers sent a newspaper front page into space and back in one minute via Telstar. Among other things, the method used in the experiment could be applied in publishing a worldwide daily newspaper, with the same edition being printed within minutes in locations thousands of miles apart. At its closest point during the experiment, Telstar passed 3,207 miles away. Its farthest point was 5,705 miles. Telstar's capability is six hundred telephone channels or one television channel.

The Governor of California talked into space to the Governor General of Stockholm, Sweden, at the opening of California's annual State Fair; thus giving it the most unusual inaugural in its long history. Surrounded by a crown of adults and children, the Governor conversed with Johan Hagander in Stockholm via a three foot communications satellite, Telstar, wheeling at twelve thousand miles an hour around the earth.

"I hope," said Governor Brown, in comments relayed throughout the Fair Grounds, "that Telstar will be an instrument of peace in the years ahead. The message came through from Stockholm 'clear as a bell.' "

Students of Bible prophecy have often wondered what means would be available in the future for the fulfillment of predictions concerning the entire world. For example, the Bible predicts the martyrdom of two special witnesses in Jerusalem, and says: "And they of the people and kindreds and tongues and nations shall see their dead bodies three days and a half, and shall not suffer their dead bodies to be put in graves" (Revelation 11:9).

Telstar is an indication of how easily such a prophecy can be literally fulfilled. And there shall doubtless be further development and perfection of Telstar.

It ill becomes atheists to laugh at seeming impossibilities; for it is true as the Lord said: "The Scripture can not be broken."

"Pin-Point" X-ray at Franklin

FRANKLIN Hospital has installed the West Coast's first polytome, an X-ray machine that rotates back and forth or in circles, to produce pictures that are revolutionizing the diagnosis of bone ailments. The machine was invented in France in 1949. Instead of producing the standard X-ray picture, which might include all the bones front to back in a chest exposure, the polytome camera can zero in on a specific area as small as the head of a pin.

Seventy-Seconds Movies

A MOVIE camera and viewing system that produces films ready for showing in only seventy seconds is being shown at the Western Electric Show in San Francisco. Developed for use in filming trace patterns on TV-like devices, the new process is self-contained and automatic, the film developing as it is fed through the system after shooting.

BEHAVIOR

Capitol for One Day

ONCE I spent the day in Lancaster, Pennsylvania. It is distinguished in a way no other city is. It was the national capitol for one day – the day when the Continental Congress, driven from Philadelphia, sat there on September 27, 1777.

But that is longer than some people rule their tongues.

The Might of Mites

HENRY GILL, night elevator operator in the Police Headquarters Building in Chicago, wiped the perspiration from his brow as he finished a trudge down from the tenth floor. "Something," he said, "is wrong with my elevator. It won't work." He and an engineer went back up, pried among the cables of the disabled machine, and then announced it was working again. Two cockroaches had become wedged in an electrical connection.

How often, in our churches and homes, has there been "something wrong" because of people who climb the miff-tree or hide in the pout closet or sulk in the tent. "To your tents, O Israel," never means the sulk tent.

History a Repeater

ARISTOTLE, the great Greek philosopher who lived more than two thousand years ago, wrote this about the young people of his time:

"Their faults are nearly all errors of exaggeration. They overdo in cases of love and in all other things. They imagine that they know everything, and stubbornly stand on their point. They like to crack jokes for joking is the bad manneredness of the well mannered."

Honey Bird

IN BECHUANALAND this bird lives. This honey bird is a creature of almost mythical behavior. African travelers state that when one of these birds sees a human being it whistles to attract attention, and then leads the way to a tree where wild bees have hived. It sits by while its human friends chop down the tree and take their fill of honey. It then proceeds to feast on the comb that is left, and especially on the young bee grubs.

We find many human counterparts of this bird – who are willing to let the "other fellow" do the work and they partake of the benefits and feast on the "honey."

Excitement and Efforts Over Elvis

A MEMPHIS newspaper, dated Dec. 6, 1959, carries the news that efforts by Carol Frazer, 17, to have a street named after singer Elvis Presley were realized. To a still uncompleted subdivision lane, the city fathers of suburban Whitehaven have assigned the name "Elvis Place." Miss Frazer said she was so excited she didn't know what to do. Probably go to a movie, she thought.

"I've seen all of them," she said, "'Love Me Tender,' 107 times, 'Loving You,' 110 times, 'King Creole,' 91 times, and 'Jailhouse Rock,' 79 times."

Carol, who moved from New Orleans to be near Elvis, lives in a tiny Memphis flat with her mother. And: twelve scrapbooks about Elvis, 40,000 pictures of him, and a man-size cardboard replica of him overlooking her bed. Give your own thought to this. Make your own comment – if you desire.

Compressed Air

A French inventor perfected a pistol that knocks out a victim with a strong blast of compressed air.

But we could find more knocked out by "hot air" from mouth and pen and printed page than ever were knocked out by a pistol strong with a blast of compressed air. "The tongue is a world of iniquity." A poison pen is pernicious pollution. A page of printed error is a vulture's perch in the parlor.

Many Folks and Much Ado

Here is the account of how women acted when holiday bargains were offered in Bronx, New York. So says the Associated Press:

"They shoved. They kicked. Some wielded elbows and occasionally a hat pin flashed. Those five thousand women shoppers wanted to get at the Washington's Birthday bargains inside a Bronx department store. And they meant it. Before they were through it was a near riot with two persons injured, including a woman who was shoved through a 5-foot-wide, 14-foot-high plate glass window. Some fifty policemen and three fire companies needed two hours to control the crowd that gathered in front of Alexander's department store, coveting such items as 29-cent tooth paste and $999 mink coats.

"Shoppers began gathering at 7 A.M. with the temperature at eight degrees, and surged forward, smashing the display window, when the store opened just before 9 A.M. Bernard Gaor, assistant manager, said the store traditionally drew throngs for its Washington's Birthday sale, but previously, nothing like this. He said that with the New York City newspapers blacked out in a strike, the store had mailed out thousands of sixteen-page shopping lists. The store's sale notice advertised electric broilers for $1.99, imported cashmere sweaters for $9.95 and phonograph records for as little as nine cents.

"Gaor said he had more than four hundred and fifty clerks on hand to handle the crowd and that the store was calling in others to work on an overtime basis. The assistant manager said, 'Ninety-nine per cent of the people here today live in the Bronx. You can tell that they are in a good mood because we haven't had any fights.' He confided, however, that several articles of wearing apparel had been damaged by overzealous shoppers.

"Casualties of the sidewalk crush were Maria Martinez who was taken to Morrisania Hospital with a lacerated scalp, suffered while being pushed through a window; and Petra Gonzales who was treated by a store nurse for cuts on her left leg. Police set up rope barriers and used loudspeakers to restore order and channel customers into the store in an orderly fashion.

"Gaor said police and firemen allowed one thousand to fifteen hundred persons into the store every hour. In the afternoon there still were eight thousand persons behind the barriers. The sidewalk in front of the store was littered with buttons from women's coats. Lying among the buttons were a high-heeled shoe and a moccasin."

Have your own thoughts about such a matter.

Unfair to Women

WRITES Clayton Rand:

"On account of a longshoremen's strike ships full of rotting bananas could not be unloaded. On account of a strike by printers for fringe benefits, newspapers denied the freedom of the press guaranteed by the Constitution are not published, to idle thousands of workers and penalize the commerce of cities. Sometimes labor grievances are downright silly, as in the jurisdictional dispute in New York City between its carpenters and plumbers over the installation of kitchen sinks in a big department project. The plumbers said fitting sink tops in place was their job, carpenters said it was theirs, and with three hundred families waiting to occupy the apartments, it took two weeks to reach this compromise. The carpenters put the sink tops in place with screws, instead of nails customarily used. Then the plumbers loosened the screws, hooked up the sinks and screwed the tops tight again.

"But the two hundred women factory workers in London who recently struck, had a real grievance. An efficiency expert had kept his eye on the girls who went to the powder room. By using a stop watch, he found that within four hours, the girls made five hundred and nine trips, each spending an average of 10.7 minutes. The men made only two hundred and thirty trips and spent only 2.5 minutes each. The strike was settled by management permitting the girls to smoke at their benches, and they promised not to wash their stockings nor give one another permanents on company time."

This makes us think of some things the Bible says about women and their "wearings."

"In that day the Lord will take away the bravery of their tinkling ornaments about their feet, and their cauls, and their round tires like the moon, the chains, and the bracelets, and the mufflers, the bonnets, and the ornaments of the legs, and the headbands, and the tablets, and the earrings, the rings, and nose jewels, the changeable suits of apparel, and the mantles, and the wimples, and the crisping pins, the glasses, and the fine linen, and the hoods, and the veils" (Isaiah 3:18-23).

Higher Education Hitting Low Key

PIANO smashing, which bids to become a fad on college campuses, came to Wayne State University with a fraternity group cast in the role of wreckers. Newsmen and television crews, plus several hundred students, saw the fraternity men smash a piano to bits in four minutes, fifty-one seconds. Wayne then claimed the record as it bettered the 4:55 mark set recently at California Institute of Technology.

Axes, crowbars, sledge hammers and other assorted weapons were used in the onslaught. The idea was to reduce the piano to such fragments that each piece could be stuffed through a circular hole, nine inches in diameter.

"The foolishness of fools is folly" (Proverbs 14:24). Yes, even among those who claim to be educated.

Bug Bite Brings $625,000

A $625,000 damage award to a railroad freight yard conductor who said he was bitten by an insect while working near a pool of stagnant water was upheld by the Supreme Court. The worker, James Gallick of Cleveland, contended body ulcerations developed from the bite and resulted in amputation of his legs. He said his employer, the B & O Railroad, was negligent in permitting the pool near its tracks.

Gallick said that while working along a track under the Columbus Road Bridge in Cleveland, he felt a bite on his left leg above the knee. He reached down, felt an insect about a half-inch thick and two inches long, squeezed it and heard it "pop," felt it roll down his trouser leg to the ground but never saw it. A jury in Cuyahoga County common pleas court awarded him $625,000. The Ohio Court of Appeals, however, set aside the award. Gallick then appealed to the highest tribunal.

Behold, what a pile of money one little bite bringeth! What profit from a little pain? Deserved profit? You answer!

Italy Boasts Tallest Dam, Most Visitors

ANYONE who calls Italy a "second class nation" is liable to be hit by a ballistic pizza. Italy now has:

The tallest dam in the world, the 860-foot-high Vajont Dam where the Piave tumbles out of the Alps.

More tourists – roughly twenty million foreigners – than any other country, spending $720,000,000 a year. Only 5% of the tourists are Americans, 25% Germans.

Two missile-firing cruisers for its revived navy.

The biggest output of films outside Asia – 270 in one year.

The biggest increase in autos, six times as many as in 1950.

A low unemployment rate.

Thinking about a nation's boasts makes us think of some Bible boasts:

"Let not him that girdeth on his harness *boast* himself as he that putteth it off" (I Kings 20:11).

"My soul shall make her *boast* in the Lord" (Psalm 34:2).

"In God we *boast* all the day long" (Psalm 44:8).

"How long shall . . . all the workers of iniquity *boast* themselves?" (Psalm 94:4).

"*Boast* not thyself of tomorrow" (Proverbs 27:1).

"Why *boasteth* thou thyself in mischief?" (Psalm 52:1).

"Shall the axe *boast* itself against him that heweth therewith?" (Isaiah 10:15).

"Thou that makest thy *boast* of the law, through breaking the law dishonourest thou God?" (Romans 2:23).

"The tongue is a little member and *boasteth* great things" (James 3:5).

"*Boasters*, inventors of evil things" (Romans 1:30).

Chewing Chips

A SIX-FOOT Scotsman laid claim to the salted potato chip eating championship of the world. Richard McLeod downed thirty bags of the crisp delicacy – total of seventy-five ounces – in fifty-six minutes. Previous claimant of the title was Bob Speele, a miner in Northumberland, whose mark was twenty-nine packets in sixty-two minutes in 1956.

Richard McLeod could not, because of this chewing of chips, be listed as "a riotous eater of flesh" (Proverbs 23:20). And we do not know if this Scotsman asked God's blessings upon the thirty bags of this crisp delicacy, but we do know that he should have given thanks to God that he suffered no physical injury from such a gormandizing feat.

Costly Capers

QUITE a stir was created in Memphis recently when the newspapers reported that young people broke enough street lights throwing missiles (sometimes whisky bottles) at lights to cost the city a thousand dollars a month – $12,000.00 a year. In speaking of this some poor soul said: "We have the wrongest set of young folks ever was!"

And his remark reminded me of a paragraph in "Light Horse Harry Lee" by Thomas Boyd – a paragraph which told of some events of 1763:

"Their horseplay included 'Strowing the entries in the Night with greasy Feathers; freezing the Bell; Ringing it at late hours of the Night – Making Squibs, & other frightful compositions with Gunpowder, & lighting them in the Rooms of timorous Boys and newcomers.' Drinking wine and spirits was not unknown. Students not only smoked but chewed tobacco. By means of telescopes they ogled women who thought themselves unobserved. They periodically set fire to the college outhouse. With drums they paraded the local strumpets through the Princeton streets. They stole hens and turkeys from the villagers' roosts and roasted them over the fires in their rooms to piece out their scanty meals. And they were lively enough to protest against bad fare by moulding an effigy of Jonathan Baldwin, the college steward, later a commissary officer in the Revolutionary army, in his own rancid butter and hanging it by the neck from the rafters of the dining-hall."

Contrast in Conduct

IN MERCED, California, an Air Force sergeant who befriended a crippled widow is heir to an Alaskan mining claim worth about forty million dollars. Sgt. Thomas L. Howlett continues to serve as a jet bomber airman at $480.00 a month. "Money has never meant much to me. However, I'm going to use some of the money to build a church and endow an orphanage."

How different the response to kindness in Wentzville, Missouri. Missouri Highway Patrolmen sought two men who repaid the kindheartedness of John Smith, farmer, near Foristell, by robbing him of $4,778. Smith reported that the men, whom he had permitted to live at his farm for two weeks, bound him in his home, took the money which he received two days before from the sale of a piece of property, and fled in an automobile.

Generous gratitude – one. Base ingratitude – the others. What a contrast!

Lost Wife Minor Matter

IN PENSACOLA, Florida, a seaman reported to the Highway Patrol office that he and his wife hitched a ride with a truck driver at Wauchula. The seaman said he went into a package store. When he returned, the driver and truck were gone. Also his wife and suitcase.

"I don't care about my wife," Patrol Radio Operator John Combs quoted him as saying, "but I do want my seaman's papers back."

Surely such cheap words testify that this young sailor knew not these Bible words: "Whoso findeth a wife findeth a good thing, and obtaineth favour of the Lord" (Proverbs 18:22). "A prudent wife is from the Lord" (Proverbs 19:14).

Kissing a Crime

IN ROME, Italy, kissing in a car is a crime. Italy's highest court has reversed itself and now says it is a crime for a couple to kiss in an automobile even if the windows are frosted over and no one can see inside. The Italian penal code outlaws public kissing. Innumerable persons have been arrested on charges of obscene behavior because police caught them kissing in parked cars. Several appealed on the grounds that a kiss in a car is not public.

Several months ago the court of cassation ruled in one case that a kiss in a car was all right if the car had blinds or if its windows were frosted over. But if a person could see into the car, the court ruled, kissing was illegal. In a decision made known recently the court said any kissing in a car is illegal.

To insert some *fun* just here will, I hope, be excusable: Two Negro boys met one day. One had been studying hygiene and hoping to display his newly acquired knowledge, said to his friend, "See here, Rastus, don't you know going aroun' kissing gals, you gonna git germs and microbes on ya?" "What care I got germs and microbes, I go 'bout kissin' my gal in a sanitary way."

"You do, hows you does it?"

"When I calls on my gal, Sal, I goes across a pasteurized lawn, I hops across propylactic steps, I dashes across a sanitary porch, I knocks on a venilated door, I trots across a renovated rug, I sets down on a medicated couch, I takes that fumigated gal on my etherized knees, and I puts my vaccinated arm around her sanforized waist, and I leans over in a Listerine breath, and I sez, 'Come on, honey, ain't you gonna kiss yo antiseptic poppy?' "

But nobody could term the kiss mentioned in Psalm 85:10 as evil: "Mercy and truth are met together. Righteousness and peace have kissed each other."

But evil are some kisses: "Faithful are the wounds of a friend; but the kisses of an enemy are deceitful" (Proverbs 27:6).

And worshipful with love were the kisses the woman gave Jesus: "And, behold, a woman . . . stood at his feet behind him weeping, and began to wash his feet with tears, and did wipe them with the hairs of her head, and kissed his feet, and anointed them with ointment" (Luke 7:37, 38).

Paul spoke of the holy kiss: "Salute one another with a holy kiss" (Romans 16:16).

Library Fine $2,956

FROM Benton, Illinois, comes the news that the Benton Public Library conducted a drive to get back into circulation overdue books. All fines were suspended during "free days." One borrower returned a novel checked out in 1879. It was eighty-one years overdue. Since the old library association's charges for overdue books were ten cents a day, it would have cost the borrower, long since forgotten, about $2,956.

Chemistry Conquests

CHEMISTRY has provided an answer to sudsy saboteurs at the Old Mill, a popular tunnel of love at the Minnesota State Fair. For the last three years, teen-age pranksters have been foaming up the Old Mill's waterway by dumping detergent at the darkened point where a huge waterwheel creates current to propel the boats.

This year, Jim Orrell, has a counter measure. He called on a University of Minnesota chemist, and has a chemical, one pint of which takes care of soapsuds in ten thousand gallons of water.

"The kids might as well save their money," says Orrell. "At the first sign of suds I come with the chemical." But Orrell admits the kids are still a harmless one-up on him. They're dropping water dye – the kind fliers use from life rafts. "It's the prettiest green you ever saw," said Orrell.

Hounds—Guns—Insanity

In Nacogdoches, Texas, one April, bloodhounds and a National Guard tank flushed out a criminally insane man holed up in the East Texas piney woods with five rifles and shotguns. The man, Ellis Whittaker, broke out of the state hospital for the criminally insane at Rusk, Texas. He shot five bloodhounds and killed a horse a deputy sheriff was riding, when they tracked him down. But when Whittaker saw the tank clanking toward him, he meekly surrendered. He was captured about twenty-two miles northwest of Nacogdoches.

Deputy Sheriff Terry Weems said more bloodhounds were brought up from the Texas state penitentiary at Huntsville and used to track down Whittaker. The dogs flushed Whittaker from his hiding place in thick underbrush. Weems said Whittaker raced out of the brush, spotted the tank and surrendered. Some forty-five state and local police were following the dogs and tank.

Whittaker got his firearms by burglarizing his brother's home in the small town of Lilbert. Whittaker had been committed to the hospital for setting his brother's house on fire. Weems said the National Guard tank was called out as a safety precaution after Whittaker killed the bloodhounds and shot the horse out from under Deputy Ray Smithhart.

Obsessed by Sex

In the Los Angeles crusade, Billy Graham said the young people of the United States are "obsessed by sex." Graham told 45,796 persons who turned out for the fourth meeting of his twenty-five-day crusade there that the obsession stems from a desire for security and that is why sixty per cent of the young people go steady. "America's worship of the goddess of sex is a daily oblation made through all the media of mass communication, invading every phase of life with the enticements of bosoms and legs and rock-and-roll sensuality," he said.

That makes us think of what Mrs. Ella Wheeler Wilcox wrote years ago:

God gave him passions splendid as the sun
Made for the lordliest purpose;
A part of Nature's full and fertile mother heart.
And now, behold what he has done:
In Folly's Court and Carnal Pleasure's Mart,
He flung the wealth God gave him at the start.

And Dr. Louis Evans has said: "We have in the United States twenty-seven million young people who are as spiritually illiterate as if they had been born Hottentots in heathen Africa."

If only we could get all of our young people to obey these words: "Remember now thy Creator in the days of thy youth" (Ecclesiastes 12: 11).

The Accused Killer

There is a rich familiarity about Byron De La Beckwith, the man accused of killing the NAACP organizer in Mississippi. What the sense of familiarity proceeds from, the reader may judge.

Beckwith was not born in Mississippi. His mother, a member of what used to be called the plantation aristocracy, married a Californian and moved with her husband to that state, where Beckwith was born. At three, Beckwith's father died and his mother returned to the ancestral town of Greenwood to raise her son, as one account has it, "amid a Southern plantation atmosphere." She died when the boy was eleven and he was placed in the home of an uncle, who saw to his schooling in the traditional way – prep school, where Beckwith was a weak scholar, then a brief attendance at Mississippi State.

His grandmother was a friend of Jefferson Davis, and correspondence between the two was preserved in the family. When Davis died, Mrs. Davis made a gift of books and china to Beckwith's grandmother, all of which was later given to the University of Mississippi.

Beckwith (called "Delay" by his friends), sometimes seemed "unusual," according to childhood contemporaries, but they dismissed it with, "Well, that's Delay." As a Marine he rose to be staff sergeant and was wounded in the Pacific.

Afterward he married into an "old family" that traced its lineage to Roger Williams, the founder of Rhode Island, but the marriage was unsuccessful. Beckwith became a tobacco salesman with the reputation of having a "gift for gab." Some of his friends regarded him as "eccentric."

He reportedly stood guard personally in the Greenwood bus station to preserve separate waiting rooms. He engaged the National Council of the Episcopal Church in a dispute over integration. He wrote and distributed handbills.

The FBI determined that fifteen thousand Golden Hawk rifle sights had been imported into this country. Five were sold in Mississippi, all accounted for but one. The fifth one was traced to Beckwith, who when he heard his house was being watched, surrendered to the FBI.

Beckwith's home was described as follows in a report to the Memphis Commercial Appeal:

> Once a showplace, the family home . . . still remains in the family. Now delapidated and weather-beaten, the three-story wood frame building, was originally furnished in priceless antiques, some of which have been distributed to other family members. Unpainted for years, strips of white paint cling to the walls with almost visible effort. The yard is unkempt and bare of shrubbery, but a political sign, "Sullivan For Me In '63," has been attached at the front entrance. Visitors described as "dismal" the interior of the house where wallpaper was sagging from the ceilings and walls.

Byron De La Beckwith was living here alone when arrested and charged with murder.

BIBLE

What Choice

"I'm glad for the Bible. It gives me a chance to see how other men chose – and the results. There's the contrast between Abraham's choice and Lot's choice before Sodom. There's Moses' choice of his fellows rather than the riches of Egypt. There's

Joseph's choice in the prison house of Potiphar, and Daniel's choice of the king's vegetables rather than his meats. Paul paid a glorious price when he chose his lot with the early Christians. Christ made marvelous choice when he set his face toward Jerusalem, at the Garden of Gethsemane, and in the Judgment Hall.

Adam's choice cost him Eden; Esau's, his birthright; Achan's, his life; Lot's, his home and herds; Absalom's, his father's throne; Saul's, his kingdom; the rich young ruler's, the companionship of Christ. Judas lost his apostleship; Demas, his discipleship. Pilate, Agrippa, and Felix chose wrong and missed immortality. Ananias' choice fooled no one but himself. Caleb and Joshua chose well, while Jonah's first choice nearly shipwrecked himself and the crew."

Ye older ones, what would your answer be as a father, as a mother, as a Christian leader, if, concerning our young people, God would say to you today, "Ask what I shall make of these young people." Would your answer prove you know how to choose the things that matter most? Would your answer prove you are a wise leader – for them?

The Hymn of the Hebrew Maid

Several have asked me who wrote the above-titled poem. Sir Walter Scott wrote it. Note how Scott knew the Bible:

When Israel, of the Lord beloved,
Out from the land of bondage came,
Her father's God before her moved,
An awful guide in smoke and flame.
By day, along the astonished lands,
The cloudy pillar glided slow;
By night, Arabia's crimsoned sands
Returned the fiery column's glow.

There rose the choral hymn of praise,
And trump and timbrel answered keen;
And Zion's daughters poured their lays,
With priest's and warrior's voice between.
No portents now our foes amaze –
Forsaken Israel wanders lone;
Our fathers would not know Thy ways,
And Thou hast left them to their own.

But, present still, though now unseen,
When brightly shines the prosperous day,
Be thoughts of Thee a cloudy screen,
To temper the deceitful ray.
And O, when stoops on Judah's path
In shade and storm, the frequent night,
Be Thou, long-suffering, slow to wrath
A burning and a shining light.

Our harps we left by Babel's streams –
The tyrant's jest, the Gentile's scorn;
No center round our altar beams,
And mute are timbrel, trump, and horn.
But Thou hast said, the blood of goats,
The flesh of rams, I will not prize –
A contrite heart, and humble thoughts,
Are Mine accepted sacrifice.

A Coleridge Comment

Grown gray, grown gray, reading the story of the Prodigal Son, Coleridge, his heart greatly moved, his throat full of sobs, said:

It finds me, it finds me,
This Divine Book is a mould that fits my heart.

The Bible is a book like the needle to the North Pole – it points to heaven. "Thy Word is a lamp unto my feet and a light unto my path."

Within that awful volume lies
The mystery of mysteries!
And better had they ne'er been born,
Who read to doubt, or read to scorn.

And those who put question-marks after the eternal affirmations of the Bible are guilty of showing forth "the dopy drivel of rheumatic brains."

The Best Purchase

John Wanamaker, world's merchant prince, companion of kings and rulers and presidents, began his career as an errand boy at $1.25 a week. He became one of the largest purchasers of merchandise the world has ever known. But, let us ask, what did he consider his greatest purchase? Hear ye him: "I have, of course, made large purchases of property in my lifetime, involving many millions of dollars, and the buildings and grounds in which we are now meeting represent a value of approximately twenty billion dollars. But it was as a boy, in the country, at eleven years of age, that I made my biggest purchase. In a little mission Sunday school of the Lutheran Church I bought from my teacher a small red leather Bible about eight inches long and six inches wide. The Bible cost me $2.75 – which I paid in small installments as I saved up my own money which I had earned."

The *Herald Tribune* of New York, commenting on this statement, said, "Later deal in millions called small compared with buying Holy Writ at eleven."

If more people really read the Bible, they, too, would have some great testimonies to make as to its worth to the individual life.

Some Carelessness

FATHER: "Why were you kept in at school?"

Son: "I didn't know where the Azores were."

Father: "In the future, just remember where you put things."

And what that father knew about the Azores is more than many know of what God's Book teaches about some things.

Beneath the Surface

RUSKIN says that many people read the Scriptures as the hedgehog gets grapes. The old monks said that this animal rolled over among the grapes and carried what happened to stick to its spines, or quills. So the "hedgehoggy" readers roll themselves over on a portion of the Scriptures and get only what happens to stick. But you can get only the skins of Bible verses that way. If we want the juice, we must press them in clusters.

Bible Statistics

BOOKS of Old Testament – 39.

Books of New Testament – 27.

Total number of books – 66.

Chapters in Old Testament – 929.

Chapters in New Testament – 260.

Total number chapters – 1,189.

Verses in Old Testament – 33,214.

Verses in New Testament – 7,959.

Total numbers of verses – 41,173.

Words in Old Testament – 593,493.

Words in New Testament – 181,253.

Total number of words – 774,746.

Letters in Old Testament–2,728,100.

Letters in New Testament – 838,380

Total number of letters – 3,566,480.

The shortest chapter is Psalm 117.

Ezra 7:21 contains all the letters of the alphabet except "j."

Esther 8:9 is the longest verse.

John 11:35 is the shortest verse.

There is no word of more than six syllables in the Bible.

Blessed Book

A YOUNG Christian, packing his bag for a journey, said to a friend, "I have nearly finished packing. All I have to put in the bag yet are a guide book, a lamp, a mirror, a microscope, a volume of fine poetry, a few biographies, a package of old letters, a book of songs, a sword, a hammer, and a set of books I have been studying." Then he placed his Bible in a corner of the suitcase and closed it.

All this – and more – is the blessed

Word of God which God has magnified above His own holy name (Psalm 138:2).

If this young man had put in a can of honey and a bag of gold, he would have included something else that the Bible is.

Splitting and Saving

THE splitting of a diamond and the saving of a fortune is now history. In New York the fabulous Vargas diamond, largest in existence, lay resplendent before a tense workman. The moment had arrived, after three months of computations, when it was to be cut into the first of two million dollars' worth of smaller stones.

The veteran cutter raised his hand. The 726 carat stone would split cleanly or would shatter into fragments. He struck a wedge sharply – once, twice, three times. The gem severed perfectly at the third blow. The cutter breathed a sigh of relief, then fainted.

Arian Grasselley, who had been living on cigars and black coffee for weeks as he thought of the ordeal confronting him, was still weak as he told of the operations which took place. He explained that his tension was unusually high because of the three blows necessary. A diamond usually splits with one blow. The ticklish work took place in the Fifth Avenue office of Harry Winston, the owner.

"All day long we had worked at grooving the stone in just the right place," Grasselley related. "When we were ready I took a square edged knife and fitted it into the groove. I did not think my usual hammer was heavy enough, so I used the axle from an old motor that was handy."

After the first blow there was a split only three millimeters deep. Grasselley struck again, and the cut deepened only a few more millimeters. The third time he hit harder. The stone split as calculated. The diamond, the third largest ever found, was discovered in 1933 by two Brazilian diamond hunters. They got $250,000 for the rough stone. Winston bought it for $700,000.

Rough and blue white, the diamond measured 2½x2x1 inch. It was heavier than the famed Jonker diamond which yielded 12 stones, the largest 126 carats. The Vargas stone, named after President Vargas of Brazil, will be cut across grain with a saw and may be split with the grain four or five times more before all the cut gems, the largest one of 160 carats, are obtained.

Fortunes in one diamond. But greater fortunes there are in single chapters, yea, in single verses of the Bible which, even as the judgments of God, are "more to be desired than gold, yea, than much fine gold" (Psalm 19:10).

Light Can Cut Diamonds

THE General Electric Company of Schenectady, New York, revealed a pencil thin beam of light which actually cut diamonds. It is called a "laser," which is the abbreviation for "light amplification by stimulated emission of radiation."

The light is compacted into the heart of a ruby, then forced out one end of it into a very narrow beam which cuts the diamonds.

This experiment points the way to high speed, inexpensive techniques for machining all sorts of extremely hard metals. The head of the general engineering laboratory said: "If we can cut diamonds, we can use the light beam to cut anything."

The diligent student of the Scriptures has known all along that a thin beam of spiritual light can cut through the hardest of hearts. For example, when the Apostle Peter and his contemporaries, on the day of Pentecost, turned the light of the Gospel upon the men who were guilty of the cold blooded murder of the Lord Jesus, they were cut to the heart and asked, "What shall we do?" (Acts 2:37). And when that hard-hearted Saul of Tarsus was exceedingly mad against the Lord and against all who believed in Him, as he was on his persecuting way to Damascus, he was stricken down by a light shining from heaven – a light above the brightness of the sun – he fell to the earth, and asked: "Who art thou, Lord?" and again, "Lord, what wilt thou have me to do?" (Acts 9).

After this blasphemous and injurious person believed, and was saved and was called to be an apostle, he wrote to the believers in Corinth: "For God, who commanded the light to shine out of darkness, hath shined in our hearts, to give the light of the knowledge of the glory of God in the face of Jesus Christ" (II Corinthians 4:6).

And to the Christians at Philippi, he wrote: "But what things were gain to me, those I counted loss for Christ. Yea doubtless, and I count all things but loss for the excellency of the knowledge of Christ Jesus my Lord: for whom I have suffered the loss of all things, and do count them but dung, that I may win Christ" (Philippians 3:7, 8).

Locusts Swarm for Miles

On April 18, 1952, the news broadcast told of a dense locust swarm which covered an area two by four miles in the southern outskirts of Addis Ababa, Ethiopia. The insects were so thick they bent the branches of trees.

All this in Ethiopia. Yet some Bible doubters and mutilators deny the account the Bible gives of locusts in Egypt in the days of King Pharaoh and God's servant, Moses.

"And the Lord said unto Moses, Stretch out thine hand over the land of Egypt for the locusts, that they may come up upon the land of Egypt, and eat every herd of the land, even all that the hail hath left. And Moses stretched forth his rod over all the land of Egypt, and the Lord brought an east wind upon the land all that day, and all that night; and when it was morning, the east wind brought the locusts. And the locusts went up over all the land of Egypt, and rested in all the coasts of Egypt: very grievous were they; before them there were no such locusts as they, neither after them shall be such. For they covered the face of the whole earth, so that the land was darkened; and they did eat every herb of the land, and all the fruit of the trees which the hail had left: and there remained not any green thing in the trees, or in the herbs of the field, through all the land of Egypt. Then Pharaoh called for Moses and Aaron in haste; and he said, I have sinned against the Lord your God, and against you. Now therefore forgive, I pray thee, my sin only this once, and intreat the Lord your God, that he may take away from me this death only. And he went out from Pharaoh, and intreated the Lord. And the Lord turned a mighty strong west wind, which took away the locusts, and cast them into the Red sea; there remained not one locust in all the coasts of Egypt" (Exodus 10:12-19).

BLESSINGS

When I Found You

IN A scrap book, years old, I found this precious poem – the name of the author not given:

When I found you – all nature seemed
    to call;
The silence of the years that crept along
Now burst into a maddening lyric song,
The very skies took on a different hue –
        When I found you.

A little rill that lay within my heart,
All frozen over with the pain of years,
Broke from its dams, and like refreshing
    tears
Swept through my being – bringing hope
    anew,
        When I found you.

The pagan "I" now stole away in shame,
The angels seemed to peep from every
    space
And all the sunbeams mirrored your dear
    face;
At last I knew that God sent rain and dew,
        When I found you.

And so you brought into my darkened soul
A wondrous light – a knowledge of great
    things;
Then all the evil spirits took to wings
And I at last to righteous things was
    true –
        When I found you.

This sounds something like the words the Apostle Paul wrote to the Philippians: "I thank God upon every remembrance of you" (Philippians 1:3).

The World Is Mine

Today upon a bus, I saw a lovely maid
    with golden hair;
I envied her–she seemed so gay–and
    wished I were as fair.
When suddenly she rose to leave, I saw
    her hobble down the aisle;
She had one foot and wore a crutch, but
    as she passed, a smile.
Oh, God, forgive me when I whine;
I have two feet–the world is mine!

And then I stopped to buy some sweets.
    The lad who sold them had
Such charm, I talked with him–he said
    to me;
"It's nice to talk with folks like you.
You see," he said, "I'm blind."
Oh, God, forgive me when I whine;
I have two eyes–the world is mine!

Then, walking down the street, I saw a
    child with eyes of blue.
He stood and watched the others play;
It seemed he knew not what to do.
I stopped for a moment, then I said:
"Why don't you join the others, dear?"
He looked ahead without a word, and then
I knew he could not hear.
Oh, God, forgive me when I whine;
I have two ears–the world is mine!

With feet to take me where I'd go,
With eyes to see the sunset's glow,
With ears to hear what I would know,
Oh, God, forgive me when I whine;
I'm blessed, indeed! The world is mine.

–Author Unknown

BROTHERLY LOVE

Campaign for Concern

PRINCE William of Orange led his people in a war that lasted thirty-seven years. King William of Spain offered him fabulous sums of money and offered to put him in line for the Spanish throne. But Prince William sent back this message which is embalmed in the hearts of the Dutch people and which illumines the pages of history: "Not for wife, nor children, nor lands, nor life will I mix in my cup one drop of the poison of treason." For his country he cared.

Let us, in wisdom and courage like unto his, show that we care for the souls of men – for the progress of our church. A campaign for *concern* we need and must have!

Chippewa Commandments

IN OSCODA, Michigan, Rev. John Siler gives the Ten Commandments the Chippewa Indians had in the long ago. They are:

1. Never steal, except from an enemy.
2. Respect the aged and harken to them.
3. Be kind to the sick and deformed.
4. Obey your parents.
5. Be modest.
6. Be charitable.
7. Be of good courage, suffer in silence.
8. Avenge personal and family wrongs.
9. Be hospitable.
10. Pray to the Great Spirit.

Many people criticize some of these Chippewa commandments and at the same time look upon God's Ten Commandments as ghostly whispers of a dead age.

Beauty Aids

A DEAR old lady was asked what she used to make her complexion so beautiful and her whole being so bright and attractive. She answered in short:

"I use for my lips, truth;
I use for my voice, kindness;
I use for my eyes, compassion;
I use for my hands, charity;
I use for my figure, uprightness;
I use for my heart, love;
I use for any who do not like me, prayer."

Try this make-up and see what it will do for you.

Gold-Frankincense

"Whoso bears his brother's burden,
Whoso shares another's woe,
Brings his frankincense to Jesus
With the man of long ago.

When we soothe earth's weary children,
Tending best the least of them;
'Tis the Lord Himself we worship,
Bringing gold to Bethlehem."

Tarragon

"TARRAGON is a perennial aromatic herb used for flavoring vinegar!"

What a sentence! Tarragon! *Perennial* tarragon! Used to flavor *vinegar!* Give us plenty of tarragon Christians! There is plenty of vinegar to work on! How we need those who are as tarragonly "sweet as the last smile of sunset," "sweet as the joy which sorrow hushes," "sweet as the look of a lover saluting the eyes of a maid," "sweet as when winter storms have ceased to chide," in order to help others to be as "sweet as the song of the wind in the rippling wheat," "sweet as tropic winds at night," "sweet as the sound of bells at evening," "sweet as the harps that hung by Babel's stream," "sweet as the life of a lily," "sweet as death – annihilating song."

What Is Love?

LET Adelaide P. Love answer that question. She says:

I asked a river, "What is love?"
And it replied: "The Sea."
I asked the question of the trees:
"The wind," they answered me.
I asked a mountain and it cried:
"The Stars!" And I asked a field of grain;
It quickly sang: "The rain! the rain!"
The shore told me it was the tide.
And when I asked my soul, it said:
"Love is the shining key
To that fair golden temple
Of my immortality."

Nisumi says: "Love, like the creeping vine, withers if it has nothing to embrace."

Reciprocity

AN OLD Negro was in the habit of using big words. Someone accused him of using them without knowing what they meant. Somebody asked him the meaning of reciprocity. The old Negro pointed to a chicken house near by, saying, "De hens over dere lay fer de white folks. I lay fer de hens. De white folks, dey lays for me. Dat is reciprocity!"

Penny Truths

A ONE-CENT piece has the United States stamp on it, and the government is back of it as truly as a ten-dollar gold piece. So with truth. God is back of all truth. But some people seem content with penny truths and never go in for ten-dollar truths. Still, in the realm of truth, many have thoughts "as trifling as hobby horses" – and speak things "empty and trifling like little dogs biting one another."

On Good Terms

RECENTLY I looked with interest on a photograph of a dog, a cat, and a canary together – and not molesting each other. The dog was in no wise perturbed by the immediate presence of the cat. The canary was sitting on the edge of a glass in which was some milk-soaked bread. And the cat was very busy trying to get the morsel of bread out of the glass.

But more wonderful the scene when neighbors who bite and scratch each other with sharp tongues live together in quiet and respect and love.

Weight Lifter

FROM Stockholm, August 25, 1953, came the word that Ivan Udodov, Olympic champion and world record holder put Russia in front in the world weight-lifting championships by successfully defending his bantam weight title.

Kamal Mahgoub of Egypt was second and Czechoslovakia's Karel Saitl third. No American was entered in the class.

Udodov won all three divisions of the competition. He pressed 204 pounds, came within one pound of his own world record in the snatch with 215 pounds and lifted 275½ pounds in the clean and jerk for a total of 694½ pounds.

Mahgoub had a total of 650⅓ pounds and Saitl, 617⅓.

But greater than the weight lifting of these three men is the work of those who, for Christ's sake, lighten the loads for the weary of earth. Greater than to say, "I lifted 200 pounds by the strength of my body" is it to say: "Unto thee, O Lord, do I lift up my soul" (Psalm 25:1). And more joyous than to testify of physical strength that lifts huge loads is it to be able truthfully to testify:

In loving kindness, Jesus came,
My soul in mercy to reclaim;
And from the depths of sin and shame,
Through grace, He lifted me.

Americanism

Dr. Henry van Dyke – some years ago – defined Americanism in these words:

"What is true Americanism, and where does it reside? Its dwelling is in the heart. It speaks a score of dialects, but one language, follows a hundred paths to the same goal, performs a thousand kinds of service in loyalty to the same ideal which is its life. True Americanism is this:

"To believe that the inalienable rights of man to life, liberty, and the pursuit of happiness are given by God.

"To believe that any form of power that tramples on these is unjust.

"To believe that taxation without representation is tyranny, that government must rest upon the consent of the governed, and that the people shall choose their own rulers.

"To believe that freedom must be safeguarded by law and order, and that the end of freedom is fair play to all.

"To believe not in a forced equality of conditions and estates, but in a true equalization of burdens, privileges and opportunities.

"To believe that the selfish interests of persons, classes and sections must be subordinated to the welfare of the commonwealth.

"To believe not that all people are good, but that the way to make them better is to trust the whole people.

"To believe that a free state should offer an example of virtue, sobriety and fair dealings to all nations.

"To believe that for the existence and perpetuity of such a state a man should be willing to give his whole service, in property, in labor, and in life."

These words remind us of what Thomas Jefferson said: "The whole government consists in being honest." And of what Cicero said: "Of all human things nothing is more honorable or more excellent than to deserve well of one's country." And of what Ovid wrote: "The love of country is more powerful than reason itself." And what Seneca wrote: "To preserve the life of citizens is the greatest virtue in the father of his country."

Overlooked and Unnamed

In that day of the great revealing of all the things of life, we shall see many of the overlooked of earth – and the unnamed. Which makes us think of what Stanton says, in "Unnamed":

Who would not wish to know the name
Of that sweet maid whose faith in God,
Long years ago, brought healing touch
To Naaman, plunged 'neath Jordan's flood?

BROTHERLY LOVE

The lad whose thoughtful mother gave
The frugal lunch, which then became
A meal to feed the hungry crowd
At Christ's command—what was his name?

That day when, at the Lord's behest,
The favoured two trailed hard the man
Who bore the water pitcher—who was he?
They are unknown;
Their deeds alone live on;
While in the record book of God
Resplendent shine their names.

So may I live, dear Lord, from day to day,
Unknown, save for the gentle touch,
Or soothing word, or helpful hand,
Content to know within the deed book
over there
My name is placed, and thou dost understand.

Kindness Pays Off

TO EX-SERVICEMAN James Kilpatrick, of Glendale, California, it was everyday kindness to share his army coffee and cakes from home with a hungry old French lady; but that kindness so impressed Mme. Jeanne Marshal, 83, of Baccarat, France, whose seven sons were killed by the Nazis, that she willed Kilpatrick $50,000 before her death in January, 1953. The bequest was totally unexpected to Kilpatrick who will use it to study music.

That reminds us of what King David, long centuries ago, said to the men of Jabesh-gilead after he was told that those were the men who buried Saul:

"And David sent messengers unto the men of Jabesh-gilead, and said unto them, Blessed be ye of the Lord, that ye have shewed this kindness unto your lord, even unto Saul, and have buried him. And now the Lord shew kindness and truth unto you: and I also will requite you this kindness, because ye have done this thing" (II Samuel 2:5, 6).

It makes us think, too, of what David said to the lame Mephibosheth as sweet memories of Jonathan surged in David's heart:

"And David said unto him, Fear not: for I will surely shew thee kindness for Jonathan thy father's sake, and will restore thee all the land of Saul thy father; and thou shalt eat bread at my table continually" (II Samuel 9:7).

This urges us to heed the words of the Apostle Paul:

"Put on therefore, as the elect of God, holy and beloved, bowels of mercies, kindness, humbleness of mind, meekness, longsuffering" (Colossians 3:12).

And to rejoice, too, in the celestial arithmetic of the Apostle Peter:

"And to godliness [add] brotherly kindness; and to brotherly kindness charity" (II Peter 1:7).

Quarrel of Tools

IN A carpenter's shop – a very noisy one—the tools were quarreling among themselves. Brother Hammer was in the chair, but the other tools had told him to leave because he was so noisy. He answered, "If I am to leave the carpenter's shop, Brother Gimlet must leave the carpenter's shop; he is such an insignificant thing, and when he has finished his work, he seems to have made so little impression." Little Brother Gimlet rose, and said, "If it is the wish of all of you that I should go, then I will do so, but Brother Screw must go, too. You have got to turn him round and round to get him into anything." And Brother Screw said, "If you wish me to go, I will, of course, go, but if I go, Brother Plane must go, too. I know he seems to be doing a lot of work, but it is all superficial; there is no depth in it." And Brother Plane said, "I will go if you wish it, but if I go, Brother

Rule must go, too. He is always telling others what to do." "Well," said Brother Rule, "I will go, but if I go, Brother Sandpaper must go, too; he is always rubbing people the wrong way."

In the midst of all the discussion, the latch of the door was lifted, and into the shop walked the Carpenter of Nazareth. He had come for His day's work. First He put on His apron, and then He went to His bench. In front of Him He had the plan of a pulpit that He wanted to make, from which He might proclaim the message of His love and grace to men. So He took up the hammer, and the little gimlet, and the screw, and He used them. And He took up the rule, and used that. And He took up the plane, and He worked with it. And He took up the sandpaper, and He rubbed off the edges. Then the time of sunset came, and the day's work was done. The Carpenter had finished the pulpit, and it was perfect. And after He had gone, the tools remained silent. They had discovered that the great Carpenter had a work for each, and that they had become workers together with the Son of God.

Some of the quarrels in homes and churches and neighborhoods and among the nations are as wicked in God's sight as the quarrel which Herodias had against the great wilderness preacher, John the Baptist, when she "would have killed him" (Mark 6:19), – because John had said unto King Herod: "It is not lawful for thee to have thy brother's wife" (Mark 6:18).

With emphasis on the word *quarrel*, we should give heed to the words written by the Apostle Paul to the Colossians:

"Put on therefore, as the elect of God, holy and beloved, bowels of mercies, kindness, humbleness of mind, meekness, longsuffering; forbearing one another, and forgiving one another, if any man have a quarrel against any: even as Christ forgave you, so also do ye" (Colossians 3:12, 13).

The Tactful Touch

An irate policyholder managed to barge unannounced into the office of an insurance executive. Without preliminary, he launched into a vehement tirade of abuse. He angrily denounced the company because his claim had not been settled his way. The official listened patiently and courteously until the caller had finished his diatribe. Then he commented smilingly, "Had I not known all the facts involved I think I would have felt as you do about it." He explained the factors that had determined the settlement. He was so tactful about it that the visitor soon recovered his composure. Although he was naturally disappointed over the disposition of his case, he seemed to understand it and left in good humor.

In its derivation "tact" is related to "touch." It suggests a sensitive understanding that prompts consideration for others. It is that poise that enables one to meet calmly difficult situations and aggravating people. Tact is that delicate and sympathetic perception of how to be gracious in dealing with others. It never connotes a compromise with conscience or a surrender to wrong. The man who can tactfully maintain his position without giving needless offense is more effective in his work and more valuable to his associates than the fellow who just blusters his way through.

A beautiful story is told of James Whitcomb Riley, to whose home one day came a hunchbacked little boy with a tear-stained face. With trembling voice he asked, "Mr. Riley, you have seen some crooked soldiers, have you not?" The famed poet looked around and saw a group of youngsters with their wooden swords and guns, intently waiting for his answer. They had told the little cripple that he could not play soldier. Mr. Riley, in whose poems is reflected the heart of childhood, replied: "Of course I have. Not many, though, because crooked soldiers are the bravest and the best and the hardest to get."

Tact is the soft touch of human kindness.

Student Shakes Way to Record

IN SOUTH AFRICA, March 16, 1963, a Capetown University medical student, John Keough, claimed the world's hand-shaking record with sixty thousand shakes in an hour. Keough said his record smashed an old mark of ten thousand, three hundred in nine hours, but did not say who set it. But, with no disparagement of Mr. Keough's feats, I say that the hand that lifts a burden from another or smooths a pillow for some sick one does more good than all the sixty thousand shakes.

$100,000 Royalty

CONGRESS has voted $100,000 to the heirs of an inventor credited by some with a major role in developing the bazooka. The House, passing by voice vote a bill already approved by the Senate, sent it to President Kennedy. It would authorize payment of $100,000 to the estate of Gregory J. Kessenich, late Army officer and civilian employe of the Ordinance Department, who designed a military rocket in 1941, and subsequently patented it.

The Army opposed the bill, saying Kessenich might be classified as *an* inventor of the bazooka rocket but not as *the* inventor. Many ideas and modifications, it said, went into the final design of a self-propelled projectile that would be fired from a hand-carried tube. Kessenich had lost a civil suit for compensation when the Court of Claims held he had no contract to be paid for his device.

More wonderfully profitable it would be if about the heirs of the bazooka "father" it could be said: "Thou shalt also be a crown of glory in the hand of the Lord, and a royal diadem in the hand of thy God" (Isaiah 62:3).

Or – if the heirs would give heed to these words: "If ye fulfil the royal law according to the scripture, Thou shalt love thy neighbour as thyself, ye do well" (James 2:8).

Two Monuments in South Carolina

IN FORT MILL, S. C., is a monument in the small park on the main street dedicated to the slaves of the Confederate people of the area. On the monument are these engraved words:

"Dedicated to the faithful slaves, who, loyal to a sacred trust, toiled for the support of the army with matchless devotion and with sterling fidelity guarded our homes, our women, and children during the struggle for the principles of our Confederate States of America, 1860-1865."

In the little town of Fountain Inn, S. C., standing on the lawn of the home of the late Robert Quillen, newspaper editor, is a monument to the first woman, the first wife, the first mother of the world – Eve. The monument to Eve was erected by Robert Quillen in 1926. This is the first and only monument in the world ever erected to the memory of Mother Eve.

We Are Like Siamese Twins

DR. DONALD Gray Barnhouse wrote the following over ten years ago:

"The oldest United States' born Siamese twins, Margaret and Mary Bigg, were wheeled into a Boston operating room for the removal of Margaret's abdominal tumor. Because they are joined at the base of the spine at an angle, both had to be strapped to operating tables, one level, one tilted. Because they have a common blood system, both had to be anesthetized, but only Margaret suffered post-operative pain and shock. The operation was successful and both are doing fine.

"As I read this item in the daily press, I thought of the way that believers are spiritually joined together. We are members of His body (Ephesians 1:23; Colossians 1:18, etc.). The Bible uses as an illustration of the relationship between believers that of the single, normal body, the relationship between the hand and the foot. But it helped me to think of this union between the two sisters that it bound them in such a way that if one suffered the other literally suffered.

"How we should react to the needs of the other believers. How we should consider their welfare. How necessary for Siamese twins not to fight with each other, not to disagree violently. How impossible for both to have their own way and go in opposite directions. As they grew together through the years it became necessary for each to establish a system of yieldedness to the will of the other so that they might be in perfect agreement on each step that should be taken. If only it were possible for believers to think of one another in such a manner. Then we would know what it means to prefer one another and to esteem others better than self (Philippians 2:3).

"Spiritually speaking, the union between believers is, positionally, the same as that between Siamese twins. But it is necessary for the Lord to exhort us to spiritual oneness. We are one – therefore we should be one. But alas! Our positional oneness often does not affect our practical oneness. We act, frequently, as though we did not have the same spiritual blood stream, were free to go our own selfish way. But this course of action must have its spiritual effect on us. We must ever study to be spiritually one with all who are truly born the second time."

Say It!

THE great servant of the Lord, B. W. Spilman, wrote this, which would lighten many loads and brighten many roads – if put into practice:

"You have a friend – a man, a woman, a boy or a girl. For some reason you love him very much. Have you ever told him so? Perhaps he would like to have you *say it.*

"Your friend has helped you along the way in the days gone by. Gratitude is in your heart. Do not let it lie buried there – *say it.*

"Some joy has come his way. You rejoice with him. But he will never know it unless you *say it.*

"An honor comes to him. He wins in the game of life, and you are glad – *say it.*

"Your friend succeeds in some task which he has undertaken. You feel a grateful pride that he has done it – *say it.*

"A sorrow comes his way. He may have lost his property. Some of his loved ones may have gone wrong. Disease may have laid its hand on him, taking away the glow of health. You would share the sorrow with him – *say it.*

"Old age, or perhaps a breakdown in the human machinery, may shut in your friend so that he can no longer fare forth among his fellows. Perhaps the end draws near. In your heart you wish him bon voyage as he nears the sunset gate. A word of kindly sympathy would brighten the way – *say it.*

"The messenger of death may have knocked at his door and borne away into the unseen world some loved one. A word of sympathy would help to lighten the load and brighten the way – *say it.*

"A personal word, a telephone call, a postcard, a letter, a telegram, and only a few minutes of time! Silent sympathy. Your own life may be better because of it; but your friend may go to the end of the journey and never know. You may add to the joy; you may lighten the load; you may brighten the way if you only take time to *say it.*"

Ten Commandments of Human Relations

1. Speak to people. There is nothing as nice as a cheerful word of greeting.
2. Smile at people. It takes seventy-two muscles to frown, only fourteen to smile.
3. Call people by name. The sweetest music to anyone's ears is the sound of his own name.
4. Be friendly and helpful. If you would have friends, be friendly.
5. Be cordial. Speak and act as if everything you do is a genuine pleasure.
6. Be genuinely interested in people. You can like almost everybody if you try.
7. Be generous with praise – cautious with criticism.
8. Be considerate with the feelings of others. There are usually three sides to a controversy; yours, the other fellow's and the right one.
9. Be alert to give service. What counts most in life is what we do for others.
10. Add to this a good sense of humor, a big dose of patience and a dash of humility, and you will be rewarded many-fold.

Four Records

OYSTER *has six hundred and twenty pearls.* A pearl oyster has been found containing six hundred and twenty pearls. An expert says it may be a record. Twenty black pearls and six hundred seed pearls were in the oyster, measuring over four square inches.

Long Spitter Misses Mark. From Raleigh, Mississippi, Farmer George Craft won the Mississippi long-range tobacco spitting championship for the seventh straight year with a shot of ten feet, six inches. Distance man Craft finished fourth, however, in the accuracy division but then even the winner, Rapp Moulder, missed the spittoon by two inches.

Champ Typist Hits 260 words per minute. From Paris: Miss Nicole Hubert of Paris has been declared the champion stenotyper of the world for typing at a speed of two hundred sixty faultless words per minute. She was among dozens of young women competing in the event held by the United Nations Educational, Scientific and Cultural Organization.

Hiccups Arrested. From Wenatchee, Washington: Ernest Benson has had the hiccups twenty-four hours a day since 1956. Doctors and homemade remedies have been no help. But Benson dares to hope he has found a cure. A store clerk told him to try black tea and he has been drinking it periodically for two days with nary a hic.

Some records good!

Some records bad, that matter little.

Our records should be records that testify that we have concern for the welfare of others.

"Cannot-ments" By Lincoln

You may be interested in *Lincoln's "Ten Cannot-ments"* which recently appeared in News Notes, a publication for employees of a company in Birmingham, Alabama:

"You cannot bring about prosperity by discontinuing thrift.

"You cannot help the small man by tearing down the big man.

"You cannot strengthen the weak by weakening the strong.

"You cannot lift the wage earner by pulling down the wage payer.

"You cannot help the poor man by destroying the rich.

"You cannot keep out of trouble by spending more than your income.

"You cannot further the brotherhood of man by inciting class hatred.

"You cannot establish security on borrowed money.

"You cannot build character and courage by taking away man's initiative and independence.

"You cannot help men permanently by doing for them what they could and should be doing for themselves."

How far would Mr. Lincoln get today with his Cannot-ments?

Reflections in Verse

In a forty-eight-page book, (the first Mrs. Conny Schaflander, Oak Park, Illinois, has had published,) we find some unpretentious poems which deal, for the most part, with unrequited or blighted love – and they stress courage and endurance in loss and other human suffering. One of the best evocations of the book's mood comes in "I Asked The Sphinx"

"What is love?
It is warmth in a cold world,
It is light in a dark world,
It is joy in a sad world,
It is over so soon.
Why is it over so soon?
Because we don't love ourselves,
Because we don't respect each other,
Because we're misers in what we give,
Because man is only human.
What makes man human?
His great intellectuality,
His great creativity,
His great adaptability,
His great need for love.
Why does man need love?
Because it's a cold world,
Because it's a dark world,
Because it's a sad world,
Because it's over too soon."

CHRIST

Monument Speaks of Substitution

Rev. W. E. Sutterfield, pastor of First Baptist Church, Palmyra, Missouri, writes this:

"Many times I have heard ministers, when discussing the doctrine of substitution in the Bible, give as an illustration the story about a man during the war between the States who offered himself as a 'substitute' for another man who had been condemned to death by a military court. One such incident happened here in Palmyra on October 17, 1862. During the war both the North and the South had troops in this area. At the time this incident happened Palmyra was practically under military law and in a state of siege. Many acts of violence, no doubt, were committed on both sides. It happened that an informer for the military power in the town at the time disappeared and the commander in charge, in order to bring about the return of the missing man and to prevent the recurrence of such incidents, ordered ten men to be shot in reprisal.

"Several men were being detained in Palmyra jail as prisoners of war at that time, and ten men were selected from among them. Of this number one was Wm. T. Humphrey, the father of several children, whose wife pleaded for his release. Because of her physical condition and because Humphrey was the father of several children, the commanding officer struck his name from the list and chose the name of Hiram Smith, a young man without a family. However, it cannot be said that Smith volunteered to take the place of Humphrey, but it is known that he did give his consent and stated that perhaps it were better for a single man to die rather than a man with a family.

"The ten men were shot on 17 October 1862 in what has come to be known as the 'Palmyra Massacre.' At Mt. Pleasant Church cemetery in Mt. Salem Association is a stone erected at the grave of Hiram Smith by G. W. Humphrey, the son of the reprieved man, and an inscription on it which reads:

This monument is dedicated
to the memoy of
HIRAM SMITH
The hero that sleeps beneath the sod here
Who was shot at Palmyra, Oct. 17, 1862
as a substitute for
Wm. T. Humphrey, my father.
—G. W. Humphrey

Depopulation when the Scourge Struck

IN 1878 the yellow fever scourge struck Memphis, Tennessee, with epidemic fury. Within two months it was to depopulate Memphis.

Two earlier disastrous visitations of Yellow Jack – in 1855 and 1873 – had left the inhabitants of the river town ripe for panic, and when, on August 14, 1878, twenty-two new cases of yellow fever followed the death of the first victim the day before, the exodus was on. Within four days – by August 18 – an estimated twenty thousand white residents fled the city. By August 15, the retreat from death had assumed stampede proportions. When the fever struck, the city's population stood at about forty-five thousand.

Before the epidemic was declared ended on October 29, coffins were stacked high on the street corners and the dead wagons rumbled in a steady parade to Elmwood Cemetery where grave diggers worked overtime.

Historians say that 5,150 Memphians died of the fever while other thousands fell ill. As a result, the city's life stopped and Memphis literally died – its charter was revoked and for many years the city remained merely a taxing district of the state.

What a beneficiary is Memphis of the sacrifices of those who discovered and eliminated the cause of yellow death that rode in on the gauzy wings of mosquitoes – and found entrance into human blood through their needle-like, death-dealing mouths.

And what beneficiaries are we all of the labor and genius of many who, for the welfare of others, counted not their lives dear unto themselves. What a beneficiary is the whole wide world of the sacrificial blood-letting and death of Jesus Christ, concerning whom these words are written:

"But we see Jesus, who was made a little lower than the angels for the suffering of death, crowned with glory and honour; that he by the grace of God should taste death for every man. For it became him, for whom are all things . . . in bringing many sons unto glory, to make the captain of their salvation perfect through sufferings" (Hebrews 2:9, 10).

Sumner's Statement

THE spiritually-minded and spiritually-aflame evangelist, Robert L. Sumner, makes this joyful statement about cancelled debts. He tells of a doctor who died in Chicago and left a will behind which completely wiped out all the unpaid medical fees owed by his patients. Dr. William V. Gooder wrote: "Having practiced medicine and surgery for forty-five years in Marengo, I hereby cancel and forgive all unpaid medical fees owed me by any and all former patients."

The attorney who filed the doctor's will estimated that the unpaid bills totaled around $25,000. The doctor, who died at 79, left an estimated $100,000 estate.

As Sumner states, the good doctor's actions completely and finally cancelled every one of the debts. No heir can ever in the future collect a single dime of the $25,000 total. The once-indebted ones are forever free from the obligations.

Sumner says: "In a much grander and nobler sense, of course, that is part of what happened on the cross of Calvary. There our staggering debt of sin was cancelled once and for all in behalf of each individual willing to accept it." "Blotting out the handwriting of ordinances that was against us, which was contrary to us, and took it out of the way, nailing it to his cross" (Colossians 2:14). That is the way Paul expresses it.

What a thrill to know that the payment accepted for sins need never be made again. Sin once forgiven is sin forever forgiven. And God never *has,* never *can,* never *will* demand two payments for one debt. And it makes us to say, in gratitude, what the Psalmist said: "My lips shall praise thee" (Psalm 63:3).

Estate of $127,000

FROM Casper, Wyoming, February 12, 1960, came the news that two "poor" maiden school teachers, whose top salary was $2,185 a year in 1945 when they retired, have left an estate of $127,000 to Casper's Presbyterian Church. Where did the extra money come from? As administrator of the estate even Casper's First National Bank isn't quite sure. The two school marms had no common stock that would pile up high returns. Most of their savings was in U.S. government Series E saving bonds. They once told a bank official they "wanted to buy bonds to help the war effort, so many of our former students are in the service."

The two teachers, Miss Marie Ross and her sister, Miss Mosa Ross, came west from Trempealeau, Wis. They have no known surviving relatives.

Mosa died in March, 1959, at 82, leaving her estate to Marie. Marie died Jan. 25, 1960, at 87, leaving the $127,000 to the church. Details came out when proceedings were filed this week in Probate Court. About $100,000 is expected to go to the church after court costs and payments of other debts. Marie taught at Hawarden, Iowa, and Mosa taught at Iowa City and Rock River and Lusk, Wyo., before they both came to Casper in 1913. The church said part of the money will be used as a memorial to the two sisters.

How great the gift these two ladies made. Millions of times greater the gift made by Jesus, God's unspeakable gift, as set forth in these words:

"For ye know the grace of our Lord Jesus Christ, that, though he was rich, yet for your sakes he became poor, that ye through his poverty might be made rich" (II Corinthians 8:9).

So much greater than any estate ever given by anyone is man's "redemption . . . according to the riches of God's grace" (Ephesians 1:7), "the unsearchable riches of Christ" (Ephesians 3:8), "the riches of the glory of this mystery among the Gentiles – Christ in you, the hope of glory" (Colossians 1:27), "all riches of the full assurance of understanding" (Colossians 2:2), and "the riches of God's goodness and forbearance and longsuffering" (Romans 2:4).

365 Tattoos

Show business has left its mark on Mrs. Ethel Vangi – a woman who was in the show business for years. She is covered from head to toe with 365 tattoos.

A retired circus performer, Mrs. Vangi was billed as "Lady Viola, the World's Most Beautifully Tattooed Lady."

Mrs. Vangi said: "Tattooing preserves the skin if you use the right ink. It is healthy for you."

And we know, having learned something of the lives of many, that sin and the follies of sin have left more than 365 marks on human beings, without bringing spiritual health to anyone.

But we rejoice that the marks of sin are not tattooably indelible when the blood of Jesus Christ is applied – because "the blood of Jesus Christ cleanseth us from all sin" (I John 1:7), and "Come now, and let us reason together, saith the Lord: though your sins be as scarlet, they shall be as white as snow; though they be red like crimson, they shall be as wool" (Isaiah 1:18).

Good for Gossip

Mr. Gossip, author of *The Hero in Thy Soul,* says:

"The gate into the boundless possibilities there are in Christ is flung wide open to the most hopeless and impossible bungler of us all. You see that poor stick lying in the dust and shriveling in the hot sun, and then that vine laden with branches loaded down with heavy clusters. That is the difference Christ can make in you and will make in you if you give Him any chance at all."

The Most Perfect Language

Many authorities on philology have claimed that the ancient Greek is the most perfect language that has ever existed in the world! But any language which confesses Jesus before the world comes near perfection in God's sight.

Narrow and Broad Roads

Until the track gauge was standardized in 1881, Illinois Central Railroad trains running between Cairo and New Orleans had to be jacked up and their wheels exchanged because of a difference in width of the northbound and southbound tracks.

But it was not as difficult to jack up these trains and exchange the wheels thereof and put a train from a broad gauge road on to a narrow gauge as it is now to get people to leave the broad road and travel on the narrow road about which Jesus so wisely spoke:

"Enter ye in at the strait gate: for wide is the gate, and broad is the way, that leadeth to destruction, and many there be which go in thereat: because strait is the gate, and narrow is the way, which leadeth unto life, and few there be that find it" (Matthew 7:13, 14).

Arms Around the Armless

THIS news from Waxahachie, Texas: District Judge R. A. Stout announced here that Louise Hood, armless baby, had been adopted by a Dallas couple. Adoption papers will be completed in about six months.

Judge Stout said the couple offered the child a home because of a deep religious feeling. He said the couple, middle aged, were of more than moderate means and desired that their identities not be revealed.

The nine-months-old child was abandoned in Ellis County by her parents. The little girl was born without arms.

When her plight became known, there were many offers to give her a home. While investigating prospects for a permanent home, county officials placed the child in the Jones Children's Haven.

A trust fund of about $3,000 has been raised for the child. Judge Stout said the couple adopting her had asked for no money and that the fund probably would be kept until the child enters school.

Job testified: "I was eyes to the blind, and feet was I to the lame" (Job 29:15). But this event shows that there are those who are and will be arms to the armless. This is something greatly commended, I am sure, by Jesus who, during the days of His flesh on earth, took little children up and put His hands on them (Mark 10:16).

Six Miles in Forty-Two Years

IN NEW YORK, November 3, 1953, Manhattan District Attorney Frank S. Hogan was holding a postcard addressed to Mrs. R. L. Bartlett. The postcard was mailed in Brooklyn – six miles away – November 5, 1911, and bore this message: "Will be down Monday about 5 P.M. Do not stay at home on my account. Hope your cold is better."

Mrs. Bartlett, who worked in the district attorney's office from 1901 to 1919, could not be located.

The deliverance of a card 42 years after it was mailed did not have much sober importance. But for one to wait forty-two years to confess Christ and start the Christian life is tragedy – because delay is really decision for the wrong way. Perilous is procrastination. How tragically true it is that with many "tomorrow and tomorrow and tomorrow creeps in this petty pace from day to day." How often we need to read and heed these words:

"Go to now, ye that say, To day or to morrow we will go into such a city, and continue there a year, and buy and sell, and get gain: Whereas ye know not what shall be on the morrow. For what is your life? It is even a vapour, that appeareth for a little time, and then vanisheth away" (James 4:13, 14).

Life From the Dead

IN HOUSTON, TEXAS, September 21, 1953, this was done: A surgeon, who had time only to grab a scalpel, removed a living baby from the womb of a dead woman in the emergency room of Jefferson Davis Hospital.

The woman, Mrs. Janna Dabney, a Negro, was a "very large woman," physicians at the hospital said, and when she was declared dead on arrival there was no outward indication she was even pregnant. But an intern put his hand on her stomach and felt the baby move. He shouted for the resident surgeon, who rushed in and performed a Caesarean section with a scalpel, the only instrument he had time to get. The surgeon—neither he nor the intern was identified—said he started the baby to breathing by sticking a tube in her mouth and inhaling and exhaling through it.

The baby is a six-pound girl. She was put into an incubator and physicians said her condition is good. They didn't know how long the mother had been dead, since, they said, she apparently died en route to the hospital. Mrs. Dabney's husband said he rushed her to the hospital when she complained of being short of breath and that she still had a pulse when she arrived.

When she grows into young womanhood, this girl baby can tell how she was born after her mother was dead. But more wonderful are the words spoken by the prodigal's father when his wandering boy came back from companionship with the hogs in the far country: "This my son was dead and is alive."

Is It I?

OUR sins were the palms that slapped Jesus, the fists that beat Him, the scourge that cut Him, the thorns that crowned Him, the nails that transfixed Him. This, in a sermon, I have said several times. The truth of it, John Trowbridge has expressed in these words:

A crown of thorns
And a purple robe—
Somebody fashioned them both.
Somebody platted the bloody crown,
Somebody fitted the gaudy gown,
Somebody fashioned them both.

A crown of thorns
And a purple robe—
And was it so long ago
They made that vesture our Saviour wore,
And wove that crown that He meekly bore?
And was it so long ago?

A crown of thorns
And a purple robe—
I read the words with a sigh:
But when I remember my own misdeeds,
My soul awakes, and my conscience pleads,
And I say to myself, "Is it I?"

Attitudes Toward the Cross

EVERY kind of disposition was represented among the witnesses of the crucifixion of Jesus. There were those who were characterized by *apathy*, or indifference, the absence of either love or hate; who were present by chance or were there in the line of their professional duties; as soldiers. There were others who were moved by *antipathy* toward Him, the rabble whose clamor for His blood subsides only at the foot of the cross. Then there were the few who bore Him *sympathy* in His dying hour and who followed Him faithfully to the end, as the disciple John and the two Marys. Even so today: every sort of attitude toward Jesus on the cross exists among the multitude of men. What is yours?

Adoption of a Son's Fiancee

IN HUNTINGTON, WEST VIRGINIA, a German woman who was to have become a Huntington couple's daughter-in-law has become their adopted daughter instead.

Miss Annelies Lange had been engaged to Mr. and Mrs. C. G. Gillette's son, William Joseph, who died of heart disease. The couple asked Annelies to make her home with them. William Gillette met Miss Lange when he was stationed in Germany during World War II.

How lovely and to be praised is this adoptive action on the part of Mr. and Mrs. Gillette. How much more to be desired on the part of sinners is adoption by the Lord.

"For ye have not received the spirit of bondage again to fear; but ye have received the Spirit of adoption, whereby we cry, Abba, Father . . . And not only they, but ourselves also, which have the first-fruits of the Spirit, even we ourselves groan within ourselves, waiting for the adoption, to wit, the redemption of our body" (Romans 8:15, 23).

How much more wonderful the adoptive relationship spoken of by the Apostle Paul:

"But when the fulness of the time was come, God sent forth his Son, made of a woman, made under the law, to redeem them that were under the law, that we might receive the adoption of sons" (Galatians 4:4, 5).

"According as he hath chosen us in him before the foundation of the world, that we should be holy and without blame before him in love, having predestinated us unto the adoption of children by Jesus Christ to himself, according to the good pleasure of his will, to the praise of the glory of his grace, wherein he hath made us accepted in the beloved" (Ephesians 1:4-6).

Correct Color Combinations

WHAT cannot man's machines do now?

William M. Stuart, president of the Martin-Senour Co., has figured out a machine that looks undramatic but does a lot of dramatic things with color. Stuart also is godfather of a comprehensive color mixing system. Colors can be put together by formula.

He called on Arthur G. Russell of the Russell Machine Co., Forestville, Connecticut, to build a machine that would mix paint automatically and accurately. Russell's result is a precisioned gadget that mixes paint in a matter of seconds. It's a pilot model.

Some 2,000 colors can be mixed with it. The machine puts the paint together by formula. Correct proportions are obtained by a unit system of 1,000 to a quart. Only 12 basic ingredients are required. Combinations are mixed from three primary hues — red, blue and yellow — and the three secondary hues of green, violet, and orange, plus a graying agent called shade-x and basic whites.

The paint is mixed and pumped to containers by pistons placed at the back of the machine. When a customer orders a color, the dial-like settings at the top are used. These are divided into 1000 unit scales and each one is assigned to a color. To get a plum color, for example, the dealer would set the machine to deliver 260 units of red, 30 units of purple, 210 units of shade-x, 250 units of mix-x and 250 units of flat. A container is placed in the center of the machine, a lever is pushed and the machine does the rest. A quart of paint is delivered in 12 seconds.

But more marvelous is the mixture of color which God makes — as Isaiah speaks the words of the Lord:

"Come now, and let us reason together, saith the Lord: though your sins be as scarlet, they shall be as white as snow; though they be red like crimson, they shall be as wool" (Isaiah 1:18).

There is the mixture of red and scarlet, with the result being whiteness like the snow.

Clue Conjecture

In Tucson, Arizona, December 3, 1953, three University of Arizona scientists declared that they believed they found a clue to the origin of an epidemic that ravaged ancient Indian settlements and sent disease raging across the earth.

A syphilis epidemic started in Europe in 1495, infecting one of every three persons, killing one in ten. The plague ravaged the Continent for seven years. Traders carried the hitherto unknown disease to China in 1505. Portuguese sailors took it to Japan in 1569. People in both countries died by the tens of thousands. Entire populations on some South Pacific islands were wiped out.

Origin of the dread killer long remained an enigma. Using a simple test of their own invention, the three scientists checked dozens of cremated skeletons from Point of Pines, an ancient Arizona pueblo that was abandoned in haste by its 3,000 residents between A.D. 1400 and 1450. Of 153 tested, 43 skeletons contained positive indications of a virulent type of syphilis. Anthropologists have long wondered why the ancient settlement was abandoned within a comparatively short time. The reason, among other possibilities, may have been a syphilis epidemic that killed more than 20 per cent of the people. Tests on skeletons of Europeans indicate that the disease was unknown on the Continent until shortly after the voyages of Columbus.

The Arizona scientists believe that America's first gift to the old world may have been the dreaded spirochete of syphilis. Columbus and his men, returning to Spain with news of their discovery, may have been the first bearers of the disease.

But there is no conjecture (and we spurn every conjectural clue) as to how the plague of sin entered our world. "Wherefore, as by one man sin entered into the world, and death by sin; and so death passed upon all men, for that all have sinned" (Romans 5:12).

By Adam the terrible death-dealing spirochete of sin entered the world. But – thank God! – we know that "as by the offence of one, judgment came upon all men to condemnation, even so by the righteousness of one, the free gift came upon all men to justification of life" (Romans 5:18).

And it's good to read:

"But not as the offence, so also is the free gift. For if through the offence of one many be dead, much more the grace of God, and the gift by grace, which is by one man, Jesus Christ, hath abounded unto many. And not as it was by one that sinned, so is the gift: for the judgment was by one to condemnation, but the free gift is of many offences unto justification. For if by one man's offence death reigned by one; much more they which receive abundance of grace and of the gift of righteousness shall reign in life by one, Jesus Christ" (Romans 5:15-17).

"For as by one man's disobedience many were made sinners, so by the obedience of one shall many be made righteous. Moreover the law entered, that the offence might abound. But where sin abounded, grace did much more abound: that as sin hath reigned unto death, even so might grace reign through righteousness unto eternal life by Jesus Christ our Lord" (Romans 5:19-21).

Light to Guide

The most celebrated lighthouse of antiquity was the one erected by Ptolemy Soter in the island of Pharos, opposite Alexandria. Josephus says it could be seen at a distance of forty-two miles. It was one of the seven wonders of the ancient world.

Of modern lighthouses, the most famous are the Eddystone, fourteen miles southwest of Plymouth; the Cordouan lighthouse, at the entrance of the Gironde in France; and the Bell Rock, which is opposite the Firth of Tay. The Bartholdi Statue of Liberty, in New York harbor, is 305 feet high. Eddystone light is 133 feet high and lights a radius of approximately 13 miles.

But more than all these lighthouses have meant to people did the pillar of fire, "a great column of brilliant light," mean to the Israelites in their journeyings. It was their necessary guide and rendezvous. And more than all lights to all peoples is Jesus who said: "I am the light of the world" (John 8:12).

The Useless Flag

Two cars of an excursion train from Kinston, North Carolina, plunged into an open draw bridge on the Elizabeth River – and eighteen of the passengers were drowned or killed. The mystery of the accident was increased by the assertion of the signal man that he had displayed his red flag in time for the engineer to stop the train before entering the open draw. Other employees corroborated his assertion. The engineer contended that it was a white flag that was shown, and he took it as a signal that the road was clear. The flag was produced and the mystery solved. It had become faded. and might in the distance have been mistaken for a white flag. Many Christians have become like a faded flag that fails to convey God's message of warning to imperiled men. Oh, the wrecks of souls that have resulted from the unfaithfulness of those whose Christianity is a faded flag. Solemn are these Bible words:

"Confidence in an unfaithful man in time of trouble is like a broken tooth, and a foot out of joint" (Proverbs 25:19).

How sad the indictment God made of His people after He made "his own people to go forth like sheep, and guided them in the wilderness like a flock," casting out the heathen before them . . . and made the tribes of Israel to dwell in their tents.

"Yet they tempted and provoked the most high God, and kept not his testimonies: but turned back, and dealt unfaithfully like their fathers" (Psalm 78:56, 57).

Oldest Tree in the World

THE world's oldest known tree is a bald cypress growing in Santa Maria del Tula, Mexico. It is said to be from 4,000 to 5,000 years old and is about 125 feet in circumference.

But, going back into the councils of eternity, and thinking of Jesus, "the Lamb slain from the foundation of the world" (Revelation 13:8), "who verily was foreordained before the foundation of the world" (I Peter 1:20), who "must have often suffered since the foundation of the world" (Hebrews 9:26), we wonder if the oldest tree is not the cross tree about which the Apostle Peter wrote, saying:

"Who his own self bare our sins in his own body on the tree, that we, being dead to sins, should live unto righteousness; by whose stripes ye were healed" (I Peter 2:24).

Peach Bark Wonder Drug

FROM Townsend, Tennessee, Hal Boyle writes of a married couple who lives in the great Smoky Mountains: Mrs. Della Effler, 69 and her husband,

"Barefoot Jerry," 71, operate a small grocery at the edge of the Great Smoky Mountains. They charge for the groceries, but Della, one of the dwindling human storehouses of old time mountain medicine, dispenses freely her cures for what ails you. Aunt Della doesn't volunteer medical advice, but won't refuse her counsel to those who ask her. Her reputation is based on her ability to get rid of warts, and there are those who dwell there in those eternal hills who swear that nobody can eradicate warts better.

" 'It's not me that takes them off,' said Mrs. Effler, 'It's the good Lord that does it. Nobody taught me how to get rid of warts. It just come to my mind.'

"Her recipe is her own secret. But she is certain the warts will come back if the patient tries to pay her, thank her – or discloses the form of treatment.

"Aside from her wart cure, Mrs. Effler is quite willing to discuss folk remedies. 'The best medicine you can give a child is to wrap an onion in a wet rag, let it cook in the ashes, then strain the juice, mix it with sugar and give it to the baby. It will put a child to sleep or cure it of a cold or the hives.'

"To help a baby cut its teeth, Mrs. Effler recommends having it wear a burdock root or a mole's foot around its neck. 'To cure thrash (a mountain term for an oral infection in infants), you have the seventh consecutive son in a family breathe in the child's mouth. Either that, or have it done by a boy or girl who has never seen their daddy. Both will work.'

"Mrs. Effler has great faith in the remedial powers of plants and trees. 'Chew ginseng root for the nerves, or boil it and chop it up to help a baby with the colic.' Her cure for an upset stomach is to scrape the bark downward off a peach tree switch, boil it and serve it as a drink. To cure diarrhea, you scrape the bark off upward.

" 'For earache,' continued Aunt Della, 'you take a stick off an ash tree, put it in the fire, catch the juice as it bubbles – and put it in the young'un's ear. Hot coffee in the ear is good, too.' Mrs. Effler said the juice of 'queen of the meadow,' a local plant, is good for the kidneys. For treating asthma in childhood, she advised: 'Cut a sourwood switch the exact height of the child, hide it where nobody will see it and where it can't get wet – and as the child outgrows the stick, she'll get well.' Aunt Della puts great store in purifying the blood by drinking spicewood or sassafras tea. 'That's what ails us all now,' broke in Barefoot Jerry, who has served a long internship in mountain medicine, 'we don't bleed enough. What makes you old is dead blood. You have to get rid of it.'

"While Mrs. Effler isn't distrustful of modern wonder drugs, she retains a quiet faith in what experience has taught her. 'Sometimes some of the old remedies will beat those the doctors have,' she said.

"Physicians might question the efficacy of some of Aunt Della's and Barefoot Jerry's remedies, but they couldn't well quarrel with the Effler family health record. The Efflers have been married 52 years. They raised eight of their nine children. And they have 49 grandchildren and 12 great grandchildren."

More wonderful by magnitudes immeasurable is what Jesus did – in answer to a question:

"And John calling unto him two of his disciples sent them to Jesus, saying, Art thou he that should come, or look we for another? When the men were come unto him, they said, John the Baptist hath sent us unto thee, saying, Art thou he that should come? or look we for another? And in that same hour he cured many of their infirmities and plagues, and of evil spirits; and unto many that were blind he gave sight. Then Jesus answering said unto them, Go your way, and tell John what things ye have seen and heard; how that the blind see, the lame walk, the lepers are cleansed, the deaf hear, the dead are raised, to the poor the gospel is preached" (Luke 7:19-22).

Antidotes for Poison

For muriatic, oxalic, acetic, sulphuric, nitric acids – take soapsuds, magnesia, limewater.

For prusaic acid – take ammonia in water, dash water in face.

For carbonic acid – use flour and water, mucilaginous drinks.

For alkalies – use vinegar or lemon juice in water.

For arsenic, rat poison, or Paris green – take milk, raw eggs, sweet oil, lime water, flour and water.

For bug poison – use whites of eggs or milk in large doses.

For chloroform – dash water in face, on head and chest. And artificial respiration.

For iodine – take starch and water and an astringent.

For mercury – use whites of eggs, milk, and musilage.

For opium – use strong coffee, hot bath, keep awake and moving at all costs.

For sin – an opiate in the will, a madness in the brain, the quintessence of all horrors, the causative element of all world suffering, a poison in the heart – apply by penitence and faith the blood of Jesus Christ, and live.

Then you will have the wholeness in your life which the poison pottage had when Elisha cast meal into the pot:

"And Elisha came again to Gilgal: and there was a dearth in the land; and the sons of the prophets were sitting before him: and he said unto his servant, Set on the great pot, and seethe pottage for the sons of the prophets. And one went out into the field to gather herbs, and found a wild vine, and gathered thereof wild gourds his lap full, and came and shred them into the pot of pottage: for they knew them not. So they poured out for the men to eat. And it came to pass, as they were eating of the pottage, that they cried out, and said, O thou man of God, there is death in the pot. And they could not eat thereof. But he said, Then bring meal. And he cast it into the pot; and he said, Pour out for the people, that they may eat. And there was no harm in the pot" (II Kings 4:38-41).

Christ — the Bible's Theme

Christ is the Bible's fullness, the Bible's center, the Bible's fascination. It is all about Jesus – in the Old Testament. The Old Testament conceals, infolds, promises, pictures, prophesies, localizes, symbolizes Christ. The New Testament reveals, unfolds, presents, produces, proclaims, universalizes and sacrifices Christ. Yes, the Old Testament and New Testament alike tell of Jesus the great Fact of history, the great Force of history, the great Future of history. Of this book it can truly be said: "The Glory of God doth lighten it, and the Lamb is the Light thereof!" The name of Jesus, the Supreme Personality, the center of a world's desire, is on every page – in expression, or symbol, or prophecy, or psalm, or proverb. Take Jesus out of the Bible – and it is like taking calcium out of lime, carbon out of diamonds. truth out of history, matter out of physics, mind out of metaphysics, numbers out of mathematics, cause and effect out of philosophy. Through this book the name of Jesus, the Revealed, the Redeeming, the Risen, the Reigning, the Returning Lord, runs like a line of glimmering light. The thought of Jesus, the Desire of all nations, threads this great book like a crystal river winds its way through a continent.

Seven Indispensable Things

1. Without shedding of blood is no remission (Hebrews 9:22).
2. Without faith it is impossible to please God (Hebrews 11:6).
3. Without works faith is dead (James 2:26).
4. Without holiness no man shall see the Lord (Hebrews 12:14).
5. Without love I am nothing (I Corinthians 13:2).
6. Without chastisement ye are not sons (Hebrews 12:8).
7. Without Me ye can do nothing (John 15:5).

Twice a Saviour

A WEALTHY family in England, many years ago, took their children for a holiday in the country. Their host toured over his estate for a weekend. The children went swimming in a pool. One of the boys began to drown, and the other boys screamed for help. The son of the gardener jumped in and rescued the helpless one. Later, the grateful parents asked the gardener what they could do for the youthful hero. The gardener said his son wanted to go to college. "He wants to be a doctor," he said. The visitors shook hands on that. "We'll be glad to pay his way through," they told him.

When Winston Churchill was stricken with pneumonia after the Teheran conference, the King of England instructed that the best doctor be found to save the Prime Minister. The doctor turned out to be Dr. Fleming, the developer of penicillin. "Rarely," said Churchill to Fleming, "has one man owed his life twice to the same rescuer." It was Fleming who saved Churchill in that pool.

Hoover and Vallee

ONCE when that much-maligned and misunderstood statesman, Herbert Hoover, was President of the United States, he said to Rudy Vallee: "Well, if you can sing a song that would make the people forget their troubles and the depression, I'll give you a medal." But Vallee did not have a song that could make men stop complaining – and start and continue singing. But there is one who can start and will keep us singing. The Psalmist spoke of him in these words:

"And he hath put a new song in my mouth, even praise unto our God: many shall see it, and fear, and shall trust in the Lord" (Psalm 40:3).

"Yet the Lord will command his lovingkindness in the daytime, and in the night his song shall be with me, and my prayer unto the God of my life" (Psalm 42:8).

"Thy statutes have been my songs in the house of my pilgrimage" (Psalm 119:54).

Wonder of Wonders

THE world is full of wonders. There are wonders in nature, science, medicine, inventions. In fact, the world is one big wonder.

Salt is a wonder. When I think that

salt is composed of two poisonous substances, I am filled with wonder. How is it possible that salt, which is necessary to life, is composed of sodium and chloride, either of which, if taken individually, would kill you? I can not answer it, neither can you. It's a wonder!

The alnico magnet is a wonder. It is the strongest magnet in the world, and yet it is composed of three nonmagnetic substances – aluminum, nickel and cobalt. Can it be explained? No. It's a wonder!

Water is a wonder. Its chemical formula is H_2O. That means it has two parts of hydrogen for each part of oxygen. Oxygen is flamable; hydrogen readily burns. Unite hydrogen and oxygen into water and you put out fires with it! That's another wonder!

Salvation is the wonder of wonders! How God can take a poor, vile, hopeless sinner and transform him into a respectable person is the greatest wonder on this earth. Is it happening? Yes, it's happening every day. On the skid rows of our cities, in the wealthy and poor homes, in jungles, in Chinese houseboats; in fact, wherever any soul wants Christ, the wonder of the new birth is taking place. People who read and believe that Christ is the Saviour as revealed in God's Word are finding that they know the Wonder of wonders.

"How shall we escape if we neglect so great salvation?" (Hebrews 2:3).

Polishing a Coffin

A ninety-two-year-old man in Stanstead Abbots, England, is the proud possessor of a solid oak coffin, which he purchased thirty-three years ago, for twenty-three pounds – about $100.

Every day since then he has visited the shed in which he keeps the coffin to give it a polishing. If he feels drowsy after shining it, he crawls into it and takes a nap.

After doing this for thirty-three years, he is satisfied that his long rest will be comfortable for his body. He said: "I even had my photograph taken in it! Wanted to see how I'd look when the undertaker lays me out. I came into the world a bit rough, as one of nine children. Now, I'm making sure I go out respectable – with an oak coffin that has solid brass handles and everything!"

The incident causes us to wonder if the aged man has had as much exercise about a satisfactory rest for his spirit and soul; for after all, the body is but the clay house in which the person lives.

A coffin is all right for the body to rest in until the resurrection; but the Lord Jesus said something about rest for the soul. He said: "Come unto me, all ye that labor and are heavy laden, and I will give you rest. Take my yoke upon you, and learn of me; for I am meek, and lowly in heart; and ye shall find rest unto your souls" (Matthew 11:28, 29).

It cost the elderly Briton about $100 to purchase a satisfactory resting place for his body; but it cost the Lord Jesus Christ the bearing of our sins in His own body on the cross – plus the endurance of God's righteous judgment against those sins. It cost Him the shedding of His precious blood for the remission of our sins (Matthew 26:28).

In resurrection, He commanded that repentance and remission of sins be preached in His name among all nations. Happy the person who can say, or sing:

I heard the voice of Jesus say,
Come unto Me, and rest.
Lay down, thou weary one, lay down
Thy head upon My breast.

I came to Jesus as I was
Weary and worn and sad,
I found in Him a resting place,
And He has made me glad!

Ten Commandments Dropped

From Ascot, England, comes the AP announcement that an Anglican minister has dropped the Ten Commandments from the church service. He says that they are not Christian. "The Commandments are Jewish – not Christian," says Rev. George Wilkins.

"Jewish?" Well – what of it? Knows not the Rev. Wilkins that the contribution of the Jewish race to Christianity is the Bible – the world's greatest Book? For the miracle Book of diversity in unity, we owe the Jewish race a great debt.

Roy Grace, writing of the Christian's debt to the Jew, said: "All that is most precious in our Christian faith and life has come to us from the Jews."

The first Christian preachers to the Gentiles were Jews. Both the Old and New Testaments were written by Jews. Jesus Christ, in whom our earthly and heavenly hopes rest, was, in His earthly origin, a Jew. A Jew among Jews was Jesus – the greatest of all Jews.

"Who are Israelites; to whom pertaineth the adoption, and the glory, and the covenants, and the giving of the law, and the service of God, and the promises; whose are the fathers, and of whom as concerning the flesh Christ came, who is over all, God blessed for ever. Amen" (Romans 9:4, 5).

Trouble in Jerusalem

Long ago this was written concerning the first Christmas: "When Herod the king had heard these things, he was troubled, and all Jerusalem with him" (Matthew 2:3).

After nearly two thousand years, there is still trouble in Jerusalem and Bethlehem – as writes Fred J. Zusy. Just before Christmas, 1949, he wrote:

"There's a sad Christmas shaping up for the little village where Christ was born. Bethlehem is jammed with Arab refugees of the Palestine war. Practically everybody is without work. The pilgrim traffic that once supported the bigger share of the population had dwindled to almost nothing. Contact with the outside world is confined almost entirely to the Red Cross trucks that cart in food supplies for the refugees, a few government and military men coming and going, and a few churchmen who now and then visit the ancient church of the Nativity. The good road that once made possible a ten-minute motor trip from Bethlehem to Jerusalem is now in Israeli hands. The only road open to Bethlehem now is a tortuous, bumpy trail winding up and around the desolate Judean hills. Located less than three miles from the boundary of the new Israel, the inhabitants of Bethlehem – although every Sunday they crowd into the church marking the stable where Christ was born – bear a deep and bitter hatred against their new neighbors."

Yes, trouble where Christ was born. Trouble is one word millions know the meaning of without the help of any dictionary.

I wish many knew the Christ who delivers from trouble. I wish many had as their own experience the blessedness described in these words:

"The Lord also will be a refuge for the oppressed, a refuge in times of trouble" (Psalm 9:9).

"For in the time of trouble he shall hide me in his pavilion: in the secret of his tabernacle shall he hide me; he shall set me up upon a rock" (Psalm 27:5).

"But the salvation of the righteous is of the Lord: he is their strength in the time of trouble" (Psalm 37:39).

Quick Arithmetic

I READ where an electronic calculating machine ten times as fast as the best now in use is under construction at the Princeton institute of advanced studies. It will be able to add and subtract in a one-hundredth of a second and multiply and divide in a ten-thousandth of a second.

The Eniac, constructed for the army at the University of Pennsylvania during the war, requires at least 1/10,000th of a second to add or subtract and but two or three thousandths of a second to multiply. It was designed, moreover, to solve problems in ballistics, which otherwise would require months of work for scores of clerks. While it can be used for other problems, it is not especially adapted for them.

The new machine was designed by Prof. John Von Neuman of the Princeton institute, one of the foremost living mathematicians. The construction of the new machine is revealed in a report issued by UNESCO, the Educational, Scientific and Cultural Organization of the United Nations, in connection with proposals to set up an international computing laboratory. The machine will be able to do about anything in mathematics – except pose the problems and supply the data – thousands of times faster than the human brain. Input and output of data will be in the form of magnetized tape, of the kind used for sound recording. It will have elaborate memory devices for storing figures and automatic checking devices to detect and locate any errors.

But even the swiftness of this machine can not equal the speed with which God removes our sins as far from us as the east is from the west – when, with repentance toward God, we "believe on the Lord Jesus Christ."

Faultless Foundation

THERE is such a thing as confusion worse than curse. Such we find when people rest their hopes in life on any foundation except the Rock of Ages.

When the Erie Railroad tracks were laid over Ararat Summit in 1875, a quarter of a mile of track and roadbed disappeared entirely, and a great quagmire occupied the place where solid ground had been before. Into it were poured ten thousand carloads of gravel and five hundred large hemlock trees, but no perceptible effect was made toward forming a foundation on which to lay a new roadbed. Finally, solid rock was found 160 feet below the surface. On this four tiers of piles, each forty feet long, were placed one on top of the other. The whole operation cost $300,000. It took fifteen hundred trees and a whole hill of gravel to make a solid bed. This was the most costly operation in the history of railroad building.

But think of the cost paid by the Son of God on Calvary in order that He might become the foundation for our faith. Happy are they who establish their eternal life on the solid Rock, Jesus Christ – and know the truth of the statement, "All other ground is sinking sand."

Only to Brides

THE town church of Friesberg, Germany, has a bridal door that has been opened only to brides for seven hundred years. But for more than seven hundred years – yea, even unto all the years that shall be until the end cometh, Jesus is the only door from famine to food in matters spiritual.

"Verily, verily I say unto you, He that entereth not by the door into the sheepfold, but climbeth up some other way, the same is a thief and a robber.

"Then said Jesus unto them again, Verily, verily, I say unto you, I am the door of the sheep.

"I am the door: by me if any man enter in, he shall be saved, and shall go in and out, and find pasture" (John 10:1, 7, 9).

Jesus is the only way – the only road from spiritual darkness to light, from spiritual deadness to life, from spiritual poverty to wealth.

To Thomas, Jesus said, and to us today Jesus says: "I am the Way – the road – no man cometh unto the Father but by me" (John 14:6). But forget not that this door is open not just to brides only, but to "whosoever will."

CHURCH

God's Machine Shop

There is a machine shop on the C. & O. Railroad that is kept immaculately white and clean inside. A long axle runs from one end of the shop to the other, high above the heads of the workmen. There are nearly one thousand wheels on it. Each wheel carries a belt connected with a machine below. Each of these machines is different. Each one has a specific job to do. Together they take a piece of raw material and make it ready for service on one of the giant mountain climbing engines.

One tremendous belt runs through a slit in the wall. It's the connecting link between the giant dynamo and that long axle. Until it moves, that machine shop stands helpless. It furnishes the power for every machine.

We are God's machines. This world is His great machine shop and we are helpless until He turns on the power. A church should be a powerhouse making available God's power to the rest of the world. We deal in power and when we, the church, cease dealing in power, there is no excuse for our existence.

Lowest Temperature

The lowest temperature ever authentically recorded in the United States was 65 degrees below zero, Fahrenheit, at Fort Keough, now Miles City, Montana, in January, 1888.

I wonder how low the temperature inside our churches would be if it were measured by our spiritual passion for the lost or by missionary zeal. A thermometer would have a hard struggle to stay above zero if the mercury in it moved according to the real concern for sin-damned and hell-doomed sinners around us – sometimes under the same roof with us, sometimes in the same office with us, sometimes dining at the same table with us.

Potent Pull

Engineers tell us that a locomotive must exert a pull of as much as thirty pounds for every ton of weight in a railroad car to start it from a standstill, and even more in very cold weather. Once the car is in motion, only about three pounds per ton may be needed to keep it moving on a straight and level track.

It takes more spiritual power, too, to start a church that is at a standstill – or even more when it has become, because of lack of the warm blood of spiritual life, "a drifting sepulchre manned by a frozen crew." Many are found guilty under Solomon's indictment: "The sluggard will not plow by reason of the cold; therefore shall he beg in harvest, and have nothing" (Proverbs 20:4).

And many never grieve over the difficulty a church faces in functioning mightily when this is true of some: "And because iniquity shall abound, the love of many shall wax cold" (Matthew 24:12).

Death Notice

Sister Old Time Prayer Meeting died recently at the First Neglected Church on Worldly Avenue. Born many years ago in the midst of great revivals, she was a strong healthy child, fed largely on testimony and scriptural holiness, soon growing into world-wide prominence, and was one of the most influential members of the famous Church family. She was a great influence for good, gathering the multitude of mankind to her bosom to hear the story of Him who wore the seamless garment; a story of never failing interest to all.

For the past several years Sister Prayer Meeting has been failing in health, gradually wasting away until rendered helpless by stiffness of knees, coldness of heart, inactivity, and weakness of purpose and will power. At the last she was but a shadow of her former self. Her last whispered words were inquiries concerning the strange absence of her loved ones, now absent from her presence, busy in the marts of trade and places of worldly amusements. Her older brother, Class Meeting, has been dead for many years.

Experts, including Dr. Works, Dr. Re-Form, and Dr. Joiner, disagreed as to the cause of her illness, administering large doses of organization, socials, contests, drives and religious education, but to no avail. A post mortem showed a deficiency of spiritual food coupled with lack of fasting, faith and change of heart. Shameless desertion and nonsupport were contributing causes. Only a few were present at her death, sobbing over memories of her past beauty and power. Carefully selected pallbearers were urged to tenderly bear her remains away but failed to appear. There were no flowers. Her favorite hymns, "Amazing Grace" and "Rock of Ages" were not sung. Miss Ima Modern rendered "Beautiful Isle of Somewhere," but none had any idea where this fancied isle might be. The body rests in the beautiful cemetery of Bygone Glories, awaiting the summons from above which shall bring her, with her blood-washed garments, into the presence of the God of Glory, spotless, blameless and full of glory. In honor of her going, the church doors will be closed on Wednesday evenings, save on the third Wednesday of each month, when the Ladies' Pink Lemonade Society serves refreshments to the members of the men's handball team.

Injections and Wrinkles

We read in a news item that injections may be used soon to erase facial wrinkles and creases. Injections of a solution of silicone fluid and fatty acids can make the face appear younger than it actually is, Dr. Harvey D. Kagan of Beverly Hills said. Kagan reported the innovation in a scientific paper prepared for ear, nose and throat physicians who perform plastic surgery. They were attending the meeting of the American Otorhinological Society for Plastic Surgery, Inc.

In addition to the cosmetic value, the process shows great promise for filling in arms and legs which have been deformed by polio, the physician said.

The fluid was formulated twelve years ago by a Japanese physician, Rin Sakurai, who claims to have performed successful therapy on seventy-two thousand persons in the past five years.

Perhaps Job would have given welcome to such injections when, with grief unassuaged, he said: "And thou hast filled me with wrinkles, which is a witness against me: and my leanness rising up in me beareth witness to my face" (Job 16:8).

Though these injections should remove wrinkles from all faces of all races, we rejoice more in the reality set forth in Paul's words: "Christ loved the church and gave himself for it – that he might sanctify and cleanse it with the washing of water by the word, that he might present it to himself a glorious church, not having spot, or wrinkle, or any such thing; but that it should be holy and without blemish" (Ephesians 5: 26, 27).

Walking

Of a certain man's walking, George Ade said: "He walks like he had gravel in his shoes." Of a certain woman, Balzac wrote: "She walked with a proud, defiant step, like a martyr to the Coliseum." Of a woman, also, Byron wrote: "She walks in beauty like the night of cloudless climes and starry skies." And Shakespeare wrote: "Walk like sprites to countenance this horror."

But Edward Payson Weston, in 1861, without writing anything, walked four hundred and forty-three miles in two hundred and eight hours to attend the inauguration of Abraham Lincoln.

Would that the spirit that possessed him to be at the inauguration would possess multitudes today as to attendance of the sanctuary of God.

COMMUNISM

Moscow Maliciousness

On the Moscow radio, March, 1963, Christian baptism was castigated as a "health menace" and "a senseless and dangerous rite." In the weekly pro-atheist broadcast, the communist commentator said that "thousands" of babies died of pneumonia following christening ceremonies and that "weak hearts" and "weak lungs" in adults had been traced to baptism in their early years.

In an all-out attack upon religious practices, the broadcast had as its theme religion's "threat" to health. Life expectancy in the time of the Czars, it said, was only 32 years because religion was widespread and baptism was administered to almost all Russians.

It added that during the communist regime life expectancy has risen to 69 years, largely because of government health services and the fact that fewer baptisms take place.

These words prove that there are people who are as dumb as a doll on a ventriloquist's knee. Moreover, they are "foolish, disobedient, deceived, serving divers lusts and pleasures, living in malice and envy, hateful and hating" (Titus 3:3), prating against Christian truth with malicious words (III John 10).

A Cuban Shocker

IN ITS Anecdote-of-the-week, the Boston *Sunday Globe* quotes Frank O. Sloane, director of research and information in the public schools of Dade County, Florida, as saying Cuban refugees report the communist government's latest campaign trick to exalt Castro and undermine the people's traditional Roman Catholic faith. A communist propagandist asks first grade children to pray to God for candy. Nothing happens. Then they must pray to Castro. During the prayer, the operator quietly places candy on each desk, then tells the students: "You see? Castro is a greater power than God."

This report, if true, shows again that the communists have no ethics and no limits to their diabolical schemes to gain their ends. It also shows that we should be extremely unwise to belittle the efforts and power of this sinister adversary, who has fortified an aggressive bastion ninety miles from our shores. It shows that nothing should be taken for granted as to the arming of Cuba no matter what might be the cost nor how closely calculated the risk.

We are made to think of what Jesus said: "It is impossible but that offences will come: but woe unto him, through whom they come! It were better for him that a millstone were hanged about his neck, and he cast into the sea, than that he should offend one of these little ones" (Luke 17:1, 2).

Comments Concerning Communism

DAVID LAWRENCE: "The basic thesis of communism is the atheistic privilege of violating written or oral pledges. Promises and assurances evidently mean nothing to the Kremlin."

Lenin: "We have to use any ruse, dodges, tricks, cunning, unlawful method, concealment and veiling of the truth."

Syghman Rhee: "Communism, Christianity and democracy cannot co-exist. We do not try to co-exist with cholera."

Dr. Fred C. Schwarz, Sidney, Australia: "Godless communism is a danger so vast and so terrible that it staggers the mind."

Jack Lotto: "The facts are clear that the God-less communist regime is interested in stamping out all religious belief."

J. Edgar Hoover, F. B. I. Director: "We Americans are face to face with a tyranny more monstrous, more devious, less understood and more deadly than any which has ever threatened civilization heretofore. In recent years, more than six hundred groups and organizations have been designated as communist front organizations by official Federal, State and Municipal agencies."

Madame Chiang Kai-shek: "I had rather die fighting communism than to live under it."

President Abraham Lincoln: "If this country is ever destroyed, it will not be from *without,* but from *within.*"

Dr. Oswald J. Smith: There is no freedom in communism."

Dr. C. H. Hamilton: "In communism, there is no freedom to travel, no freedom to strike, no freedom of the press, no freedom in religion. Communism denies the existence of God."

But so do some men of prominence in the United States of America. Dr. Wilbur Smith writes: "We are living in an age of world-wide darkness and unbelief. Approach a person today in one of our own universities or in one of the cities of Europe or the Far East, and he is all too likely to say, 'I don't believe in God.'"

Anne Roe, in *The Making of a Scientist,* says: "Fifty-four great scientists work in our country, and only three have anything to do with any religious group. The other fifty-one are wholly alienated from any church."

Dr. Harlow Shapley, for thirty years head of the Department of Astronomy of Harvard, is an agnostic. In Shapley's book, *Science Ponders Religion,* published in 1960, are essays by eighteen well-known scientists of our country, all eighteen agree that there is no personal God and no life after death.

In Berland's *Scientific Life* is the statement: "God is a general expression for the created universe. God is a convenient fiction to work with."

Prof. Stace of Princeton has been teaching philosophy to young men for thirty-five years. He says, in his book, *Time and Eternity:* "God is a superstition and he is the great unknown. There is no supernatural Being and no eternal God."

Another professor in a large institution says: "The Christian religion is a compensatory fiction for an inner feeling of inferiority – a defense mechanism, an importation of symbols into a world of fact."

And Julian Huxley, once Director General of UNESCO, said: "Science and knowledge have brought the world to the stage where God is no longer a useful hypothesis. While a faint trace of God still broods over the world like the smile of a cosmic Cheshire cat, science and knowledge will soon rub that faint trace away."

Remember, all of these statements are published in America – not Russia.

Funeral Rights Denied

Place – Moscow. Date – August 16th, 1963. Moscow's Orthodox Jews claim their dead are being denied a burial in consecrated ground – instead are being interred in a civil cemetery among atheists and gentiles. It is the first time in memory, they say, that Jews have been denied the right to be laid to rest in the tradition of their faith.

Peking Farce

Communist China staged a rally in Peking in support of American Negroes in their "struggle for civil rights." This was an insult to the intelligence and legitimate aspirations of American Negroes. The Red Chinese government operates the most brutal and oppressive tyranny in the world, which denies civil rights to its seven hundred million people, including the ten thousand compelled to attend the rally and hypocritically applaud the hypocrisy of Premier Chou En-lai, the principal speaker.

Bibles and Christianity Condemned in Red China

A renewed attack on Christianity and the Bible by the Chinese communists has been interpreted by students of Chinese affairs as fear that continued existence of Christianity in China is a danger to the Peking regime.

After a long silence, observers noted, a major Chinese communist organ, Jenmin Jih Pao, appeared with a long editorial which condemned the Bible and Christianity as tools of the "exploiting class" to undermine Marxism.

The editorial recommended that its readers study a Red treatise on religion published in the Soviet Union forty years ago and issued by the Chinese under the title, "What Kind of Book the Bible Is."

Jenmin Jih Pao observed that the author "follows Lenin's directive to call on the most backward masses to treat the question of religion consciously and to criticize religion consciously."

Close observers of Red China said the editorial appeared to point up an analogy between the situation in Russia in 1922 and happenings in China today. If this is correct, they said, then Christianity must still be considered an influence of some importance in China.

DEATH

Death Rejects a Bribe

A SINGLE sentence or a gesture may reveal more of a man's character than a full-length biography. There was Dutch Schultz, the gangster, for instance.

Fatally shot, he was still able to reach into his pocket when he arrived at the hospital.

"Here's something for you, pal," he said. "Take good care of me." He pressed into the hand of the interne who bent over him a roll of bills – $725.

A natural and revealing gesture. Hadn't money always done its stuff? Did it ever fail him in a tight place? Wouldn't it buy anything, from "protection" to a champagne dinner? Why suppose that it wouldn't also bribe death?

We seem to see Dutch Schultz standing before the pearly gates, plucking a sleeve of the good, gray-bearded figure who guards the portal. "Here's something for you, pal," he says. "Take good care of me."

What a surprise it must have been when his hand came away empty from the shroud that had no pockets, and he realized at last that there are some situations in which money doesn't talk!

We read in the Bible:

"Be not thou afraid when one is made rich, when the glory of his house is increased; For when he dieth he shall carry nothing away: his glory shall not descend after him" (Psalm 49:16, 17).

Bankruptcy by Death

ON AUGUST 17, 1953, in Alaska, Ellis A. Hall, Albuquerque, New Mexico, oilman died in a plane crash. With him died his two daughters and 17-year-old Patrick Hibben. The plane apparently disintegrated in the air after being buffeted by strong winds. On November 3, 1953, the estate of Mr. Hall was appraised. The value of his estate according to the appraisal filed in probate court was $4,250,022.11.

Mr. Hall took nothing of his estate with him. How true is the statement that all men hold in their cold dead hands is what they gave away.

Ecclesiastes 5:15: "There is nothing in his hand. As he came forth of his mother's womb, naked shall he return to go as he came, and shall take nothing of his labour, which he may carry away in his hand."

Psalm 49:16, 17: "Be not thou afraid when one is made rich, when the glory of his house is increased; for when he dieth he shall carry nothing away: his glory shall not descend after him."

It is good for us to read often these words:

"But godliness with contentment is great gain. For we brought nothing into this world, and it is certain we can carry nothing out. And having food and raiment let us be therewith content. But they that will be rich fall into temptation and a snare, and into many foolish and hurtful lusts, which drown men in destruction and perdition. For the love of money is the root of all evil: which while some coveted after, they have erred from the faith, and pierced themselves through with many sorrows. But thou, O man of God, flee these things; and follow after righteousness, godliness, faith, love, patience, meekness. Fight the good fight of faith; lay hold on eternal life, whereunto thou art also called, and hast professed a good profession before many witnesses" (I Timothy 6:6-12).

Shiloh

ONCE, as I went over the Shiloh battlefield, where on April 6, in the Sixties, the fighting was fierce and blood flowed with tragic freeness, I recalled the following bit of beautiful verse by Agnes Kendrick Gray. This:

Only the seasons and the years invade
These quiet wheatfields where the Armies crashed,
And mocking birds and quail fly unafraid
Within this forest where the rifles flashed.
Here where the bladed wings of death have mown
And gleaned their harvestry of golden lives,
The fruitful seeds of corn and wheat are sown,
And where the cannon smoked, an orchard thrives.

Long are the war years over, with their pain,
Their passionate tears and fury, and the sun
Lies hot and yellow on the heavy grain,
And all the fighting on these fields is done.
But in their peace, the quivering heart recalls
The youth that bled beside these old stone walls.

How Dead Are You?

A CERTAIN Missouri editor refuses to publish obituary notices of people who, while living, failed to subscribe to his newspaper, and gives this pointed reason: "People who do not take the home town paper are dead anyway, and their passing away has no news value."

If you never play for the fun of playing, your youthful spirit is dead.

If you do not take time occasionally to enjoy a beautiful picture, an inspiring sunset, noble music, you are dead to art.

If you have only business dealings with people you meet, you are dead to fellowship and friendship.

If you cannot tell the difference between the fragrance of an orange grove and a smoke-filled car, your sense of smell is dead.

If you never pray except when in trouble, your religion is dying.

If you do not breathe deeply and

assimilate your meals properly, your body is dying.

We are alive in proportion to the variety and vitality of our interests; our responsiveness to our surroundings.

Be alive!

Don't be guilty of being dead while alive – as were the church folks in Sardis: "These things saith he that hath the seven Spirits of God, and the seven stars; I know thy works, that thou hast a name that thou livest, and art dead" (Revelation 3:1).

In Jude 12, we read of those who are as "trees whose fruit withereth, without fruit, twice dead." Yes – we ask – how dead are you?

Huge Wardrobe

THE personal wardrobe of one of Chicago's wealthiest women – an estimated twenty-five thousand pieces of apparel – has been sold at public auction for $40,000.

The wardrobe, owned by the late Mrs. Violet Bidwill Wolfner, was sold at a three-day auction by order of Cook County probate court. The clothes included more than one thousand dresses – with a purse to match each dress – some five hundred coats and fifteen hundred pairs of shoes. The highest price paid for any item was $1,250 for a full length mink but many dresses and coats sold for fifty cents.

Mrs. Wolfner was sixty two when she died in Miami Beach, Florida, in 1962. She left an estate of $3.1 million to her two adopted sons.

She left an estate. Yes, she *left* it all – and only a few pieces of her twenty-five thousand pieces of apparel were used for her burial.

How all men and women should give heed to the Psalmist's words: "Be not thou afraid when one is made rich, when the glory of his house is increased; for when he dieth he shall carry nothing away: his glory shall not descend after him" (Psalm 49:16, 17).

Capone's "Take"

WRITER Bert Bacharach tells us that the highest income made in any year by an individual was Al Capone's "take" in 1927 – reputed to have been one hundred and five *million* dollars.

But his "*take*" when he died was nothing – *zero*. No money was in his shroud – his hands were empty – even as the hands of all the poor and all the rich are empty when burial is accomplished.

Ten Thousand Deaths

THE death toll from East Pakistan's cyclone mounted steadily, and authorities feared it would rise to above ten thousand. Delayed reports from the stricken areas along a 178-mile stretch of the Bay of Bengal told of widespread death and destruction and fears of spreading disease.

Officials said the reports indicated the final death figure from the cyclone and tidal waves would be between ten and fifteen thousand.

Press reports estimated that two million other persons were made homeless.

Still unknown was the fate of a million inhabitants of five hundred offshore islands, many of which were said to have been swept away by the tidal upsurge. The cyclone, which formed in the Bay of Bengal and first hit the coast about midnight, cut a forty-mile-wide path of destruction from Feni, eighty-five miles southeast of Dacca, south to Cox's Bazar in the Chittagong district.

Hunger Record

FROM Wiesbaden, Germany, November 15, 1953, comes the news that Willy Schmitz, a professional hunger artist, claimed a new world record for fasting – 80 days and five hours. He claimed he had only mineral water and cigarettes and that his weight dropped from 158 pounds to 92.

He climbed out of a glass cage completely exhausted and was taken to the hospital. He told reporters the previous world record was 80 days and one hour, held by an Indian fakir Reykan, whom he will meet next spring in Venezuela in a fasting duel.

Germans paid a mark (23.8 cents) to see Schmitz during the fast – his tenth in twenty-seven years.

I wonder if some folks do not set a record for long lapses as to feeding upon the Word of God that will go beyond this record of refusing to eat. Sad it is that many hunger not for the Word of God.

A Book and a Buyer

ON DECEMBER 1, 1959, Hans P. Kraus bought the copy of the 13th century illuminated Apocalypse. We read this about the book and the buyer: A New York book collector paid a record $182,000 for a 13th century illuminated manuscript of the "Magnificent Apocalypse" at an auction of 46 manuscripts. Sotheby's Auction house said that the price paid by Hans P. Kraus was a world record for any illuminated manuscript sold at an auction. The entire sale brought $820,484. It was the second of three sales of the manuscript collection of the late saucemaker Dyson Perrins.

The manuscript Kraus bought was believed to have been written and illuminated by the Benedictine Abbey of St. Albans, England. The illumination is overlaid in gold leaf. It is called the "Fra Angelico of English Painting" because of the delicacy and colors of its figures. Apocalypse is the last book of the New Testament, otherwise called the Revelation of St. John the Divine.

Worth more than this high-priced copy in the hand are the verses held in the heart and put into practice in the life:

"Blessed are they that do his commandments, that they may have right to the tree of life, and may enter in through the gates into the city" (Revelation 22:14).

Drastic Movie Laws

A RIGID motion picture censorship bill passed in South Africa some months ago. Among the things forbidden are:

Impersonation of the king.

Holding up to ridicule or contempt any member of the king's military or naval forces.

Treatment of death.

Nude human figures.

Passionate love scenes.

Illustrating night life.

References to controversial or international politics.

Antagonistic relations between capital and labor.

Disparaging public characters.

Creating public alarm.

The drug habit, white slave traffic, vice, or loose morals.

Religious convictions or feeling of any section of the public.

Ridicule or contempt.

Juvenile crime and, in case of older persons, brutal fighting, drunkenness, and brawling.

Pugilistic encounters between Europeans and non-Europeans.

Intermingling of Europeans and non-Europeans.

Rough handling or ill-treatment of women and children.

America might learn something from South Africa.

Palmyra Palm

We are told that the palmyra is the most useful plant in the world. Upward of eight hundred uses are recorded for its various parts.

Are we palmyra Christians – good for many things? Are we possessed of the spirit that will make us good for many things – or good for nothing?

It was D. L. Moody who quoted from a tombstone these words:

For the Lord Jesus Christ's sake,
Do all the good you can,
To all the people you can,
In all the ways you can,
As long as ever you can.

If that were engraved on our hearts and were to find expression in our lives, we would be palmyra-palm servants of Christ.

Forgetting and Remembering

Miss Edith Fulton, in *Contemporary Verse,* dipped her pen in black ink and touched it lightly to paper and left this gleaming jewel:

You I forgot as winds forget,
When they are still,
The aromatic breath of trees
High on a hill;

You I lost as leaves are lost
From yellow trees,
Like little lonely ships that sink
In winter seas;

I find you deathless when I hear
One morning lark,
Or breathe the stab of lilacs lost
In April dark.

The Inn-Keeper's Lament

A sermon sweet and a sermon sad did Guest preach in the two verses showing the tragedy of no room for Christ:

All my patrons now are dead
And forgotten, but today,
All the world to peace is led
By the ones I sent away.

It was my unlucky fate
To be born that inn to own,
Against Christ I shut my gate:
Oh, if only I had known!

Confederate Commendation

I lived in Charleston, S. C., for two years. In this quaint city, carved upon a memorial stone to a Confederate soldier, are these words:

The Hour of Conflict,
The Day of Defeat,
The Years of Oppression
Brought to his Courage
No slackness;
And to his Loyal Service
No Abatement.

Would that such glorious words could be written of every one who claims to be a citizen of these United States, or who names the name of Christ!

Kissing and Making Up

I don't know who said it. But some fellow said that nowadays when sweet young things kiss and make up, she gets the kiss and he gets the make-up. But I think the lovers of Tennyson would not find fun in that – when they recall Tennyson's exquisite "we fell out . . . and kissed again with tears."

Beth Borton's Best

BETH BORTON has written many beautiful things. But I doubt if she will surpass, for lift and imagery, the following lyric, which won a first-page:

Thou art the breath of my body,
  Thou art the core of my heart.
Life is a desert without thee,
  Heaven's wherever thou art!

Chorus of flutes by a fountain,
  Silvery bells in the night,
Murmur of rain on the mountain. . . .
  These are thy voice, my Delight!

Lean to me from the dark casement;
  Loose thy gauze veil from thy eyes. . . .
Thou art a breeze sweet with rose-scent,
  Thou art a cloud from the skies!

Moonstone and opal and ruby,
  Silk from a far caravan,
Perfumes and sweets I will give thee –
  These . . . and the love of a man!

That is about as pretty as what Shakespeare wrote:

Except I be by Sylvia in the night,
There is no music in the nightingale;
Except I look on Sylvia in the day,
There is no day for me to look upon.

By One Vote

THE bullet that ended Lincoln's life made a President of shy Vice-President Andrew Johnson and pitchforked him into the reconstruction welter of amnesty, enfranchisement of blacks, disfranchisement of whites, carpetbaggers, scalawags, Ku Klux Klan, Knights of the White Camelia. This lenient Johnson fought Congress for cracking down on the South; was impeached, tried by the Senate. Conviction required two-thirds vote; Johnson escaped by one vote.

But Johnson learned how to live with some inferiors as he wanted superiors to live with him.

The votes of veering crowds are not
The things that are more excellent.

Franklin's Philosophy

BENJAMIN FRANKLIN, using poor Richard, the imaginary maker of his Almanac, as a mouthpiece, taught a philosophy of common sense. In his autobiography, he told a story of a hatter in Philadelphia who desired to place a signboard over his shop. He wrote it down, "John Brown Makes and Sells Hats for Ready Money."

"Oh, dear!" said a friend to whom he showed it, "cut out 'Makes and.' Nobody cares who makes the hat so long as it is good." Then the sign read, "John Brown Sells Hats for Ready Money."

"Dear me!" exclaimed another friend whom he consulted. "Why, this is an insult to the community! 'Ready money,' indeed! Strike it out!" The sentence then read, "John Brown Sells Hats."

"Absurd!" cried a third friend, as he burst into roars of laughter, "do you suppose people will expect you to give hats away? There is no need to say they are for sale! Why 'sells hats'?"

Again he went to the sign-writer and ordered him to paint the board bearing the simple legend, "John Brown, Hats." The tabloid was complete; that told all that really needed telling.

With such wisdom Jesus agreed, when He said that our talk ought to be Yea, yea, and Nay, nay. If we have any honor or character, oaths are not needed to emphasize the truth we have to tell.

"But I say unto you, Swear not at

all; neither by heaven; for it is God's throne: nor by the earth; for it is his footstool: neither by Jerusalem; for it is the city of the great King. Neither shalt thou swear by thy head, because thou canst not make one hair white or black. But let your communication be, Yea, yea; Nay, nay: for whatsoever is more than these cometh of evil" (Matthew 5:26, 37).

Torrey Talking Tenderly

"It is easiest to lead a child from five to ten years to a definite acceptance of Christ."

"I rejoice in the work done by rescue missions, where we see the wrecks of manhood and womanhood changed into noble men and women. But this is not the work that produces the most satisfactory Christians. The younger we get a child to accept Christ and begin Christian training, the more beautiful the product."

"The overwhelming majority in our churches today were converted before twenty-one years of age."

"Whatever your church does, let it do its full duty by the children."

"Every thorn that pierced Christ's brow pierced the heart of God."

"I implore you to get ready."

Torrey Talking Triumphantly

"I am ready to meet God face to face tonight and look into those eyes of infinite holiness, for all my sins are covered by the atoning blood."

"There is One who knows, and He sympathizes with you – God."

"There is more joy in Jesus in twenty-four hours than there is in the world in three hundred and sixty-five days. I have tried them both."

"I would rather go to heaven alone than go to hell in company."

"I sit at God's table – and it is just groaning with good things."

"God's Word is pure and sure, in spite of the devil, in spite of your fear, in spite of everything."

When we consider the truth of the statements quoted – statements from one of the great gospel evangelists of the years gone by – we can say that never once was Torrey's talking like that of which William Byrd wrote: "Our talking with the ladies, like whip syllabub, was very pretty, but had nothing in it."

Nor do we painfully have to acknowledge that his talking is akin to the talking Dr. Johnson describes: "A transition from an author's book to his conversation is too often like an entrance into a large city, after distant prospect. Remotely, we see nothing but spires of temples and turrets of palaces, and imagine it the residence of splendor, grandeur, and magnificence; but when we have passed the gates, we find it perplexed with narrow passages, disgraced with despicable cottages, embarrassed with obstructions and clouded with smoke."

But rather is it like what Richard Le Gallienne calls "music set on fire." Nor are the objectives of the great preacher to be described in these words:

His talk is like a stream which runs
With rapid change from rocks to roses;
It slipped from politics to poems;
It passed from Mahomet to Moses;
Beginning with the laws that keep
The planets in their radiant courses,
And ending with some precept deep
For dressing eels or shoeing horses.

But how many who came, under his preaching, out of their bondage, sorrow, and night into Christ's freedom, gladness, and light, can testify that his preaching was in the power and demonstration of the Spirit of God – which is saying more than to say that his talking was "like the procession of a Roman triumph, exhibiting power and riches at every step – glittering with the spoils of a ransacked world"!

Monument to a Man's Leg

It was erected to the honor of Benedict Arnold on the Saratoga battlefield. It was designed by the noted sculptor, Bissell. The monument was erected as a result of a story General J. Watts Depeyster heard about Arnold. After the Revolutionary War, the story goes, an American who knew Arnold before the latter's attempted betrayal of West Point and subsequent flight to England, was visiting in London where he happened to meet the one-time idol of the Continental Army.

"What do the American people think of me?" Arnold asked.

"The American people," he replied frankly, "would like to raise a monument on the Saratoga battlefield to that left leg of yours that was wounded in the charge on the Breyman redoubt at the battle of Saratoga, and then they would like to hang the rest of your body in effigy."

General Depeyster was one of the first writers who credited Arnold with winning the battle and erected the monument at his own expense. Benedict Arnold's name appears nowhere in the inscription on the side opposite the boot. The inscription reads:

> In memory of the most brilliant soldier of the Continental Army, who was desperately wounded on this spot, the sally port of Burgoyne's great (western) redoubt, 7th October, 1777, winning for his countrymen the decisive battle of the American Revolution, and for himself the rank of major general.

One cannot help but think just here of what Swift wrote: "Praise is like ambergris; a little whiff of it, and by snatches, is very agreeable; but when a man holds a great lump of it to his nose, it is a stink and strikes down."

If sadness because of Arnold's treachery could have brought him to life and to his former place of honor, he would have known resurrection and honor years ago.

Paleface Pertinacity

The coach of the great Indian football team on which Jim Thorpe played tells of a case of "paleface pertinacity." He spoke of Vic Kennard, whose trained toe won for Harvard over Yale in a historic encounter. All through one summer he practiced drop-kicking day after day and at night he spent hours letting the ball fall to the floor, studying its rebound and calculating the right distance from his foot. That fall Kennard kicked sixty successive goals in practice from varying distances and angles. Put in against Yale in the last quarter when a field goal was needed to win, Kennard delivered.

If against the evils of our day and in becoming efficient in the Lord's work, we should train ourselves as did Vic Kennard, we would possess continents where now we possess corners for God.

Loving Her Husband

In February, 1938, the widow of Gen. Philip H. Sheridan died in Washington. Gen. Sheridan died in 1888. And from then until her death his widow lived quietly in a house filled with memories and mementoes of her famous husband.

When it was rumored in 1908 that she might remarry, she declared: "I would rather be the widow of Phil

Sheridan than the wife of any living man."

At a time when too many women and men appear to look upon marriage as a garment to be put on and off as easily as an old coat, this remark by the daughter of a long line of soldiers and the widow of one of the greatest cavalry commanders of all time should be placed among the golden words.

What wonders would be wrought in this world today if matrimonial love-loyalty prevailed — love-loyalty and loyal-love as "inexhaustible as the hoard of King Nibelung, which twelve wagons in twelve days, at the rate of three journeyings a day, could not carry off."

$5,000 to Bootblack

THE will of Manufacturer Frederick McOwen left five thousand dollars to Joseph Gonelli, the bootblack who had shined McOwen's shoes every day for nearly fifty years.

It was Publilius Syrus who wrote: *Beneficium dignis ubi des, omnes obligas*—"Where you confer a benefit on the worthy, you oblige all men." And it was Cicero who said: "He ought to remember favors on whom they are conferred. He who has conferred them ought not to bring them to mind."

Remarkable Record

A MEDAL was presented to Miss Jennie C. Powers, of Philadelphia, Pa., for having attended Sunday school without absence for fifty-six years and four months, with a total of two thousand, nine hundred and twenty-eight observances, beginning at babyhood. This is regarded as a world's record for Sunday school attendance. Would that more would have interest in making worthy records in Sunday school attendance. Too many look upon Sunday school attendance as a thing "trivial as a parrot's prate" — "trivial as the giggle of a housemaid."

Kingly Praise for a Duke

WHEN Dr. C. W. Duke, for years pastor of the First Baptist Church, of Tampa, Florida, died in 1936, the following great tribute was paid to him by a friend, a tribute which we pay tribute to by giving it space here:

C ARDINAL in his doctrine,
C ANDID in his speech,
C HRIST-LIKE in his bearing,
C ALLED of God to preach.

W ORLD-WIDE in his vision,
W ITNESSING for Christ,
W ILL of God his passion,
W INCING not at price.

D O GOOD was his motto,
D EAL kindly was his creed,
D ESPISE not the lowly,
D ENY none in need.

U NRIVALED in his eloquence,
U NASSUMING in his art,
U NBIASED in his thinking,
U NDERSTANDING in his heart.

K INGLY in his style,
K EEN in his humor,
K INDLY in his smile.
K NIGHTLY in his manner,

E STEEMED by the masses,
E NVIED by the few,
E TERNAL is his memory,
E NSHRINED in hearts true.

Bits About Bok

EDWARD BOK's first job was cleaning the show windows of a bakery for fifty cents a week. When he was twelve, he was an office boy in the Western Union Telegraph Company. At nineteen, he was a stenographer. At twenty-six, he was editor of the *Ladies' Home Journal!*

Courtship and Marriage

GARIBALDI, Italian patriot, heard, through one of his soldiers, of the beauty, bravery, and self-sacrifice of the daughter of a certain rich man – Anita, by name. Drawing rein before the door of the shop, he sent one of his men into the store to buy a trifle. In the upper window stood Anita. Each looked into the soul of the other. But let Hillis describe it:

"Suddenly Garibaldi said, 'Senorita! I have never seen you before. I do not know your name, but you belong to me! Sooner or later you will come to me.' Anita arose. She leaned out of the window. In a low voice she said, 'Shall I come now?' And Garibaldi answered, 'I will ride up the street and return within a moment. Be ready at this spot.' There was just time for Anita to grasp a cloak and a few articles of clothing. A moment later, down the street on a gallop came Garibaldi, followed by his soldiers. Anita was standing on the stone step. As Garibaldi dashed by, he put out his right arm, swept her against his horse and up to the front of the saddle and dashed away for a ten-mile gallop to a little church whose frightened priest refused to perform the marriage ceremony without publishing the banns for the next two Sundays. Anita's father was of the other political party and the soldier knew that the consent would never be given. Garibaldi laid two revolvers upon the altar and said quietly, 'Father, the service will proceed immediately.' And so they were married."

And their married life was happy. And, considering the beauty and sweetness of the married love and life of many, how entrance into blasphemy is what Thomas Flatman wrote:

Like a dog with a bottle fast tied to his tail,
Like vermin in a trap or a thief in jail,
Like a Tory in a bog
Or an ape with a clog.

You Alone

How many things are there in this world that you now enjoy would be yours if you were cast upon your own resources? Would you know how to make an automobile? Or build a home? Or make a pane of window glass? Could you make a locomotive, or run one if it were given you? Could you make a piano or organ or violin? How infinitely poorer the world would be if it had to depend on you alone! But you share in all the gain of a thousand generations. What return are you making for these inestimable gifts? Are you having your share in handing down many blood-bequeathed legacies unreduced in quality and in quantity? Are you doing more than "a walnut rolling in an empty barrel?"

In New Hampshire

DURING a visit to New Hampshire, I visited the home of Daniel Webster. As I looked upon that home where his boyhood feet pattered about, and upon the hills where the echoes of his boyish voice were heard, I thought of what he said in speaking on the love of home.

Listen!

"It is only shallow-minded pretenders who either make distinguished origin a matter of merit, or obscure origin a matter of personal reproach. Taunt and scoffing at the humble condition of early life affects nobody in America but those who are foolish enough to indulge in them, and they are generally sufficiently punished by public rebuke. A man who is not ashamed of himself need not be ashamed of his early condition. It did not happen to me to be born in a log-cabin; but my elder brothers and sisters were born in a log-cabin raised among the snow-drifts of New Hampshire, at a period so early that when the smoke first rose from its rude chimney and curled over the frozen hills, there was no similar evidence of a white man's habitation between it and the settlements on the rivers of Canada. Its remains still exist; I make it an annual visit. I carry my children to it, to teach them the hardships endured by the generations which have gone before them. I love to dwell on the tender recollections, the kindred ties, the early affections, and the touching narratives and incidents which mingle with all I know of this primitive family abode. I weep to think that none of those who inhabited it are now among the living; and if ever I am ashamed of it, or if ever I fail in affectionate veneration for him who reared it and defended it against savage violence and destruction, cherished all the domestic virtues beneath its roof, and, through the fire and blood of a seven years' revolutionary war, shrunk from no danger, no toil, no sacrifice, to serve his country and to raise his children to a condition better than his own, may my name and the name of my posterity be blotted forever from the memory of mankind!"

In Vermont

When in Vermont, I was near the spot where Calvin Coolidge took the oath of office as President of the United States, one night by the light of a kerosene lamp, his father, administering the solemn oath. I recalled Coolidge's "Eight Commandments of Public Service." Here they are:

"Do the day's work."

"If it be to protect the rights of the weak, whoever objects, do it."

"If it be to help a powerful corporation the better to serve the people, whatever the opposition, do that."

"Expect to be *called* a standpatter, but don't *be* a standpatter."

"Expect to be *called* a demagogue, but don't *be* a demagogue."

"Don't hesitate to be as revolutionary as science."

"Don't hesitate to be as reactionary as the multiplication table."

"Don't expect to build up the weak by pulling down the strong."

In Albany

In rambling around Albany, N. Y., recently I saw where Robert Fulton's little teakettle of a steamboat stopped as it struggled up the Hudson River from New York to Albany in three days. And, thinking of that voyage, I was reminded of the first *steamboat* passage ever paid in the history of the world.

Here are the details:

A man went on board the boat, and inquired for Mr. Fulton. He was directed to the cabin, where he met a plain-looking but gentlemanly-appearing man, wholly alone.

"Mr. Fulton, I presume?"

"Yes, sir."

"Do you return to New York with this boat?"

"We shall try to get back, sir."

"Can I have passage down?"

"You can take your chance with us, sir."

"How much is the passage money?"

After a moment's hesitation, he named the sum of six dollars and the coins were laid in his hand.

Four years later, Mr. Fulton met this man and took him to lunch. As they discussed many things, Mr. Fulton ran rapidly and vividly over his experiences of the past few years. He spoke of the world's coldness and sneers, of the hopes, fears, disappointments, and difficulties which had followed him through his whole career of discovery up to his final crowning triumph of success.

"I have again and again recalled our first meeting at Albany," Mr. Fulton said, "and the vivid emotions caused by your paying me that first passage money. That, sir, seemed then, and still seems, the turning point in my destiny – the dividing line between light and darkness – the first actual recognition of my usefulness from my fellowmen. God bless you, sir! That act of yours gave me the courage I needed."

Ten Minutes and a Life

We are breeding what we are in other people. It matters what we are to everybody with whom we come in contact. Dr. Scherer says he knows a man who spent his life in sacrificial devotion because for less than ten minutes he watered his horse at the same trough where Brainard Taylor was watering his. Makes us think of the life of a woman whose life was changed from something sordid and calloused into something beautiful and tender because she met Jesus at Jacob's well – met Him for just a few minutes one day, long ago. Has such been so of us as to anybody who met us for just a few minutes?

Heroic Helen's Happy Heart

The following sentences ring like jewels of gold falling down stairways of pearl. From these we get a glimpse of Helen Keller's happy heart:

"Is it not true that my life, with all its limitations, touches at many points the life of the World Beautiful? Everything has its wonders, even darkness and silence, and I learn whatever state I may be in therein to be content. Sometimes, it is true, a sense of isolation enfolds me like a cold mist as I sit alone and wait at life's shut gate. Beyond there is light and music and sweet companionships, but I may not enter. . . . Silence sits immense upon my soul. Then comes Hope with a smile and whispers, 'There is joy in self-forgetfulness.' So I try to make the light in others' eyes my sun, the music in others' ears my symphony, the smile on others' lips my happiness."

A Portrait

George Ryan, in *The Boston Herald*, says in his poem, "The Portrait," this:

He is, it seems, the sort of man
  To ponder public questions,
Or quickly formulate a plan,
  Or offer sane suggestions.
He never hints the vaguest doubt
  On money or inflation;
Indeed, he faces them without
  The slightest consternation.

He's ever ready to explain
  With reasons circumstantial,
How best the nations might regain
  Their equipoise financial.
He has a theory complete
  Of where we must advance to;
He'd put the world upon its feet,
  If he but had the chance to.

But tho' perhaps he's found the way,
  As frequently he shows me,
I'd feel more certain, if he'd pay
  The sixteen bucks he owes me.

Bowler's Woe

This woe came to Julian Levitch in Memphis, Tennessee. A wobbly No. 5 pin that stayed up prevented this magnificent bowler from being $10,000 richer. Levitch threw eleven straight strikes at Park Bowling Lanes on a

Saturday night and on his final ball, one pin swayed but wouldn't fall. He ended with 299. The Park Bowling Lanes has a standing offer of $10,000 to any player — in open or league competition — who bowls the perfect 300 game.

Thus we see the value of one for good or evil. The Bible says: "One sinner destroyeth much good" (Ecclesiastes 9:18).

Vacuum Tube

DR. LEE DE FOREST, Los Angeles, celebrated his 80th birthday August 26, 1953. He is called "the father of radio" — because he was the inventor of the vacuum tube which made radio, television, radar, and talking machines possible. He said he was not attempting to improve the electron tube.

"I'll let the new men take over that work," he said. Mr. De Forest has spent the last few years experimenting on ways of obtaining usable electric current from the heat of metals.

"The [vacuum] tube has far surpassed my wildest hope," he said. "I regard it as a magic key that has unlocked vast treasures and the treasures are widening year by year."

How long Dr. De Forest will live in the flesh, I know not. But he will live as long as the world lasts and in all corners of ali the continents of earth. Because his electron tube functions, he will live in that electron tube.

Baseball Stories

IN SPOKANE, WASHINGTON, died Leon Cadore — once the roommate of Casey Stengel. Cadore pitched the longest baseball game in major league history — twenty-six innings for the Brooklyn Dodgers against Boston, May 1, 1920.

Some of the ballplayers were having a gabfest and one asked what Cobb would hit today. A pretty fair sticker said: "Oh, about .315 or so." The questioner said: "Yea, but his lifetime average is .367!" The other guy laughed and said: "But you got to remember, Ty is 71 years old now."

Which reminds you of the remark Whitey Ford of the Yankees made about Cobb a couple years back when they appeared in an old-timers' game at Yankee Stadium. Cobb looked pretty good at the plate, swung well and beat out a hit. "He looks pretty good," said Ford. "But I'd say that he has slowed up at least a step."

Once, years ago, "Shoeless Joe Jackson," spoken of by Ty Cobb as the greatest natural hitter in the baseball world, came in from the outfield complaining in these words: "Glass in that outfield." The manager asked: "Cutting your feet, Joe?" "No," said Joe, "but it's roughin' up the ball something terrible!"

Great men these in the baseball world. We need men great in the field of life — great in character, great in spirit — who live above pettiness and the blight of prejudices.

Eight Lessons Learned

ON THE back of an envelope found among his effects after his death in a plane crash, former Atomic Energy Commission Chairman, Gordon Dean, had scrawled:

1. Never lose your capacity for enthusiasm.
2. Never lose your capacity for indignation.
3. Never judge people, don't type them too quickly; but in a pinch always first assume that a man is good and that at worst he is in the gray area between good and bad.
4. If you can't be generous when it's hard, you won't be when it's easy.
5. The greatest builder of confi-

dence is the ability to do something – almost anything – well.

6. When that confidence comes, then strive for humility; you aren't as good as all that.

7. And the way to become truly useful is to seek the best that other brains have to offer. Use them to supplement your own, and give credit to them when they have helped.

8. The greatest tragedies in world and personal events stem from misunderstanding.

Gordon Dean lived by that splendid testament.

Unfinished Cathedral

The query comes: How long is Life?
Threescore and ten, the Good Book
reads,
Is time enough for men to write
The record of his life in deeds.

Threescore and ten–how fast they fly!
Threescore and ten–they're almost
gone!
And I, who dreamed of castles high,
Have only laid the cornerstone.

–S/Sgt. Jarvis D. Anderson

Walking

In an old scrapbook, made in 1911, I find something about some walking records.

A thousand miles in a thousand consecutive hours, walking one mile each hour is the record made by Charles F. Morse, at Jackson, Michigan. He started at 1 p.m., January 11, 1897, and ended at 4 a.m., February 22, 1897 – the track thirty-nine laps to the mile.

The greatest distance walked without a rest was 121 miles, 385 yards – by C. A. Harriman, California.

There was a walk from the Atlantic to the Pacific Ocean. John Ennis started with a plunge in the surf at Coney Island, New York, Monday, May 23, 1910.

He arrived at the Cliff Hotel, San Francisco, August 24, 1910, and took a plunge in the ocean before a crowd of admirers. Before him a Mr. Weston had walked the same distance, but Ennis lowered Weston's record by twenty-five days. Ennis, like Weston, did not walk on Sunday.

But more interesting and certainly more significant the walking the Bible speaks of:

"And Enoch walked with God: and he was not; for God took him" (Genesis 5:24).

"These are the generations of Noah: Noah was a just man and perfect in his generations, and Noah walked with God" (Genesis 6:9).

"For the children of Israel walked forty years in the wilderness, till all the people that were men of war, which came out of Egypt, were consumed, because they obeyed not the voice of the Lord: unto whom the Lord sware that he would not shew them the land, which the Lord sware unto their fathers that he would give us, a land that floweth with milk and honey" (Joshua 5:6).

"And he did that which was right in the sight of the Lord, and walked in all the way of David his father, and turned not aside to the right or to the left" (II Kings 22:2).

"But sought to the Lord God of his father, and walked in his commandments, and not after the doings of Israel" (II Chronicles 17:4).

"Judge me, O Lord; for I have walked in mine integrity: I have trusted also in the Lord; therefore I shall not slide" (Psalm 26:1).

"Blessed is the man that walketh not in the counsel of the ungodly, nor standeth in the way of sinners, nor sitteth in the seat of the scornful" (Psalm 1:1).

Dumb Bell

I SPEAK not of a person who is lacking in intelligence or who lacks ability to speak. But I speak of the five-ton fire bell once used to sound fire alarms for the whole city of Hartford, Connecticut, now belonging to the Connecticut Historical Society. The bell was cast in 1881. At that time it cost $4,000. Since then repairs have cost $1,000.

But how akin to that bell of metal that used to sound alarms are the men and women of flesh and bones and blood who speak no more against evils that would lead our greatest graces to the grave and leave the world no copy. "Let the redeemed of the Lord *say* so."

Shoe Output

SHOE manufacturers report that more than four hundred million pairs of shoes are manufactured in factories in the United States each year.

Think of the places where those shoes were carried by the feet of those who wore them. To taverns, to saloons, to churches, to schools, to streets, to fields, to mountains, to mines, to stores, to hotels, to dance halls, to cabins, to palaces, to all the places where human feet go.

And how little approved of God were many places where those shoes were taken by the feet that wore them and by the folks to whom the feet belonged.

Moreover, we should be greatly sobered by the thought that the footsteps made inside and outside, by day and by night, in all places were counted by the Lord. Knowing that, we can wisely ask the questions which Job, in his eighth answer, asked:

"I made a covenant with mine eyes: why then should I think upon a maid? for what portion of God is there from above? and what inheritance of the Almighty from on high? Is not destruction to the wicked? and a strange punishment to the workers of iniquity? Doth not he see my ways, and count all my steps? If I have walked with vanity, or if my foot hath hasted to deceit; let me be weighed in an even balance, that God may know mine integrity. If my step hath turned out of the way, and mine heart walked after mine eyes, and if any blot hath cleaved to mine hands; then let me sow, and let another eat; yea, let my offspring be rooted out" (Job 31:1-8).

Emphasis on Eyes

DO YOU ever watch the eyes of people as you meet and talk with them? The eyes usually tell the story of interest and devotion or otherwise. There is an entrancing story of Old Quebec written by William Kirby and entitled, *The Golden Gog*. In it he discusses in a most appealing way "The Men of the Old Regime," and follows with an entrancing chapter on "The Walls of Quebec." In that chapter he describes the heroine of the story, Amelie deRepentigny. It is morning and the young (old) city is at work upon the protecting walls, for ominous war signs reflect against the horizon. Among the beholders is the young woman named above. Here is Kirby's description of her:

"Her hair was very dark and thick, matching the deep liquid eyes that lay for the most part so quietly and restfully hidden beneath their long, shading lashes. Eyes gentle, frank and modest – looking tenderly on all things innocent, fearfully on all things harmful . . ."

That's far enough! "Looking tenderly on all things innocent, fearfully on all things harmful!" Should that always be true of our eyes, what a fine witness for good our eyes (and lives) would be!

How we need to remember the words of Jesus:

"The light of the body is the eye: if therefore thine eye be single, thy whole body shall be full of light. But if thine eye be evil, thy whole body shall be full of darkness. If therefore the light that is in thee be darkness, how great is that darkness!" (Matthew 6:22, 23).

How we need, too, to rejoice in the precious promise written from the Lord by Isaiah:

"He that walketh righteously, and speaketh uprightly; he that despiseth the gain of oppressions, that shaketh his hands from holding of bribes, that stoppeth his ears from hearing of blood, and shutteth his eyes from seeing evil; he shall dwell on high: his place of defence shall be the munitions of rocks: bread shall be given him; his waters shall be sure" (Isaiah 33:15, 16).

Sun Goes Out

LOWELL THOMAS, a great news commentator, speaks of such a day. In these atomic times, when so many people are trembling about the "ultimate disaster," I find that there is a sort of steadying strength in the following story:

It was on May 19, 1780 – during the anxious days of our Revolutionary War—that darkness came at noon. The bats flew and chickens roosted. It was some sort of meteorological phenomenon that seemed to bring the day to an end when the sun was at zenith. Panic broke out, and people thought that the end of the world was at hand.

At Hartford, Connecticut, the State Legislature was in session and, when the darkness came at noon, the meeting of the Lower House broke up in alarm. In the State Senate, a motion of adjournment was made, so that the legislators could meet the Day of Judgment with whatever courage they could manage to summon.

But the motion was opposed by Abraham Davenport, a Yankee Selectman and Judge, friend and advisor of George Washington. Abraham Davenport faced the panic about the End of the World with the best of Yankee heart and head.

He arose, and addressed his legislative colleagues. "I'm against this adjournment," he said. Then he explained with a logic of courage:

"The Day of Judgment," he said, "is either approaching or it is not. If it is not, there is no cause for adjournment. If it is, I choose to be found doing my duty. I wish, therefore, that candles may be brought."

Of course, this was not the only time that people have beheld what seems to be the ultimate disaster. In the past they have trembled in the presence of such nightmares as the invasion of the Huns led by Attila the Scourge of God, or the rage of plagues like the Black Death, or the predicted End of the World in the year 1000.

But in all history it would be hard to find a better example for our times than the sturdy figure of Abraham Davenport. At a time when we are all haunted by doubts and questions about the possibility of atomic war and trying to decide what course to take, he gives us the only possible answer: "I choose to be found doing my duty."

Poor With Plenty

FROM St. Louis comes the news that Miss Caroline Rippe, 87 years old, who, with her 75-year-old brother,

William, was found a year ago living in a state of neglect in their six-room house on Douglas road in northern St. Louis County despite an estate later valued at more than $70,000, died in the Halls Ferry Memorial Hospital, where both had been placed by county authorities.

Almost $5,000 in cash was found about the home by authorities who were called by a physician after he found the pair sleeping on the floor. The Public Administrator's office later estimated their assets at $72,525.

More foolish than these two who died in poverty with plenty to sustain them are those who lay not up treasures in heaven where moth and rust do not consume and where there are no thieves to break through and steal. As seriously as ever in the world's history do men need to heed the words of Jesus:

"Lay not up for yourselves treasures upon earth, where moth and rust doth corrupt and where thieves break through and steal: But lay up for yourselves treasures in heaven, where neither moth nor rust doth corrupt, and where thieves do not break through nor steal: for where your treasure is there will your heart be also" (Matthew 6:19-21).

Leader Wins Respect

A SEER who saw clearly, a great mind that thought profoundly, a great heart that felt deeply was South Carolina's John C. Calhoun. When he was a young lad at college, he did not have part in many of the social and casual occurrences of the campus. One day Calhoun was asked why he did not participate in these campus matters. Calhoun replied: "One day I must represent my great state in the halls of the National Congress – and I am seeking to make these years contribute their best produce to those peaks of demand experience."

And thus, with his self-discipline and patriotic passion, Calhoun became a man of giant power – "winning the admiration of his own and succeeding generations."

When God says: "Come now therefore, and I will send thee," men and women ought to be ready – remembering the "now" of that statement.

Myself

EDWIN L. SABIN gives us this choice poem:

An enemy I had whose mien
  I stoutly strove to know,
For hard he dogged my steps, unseen,
  Wherever I might go.

My plans he balked, my aims he foiled,
  He blocked my onward way.
When for some lofty goal I toiled,
  He grimly said me nay.

"Come forth!" I cried, "lay bare thy guise!
  Thy features I would see!"
But always to my straining eyes
  He dwelt in mystery.

One night I seized and held him fast,
  The veil from him did draw,
I gazed upon his face at last . . .
  And lo! myself I saw.

Which reminds us that D. L. Moody once made this confession: "I have more trouble with myself than any other person."

One

ONE mischievous boy can break up a school. One false alarm can cause a panic. One match can start a conflagration. One false step can cost a life or ruin a character. One broken wheel can ditch a train. One quarrelsome worker can create a strike of ten thousand men. One undiplomatic word can provoke a war involving thousands of lives and destruction of millions of dollars in property. One hasty act of legislation can entail untold hardships. One wayward daughter can break a mother's heart. One lie can destroy a person's character. One false witness can send an innocent man to jail. One vote can decide an election. One kind word at the right time may save a person from suicide. One sermon may fire a man's soul and set the course for his future life. One drink may start a person on the road to alcoholism. One wrong example may lead dozens down the wrong path. One decision for Christ will determine future destiny.

And the Bible says: "One sinner destroyeth much good" (Ecclesiastes 9:18).

Yes, just as *one* broken link can make a chain useless, just as *one* leak can sink a ship, just as *one* worm can spoil an apple. But we are glad to note that *one* can do *good*, as when *one* good word maketh a heavy heart glad (Proverbs 12:25), as *one* faithful ambassador is health (Proverbs 13:17), just as *one* word spoken in due season – how good is it (Proverbs 15:23), just as *one* word fitly spoken is like apples of gold in pictures of silver (Proverbs 25:11).

Churchill Comments

COLUMNIST George Boswell writes wisely of Winston Churchill whose phrases stirred the world. Approval of honorary citizenship by the U. S. House of Representatives brings back a wave of memories of this great man who more than any other rallied the world to resist and defeat the onslaught of Hitler's Nazis. One of the most vivid phrase makers of this century, his writings and speeches already have become a permanent part of our literature.

Some may remember that it was he who described the post-war Soviet line from the Baltic to the Adriatic as "the Iron Curtain." We often hear quoted his eloquent words when he became prime minister in 1940: "I have nothing to offer but blood, toil, tears, and sweat." Let's recall other statements that will long survive him.

On the resistance to Hitler during the bloody Battle of Britain: "If the British Commonwealth and Empire last for a thousand years, men will still say, 'This was their finest hour.' "

On Hitler's threat to invade Britain: "We shall fight on the beaches; we shall fight on the landing ground; we shall fight in the fields; and in the streets: we shall fight in the hills; we shall never surrender."

Recalling these experiences on his eightieth birthday, November 30, 1954, he said: "It was the nation and the race dwelling all around the globe that had the lion's heart. I had the luck to be called upon to give the roar. I also hope that I sometimes suggested to the lion the right place to use his claws."

Here are some of his statements on the Cold War: In New York, Oct. 14, 1947: "Great wars come when both sides believe they are more or less equal and when each one thinks he has a good chance of victory."

Before the House of Commons, Dec. 10, 1948: "What are these major themes of foreign policy? The first is an ever closer and more effective relationship or, as I like to call it, 'fraternal association' with the United States . . . in the ever closer unity of the English-speaking world lies the main hope of human freedom and a great part of the hope for our own survival."

In a speech on European unity at Strasbourg, Aug. 12, 1949: "If we are to achieve our supreme reward, we must lay aside every impediment and conquer ourselves. We must rise to a level above the passions which have laid all Europe in ruins. Old feuds must die. Territorial ambitions must be set aside. National rivalries must be confined who can render the truest service to the common cause."

From a speech in Commons on March 1, 1955: "It may well be that we shall, by a process of sublime irony, have reached a stage in this story where safety will be the sturdy child of terror and survival the twin brother of annihilation."

Reading these and others of his words of great wisdom, one can only conclude that the present generation of leadership has yet to produce a Churchill.

Who does not recall Mr. Churchill's words when the bombs were falling the thickest? When he said: "You ask, what is my policy? I will say, it is to wage war, by sea, land and air, with all our might and with all the strength that God can give us. You ask, what is our aim? I can answer in one word: Victory — victory at all costs, victory in spite of all terror; victory, however long and hard the road may be, for without victory there is no survival."

Further, after declaring to his people that he had nothing to offer but "blood, toil, tears and sweat," he again made the pronouncement that will be remembered as long as history is written: the statement which we have quoted above which he made at the time Hitler threatened to invade Britain.

Listen to these words about words from God's Book:

"The words of a wise man's mouth are gracious; but the lips of a fool will swallow up himself. The beginning of the words of his mouth is foolishness: and the end of his talk is mischievous madness" (Ecclesiastes 10:12, 13).

"Bow down thine ear, and hear the words of the wise" (Proverbs 22:17).

Resolutions Concerning Myself

I WILL be joyful, that life may give me wings.

I will be courageous, that there shall be no binding fears.

I will be balanced that neither work, nor play, nor rest, nor worship shall lose its proper share.

I will be self-reliant, that thoughts of failure shall not hold me back.

I will be self-controlled, that emotions shall not be dominant.

I will be intelligent that straight thinking and knowledge shall direct all actions.

I will be healthy, that my body shall not fail to respond.

I will be clean, in spirit, mind and action, that there shall be no shame.

I will be good-tempered, that annoyance shall not irritate.

I will be patient, that discouragement shall not seem final.

I will be persistent, that the will may carry through to completion.

I will be prepared, that emergency shall not find me in confusion.

Paul, the great apostle, who left a trail of gospel glory across the Gentile world wrote: "With the mind I *myself* serve the law of God" (Romans 7:25).

"I could wish that *myself* were accursed from Christ for my brethren, my kinsmen according to the flesh" (Romans 9:3).

"I have made *myself* servant unto all" (I Corinthians 9:19).

"But I determined this with *myself*" (II Corinthians 2:1).

"In all things I have kept *myself* from being burdensome unto you, and so will I keep *myself*" (II Corinthians 11:9).

Wishbones — Jawbones — Backbones

THE body is made up largely of bones — about two hundred of them classified according to shape. Your church is also made up of bones, classified according to use. There are three kinds. First, *Wishbones*. You know this kind. They wish for greater things in the church. They wish for success in the Sunday school. They wish for larger attendances. They wish for more souls to be saved. Wishbones? They're lazy. They're languid. They're listless. The only things they deny themselves of are work and effort to make their wishes come true. Rocking-chair Christians! Drawing-room Christians!

Then there are the *Jawbones*. Nothing slow or listless about this kind. They work up and down at great speed. They criticize. They gossip. They pick flaws. They tell how it should be done. In their wake follow dissension, discouragement and disease. Verily, it taketh a Samson to handle this class and turn them to some good use!

But the third class is the one we like to think of — they are the *Backbones*. There is work to be done; the Backbones do it. There is a healthy target to raise; the Backbones raise it. There are meetings to attend; the Backbones are there. O Backbones! If we were poets we would write about thee! If we were singers, we would chant thy praises! If we were artists, we would paint thy lovely likeness! But being only ordinary humans, we can only love thee!

Verbal Flowers

WHEN Bethel Thomas Hunt, Sr., died in Memphis in 1955, an editor threw these verbal flowers the day of his burial:

"Bethel Thomas Hunt, Sr., nationally known industrial realtor, who died here Friday night, was not a man who would appreciate a requiem of words. He was a man who believed that the work a man does, the good he accomplished are the best testimonies he can leave behind. And Bethel Hunt's accomplishments were many. He was a leader in the real estate and insurance fields. He might have been described as a one-man chamber of commerce for he, as much as any one person, or probably any one group, was responsible for the industrial growth of Memphis.

"To some persons, Bethel Hunt might at times have seemed abrupt. But, the fact of the matter is, he was a shy man who overcame his shyness to become one of Memphis' great salesmen. He was a man who thought big. Sale of a single lot or a single house bored him. He preferred the challenge of great dreams; great efforts and great accomplishments. He was generous in the manner prescribed by the Scriptures and endorsed by the Presbyterian faith, which he professed — the generosity of modesty and secrecy. He believed that people should be helped by being allowed to help themselves, and no one will ever know the doors of opportunity he secretly unlocked for others."

The editor could justifiably have used these Bible words in writing of this business man: "Not slothful in business, fervent in spirit, serving the Lord" (Romans 12:11).

Senator's Prayer for His Pastor

SENATOR ROBERT S. KERR of Oklahoma was a member of the First Baptist Church of Oklahoma City. He was a long-time Sunday school teacher and Christian philanthropist. He gave more than one-million dollars to Baptist institutions in Oklahoma.

His pastor, Dr. H. H. Hobbs, in his tribute to his friend at the memorial service in the church, quoted a prayer the senator had published many years before called "A Prayer for My Pastor":

"Our Father, let me be a pillar of strength to help hold him up and not a thorn in his back to pull him down. Let me support him without striving to possess him. Let me lift his hands without placing shackles around them. Let me give him help that he may devote more time in working for the salvation of others and less time in gratifying my vanity. Let me work for him as the pastor of all the members and not compel him to spend precious time in bragging on me. Let me be unselfish in what I do for him and not selfish in demanding that he do more for me. Let me strive to serve him and the church much and be happy as he serves me less and the church and others more."

Robert Burns' Pen and Whip

Here Stuarts once in glory reigned,
And laws for Scotland's weal ordained;
But now unroofed their palace stands,
These scepter's swayed by other hands;
The injured Stuart line is gone,
A race outlandish fills their throne—
An idiot race to honor lost,
Who know them best despise them most.

THESE lines were scratched with a diamond on a pane of glass in a window of the Inn at which Robert Burns stayed—on the occasion of his first visit to Stirling. They were quoted to his prejudice at the time, and no doubt did him no good with those who could best serve his interests. On his next visit to Stirling, he smashed the pane with the butt end of his riding whip. But smashing the pane did not do away with the resentful thoughts which he caused others to have against him.

When Lincoln Prayed

GENERAL DANIEL E. SICKLES has recorded for us this intimate revelation from the heart of the Great Emancipator. The General had been severely wounded on July 2, 1863, and after suffering the amputation of a leg, was removed to Washington where he was visited by the President. We quote from General Sickles:

"Mr. Lincoln, we heard at Gettysburg that here at the capitol you were all so anxious about the results of the battle that the government officials packed up and got ready to leave at short notice with the official archives."

" 'Yes,' he said, 'some precautions were prudently taken, but for my part I was sure of our success at Gettysburg.' 'Why,' I asked, 'were you so confident? The Army of the Potomac had suffered many reverses.'

"There was a pause. The President seemed in deep meditation. His pale face was lighted up by an expression I had not observed before. Turning, he said:

" 'When Lee crossed the Potomac and entered Pennsylvania followed by our Army, I felt that the crisis had come. I knew that defeat in a great battle on Northern soil involved the loss of Washington, to be followed, perhaps, by the intervention of England and France in favor of the Southern Confederacy. I went to my room and got down on my knees in prayer. Never before had I prayed with so much earnestness. I wish I could repeat my prayer. I felt that I must put all my trust in Almighty God. He gave our people the best country ever given to man. He alone could save it from destruction. I had tried my best to do my duty and found myself unequal to the task. The burden was more than I could bear. God had often been our Protector in other days. I prayed that He would not let the nation perish. I asked Him to help us and give us the victory now. I felt that my prayer was answered. I had no misgivings about the result of Gettysburg.' "

God preserved the nation a hundred years ago in answer to prayer. He is the same Almighty One now as He was then. We thank President V. Raymond Edman of Wheaton College for giving us this incident.

Along with Lincoln's prayer, we give a letter Lincoln wrote June 13, 1860, accepting the nomination:

"Imploring the assistance of Divine Providence, and with regard to the views and feelings of all who were present at the convention; to the rights of all the states and territories and the people of the nation, to the inviolability of the Constitution and the perpetual union, harmony, and prosperity of all, I am most happy to cooperate for the practical success of the principles declared by the convention."

The Tribune said: "The letter is plain, straightforward, and unmistakable evidence of the honesty and fair dealing of the man. It has not a word too much; it is not a line too short; it expresses just what he means."

Tallest Tree

THE tallest tree in the world is believed to be a 368-foot California redwood in Humboldt County, California. This tree, according to American Forest Products Industries, tops the old Founders Tree, which lost seventeen feet in a storm a few years ago.

More wonderfully blessed it is for us – as we think of this tall tree – to remember the words of Jesus:

"Even so every good tree bringeth forth good fruit; but a corrupt tree bringeth forth evil fruit. A good tree cannot bring forth evil fruit, neither can a corrupt tree bring forth good fruit. Every tree that bringeth not forth good fruit is hewn down, and cast into the fire. Wherefore by their fruits ye shall know them" (Matthew 7:17-20).

"For a good tree bringeth not forth corrupt fruit; neither doth a corrupt tree bring forth good fruit. For every tree is known by his own fruit. For of thorns men do not gather figs, nor of a bramble bush gather they grapes" (Luke 6:43, 44).

A Beautiful Tribute

A SHORT time before Dr. Hight C. Moore, writer superior, died, he paid this tribute to Mrs. Robert Logan Patton:

"Queen of a happy home in the Highlands of North Carolina, she attained and maintained the Worthy Woman's Maximum Standard of Excellence:

"A daughter who honored her father and mother and realized the promise that her days should be long;

"A daughter-in-law unforsaking as Ruth in the lonely hour and faithful to her entrustment of loved ones;

"A sister as devoted as Miriam to Moses on the banks of the Nile;

"A sister-in-law truly filial with hands clasped and heart-strings knit together in reciprocal love;

"An aunt as loyal as Jehosheba to Joash whom she hid six years in the house of God;

"A wife whose husband, known in the gates and honored among the elders of the land, trusted in her and praised her, saying. 'Many daughters have served worthily, but thou excellest them all';

"A mother whose children rise up and call her blessed because she, like Hannah, lent them to the Lord and trained them up in the way they should go;

"A mother-in-law unsurpassed by her who irradiated and immortalized Peter's home;

"A grandmother like Naomi who fondled newborn Obed as a restorer of life and a nourisher of old age;

"A great-grandmother witnessing the mercy of God to her fourth generation;

"A Christian like Mary of Bethany, filling her house with the fragrance of spikenard devotion to Christ;

"A church member like Lydia, given to hospitality for the furtherance of the Gospel;

"A minister's wife like Phebe, the deaconess who was the helper of many, including the Apostle Paul;

"A friend and neighbor like Dorcas full of good works and alms deeds which she did;

"A citizen of the commonwealth and the kingdom, rendering to Caesar the things that are Caesar's and to God the things that are God's;

"A widow for thirty years, resourceful like the widow of Zarephath whose jar of meal wasted not, neither did her cruse of oil fail; liberal like the widow who cast her two mites into the temple treasury; and worshipful like Anna looking for the Lord."

This deserved tribute by a great man to a great woman makes me think of Solomon's words:

"Favour is deceitful, and beauty is vain: but a woman that feareth the Lord, she shall be praised. Give her of the fruit of her hands; and let her own works praise her in the gates" (Proverbs 31:30, 31).

Beautiful Resolutions

These resolutions were adopted by Dr. James Clemant Furman, first president of Furman University, when a young man of nineteen, and are appropriate in connection with every observance of Founder's Day at Furman University:

"Resolved, never to speak ill of an individual but to call to mind my own sins and imperfections and be silent.

"Resolved, when my heart feels cold and languid, to strive earnestly in prayer to God for deliverance from such a state and for the abiding influence of His Holy Spirit; and to enquire into the causes which have produced this effect upon me and to guard against them in the future.

"Resolved, never to go to bed without having endeavored to learn something more of God as He is revealed in the Holy Scriptures than I knew when I rose in the morning.

"Resolved, never to smile at anything profane or irreligious.

"Resolved, to keep in mind during the business of the day the good resolutions which I may have formed for my assistance so that if I neglect them, I may humble myself and in my retirement earnestly seek pardon from God.

"Resolved, to say nothing to irritate the feelings of anyone and especially of my relations and friends.

"Resolved, to leave as soon as possible any company which might draw off my thoughts from the things of eternity.

"Resolved, never to neglect to devote a certain portion of every twenty-four hours to secret meditation and prayer.

"Resolved, never to halt in doing anything of which I am convinced that it is duty."

EXAMPLE

Pitch Battle

THE piano tuners of America have done the nation a service in uncovering a plot to destroy the integrity of "A" above middle "C." As you probably know, "A" is an unvarying, unshakable, indestructible note of four hundred, forty vibrations per second. For forty-three years, the 440-vibration note has been the only "A" above middle "C" recognized by the United States Bureau of Standards. It is a global pitch, so basic that radio and television and electric companies use it for power calibration. However, two of the nation's top symphony orchestras have given "A" a slightly sharper edge. They are tuning their instruments from 442 vibrations per second, simply to achieve more "brilliance" in stereo and high-fidelity reproduction. The piano tuners claim the higher note puts their very lives in jeopardy. Just with a true "A" the tension on a piano's two hundred twenty strings builds up to twenty tons, and the stress of added brilliance will make a lot of old, tired pianos explode. All thinking men will rally to the side of the authentic government-guaranteed, tried and true "A" – the side of uprights and uprightness, non-explosive.

I Resolve

THE following resolutions were found among the papers of Henrietta Hall Shuck, first American woman missionary to China, who served from 1835 to 1845 as a pioneer Christian leader:

1. I will endeavor always to observe strictly the golden rule, "to do unto others as I would have them do to me."

2. I will speak no ill of anyone. If I can say no good concerning persons, I will remain silent.

3. I will mind my own business, and not interfere with the concerns of others.

4. I will pay particular attention to the rule laid down by my medical adviser, with regard to diet and exercise.

5. My children are given me to train for heaven. They shall have my vigilant attention.

6. The duty of a wife is to love and obey. My husband shall find me ever endeavoring to practice these duties, and shall receive from me, at all times, a hearty acquiescence in his wishes.

7. My duty to the lost around me shall be strictly observed.

8. I will try to exercise patience and self-denial.

9. I will watch over my temper, and endeavor to be amiable.

10. I will love my missionary friends, and be merciful and kind to all, especially to the sick and distressed.

11. I will cherish a forgiving spirit, and will return good for evil.

These rules I will pray over twice, at least, every day. I look to the Lord to strengthen me in keeping them. Whenever I find I have deviated from any one of them, I will note it down, and thereby acquire the habit of marking my own faults.

Any comment on these would be as man's woeful inadequacy to fully depict with words the beauty of the Taj Mahal in India.

Idealizing Money

READ this editorial from *The Christian Index:*

"What is money? Did you ever hold your earning in hand at the end of the week or month – solemnly asking yourself that question meanwhile? You know the cost of it.

"It cost years of preparation, it cost hard words from hard-boiled bosses; maybe five days or more from home each week; maybe humiliation as others were lifted to positions above you; possibly discharge until 'you were needed again.' If your position is secure today, and your money sure, chances are that you went through the rubbers back yonder.

"But, back to the question, What is money? The dictionary says: 'A system of coinage'; also: 'A common medium of exchange in trade.' That definition is disappointing, seeing that our money cost so much sacrifice, mental ingenuity, weariness of the flesh, untiring vigilance, misunderstanding in the family, quarrels among one's friends – all or some of which may bob up any time without notice.

"After Clarence Darrow had won a lawsuit for a lady in Chicago, a story says, his ebullient client rushed up to ask, 'Mr. Darrow, how in the world can I repay you for what you have done for me?' The materialistic-minded attorney replied, 'Lady, since the ancient Phoenicians introduced the coinage of money, that has been a useless question.' That was Clarence Darrow, if it was.

"Let's turn to some more uplifting conceptions of money. The late Jim Anderson of Knoxville, used to put a check for $750.00 on the collection plate every Sunday morning. He said it put the joy note in his singing – for he felt he was sharing with the missionary in earth's remotest station; and with the suffering patients in our Baptist hospitals everywhere; and with the poor boys and girls who were struggling to get an education in order to serve Jesus better; and that he was helping to tie up his church every Sunday with every agency that is supported and directed by the Southern Baptist Convention.

" 'Brother Jim' as he was affectionately called, believed that by idealizing money, cotton could be transmuted into character, lumber could be converted into life and merchandising could be made to signify the making of manhood and womanhood."

Statements About and By Stagg

Amos Alonzo Stagg – born August 16th, 1862, – America's patriarch of sports, reached his 100th birthday in 1962. A man who was revered as a great athlete, became even greater as a dedicated teacher of men. Twelve dinners were scheduled throughout the country to pay homage to this man from a humble origin who is honored by the National Football Foundation and Hall of Fame as player, coach, and "the game's greatest teacher."

As a youngster, Stagg was intrigued by the history of ancient Spartans, their discipline, self-denial and independence. He determined that he would face life on his own resources, physical, financial and spiritual. He was the son of a cobbler and had little hope of going to college. But a teacher saw him as a fine student and fine athlete and encouraged him. He tried and qualified for Yale.

He became the best collegiate baseball pitcher of the era and a member of Walter Camp's first All-America Football team as an end in 1889. Stagg had studied for the ministry but felt he didn't have the right speaking voice for that.

"I felt specially called to preach," he said, "but I decided to do it on the athletic fields."

His coaching career spanned seventy years, extended from coast to coast and influenced the lives of thousands who became leaders of their day.

In 1892, he was invited by President William Rainey Harper of Chicago to become the first athletic director at that new institution, coaching all sports. In accepting, Stagg wrote: "After much thought and prayer, I have decided that my life can best be used for my Master's service in the position which you have offered."

Stagg well knew the value of money although it never played an important part in his life. In his forty-one years at Chicago, his salary never exceeded $8,500 a year, yet one time he turned down an offer of $350 for a single speech because it would mean missing a day of football practice with his squad. This was the same man who made luncheon and dinner several times in college on five cents worth of soda crackers.

Stagg never drank, smoked or swore. He'd call an erring player a jackass, double jackass or even a triple jackass.

And comments I could make about this man who was a maker of men, might be as man's mean paint on God's fair lily.

Manner of Walk Detected

The Army recently announced development of an ultra-sensitive radar which can spot "the slightest movement" behind enemy lines and even distinguish between a walking man and woman. A soldier crawling on the ground two miles away cannot only be "seen" but "heard."

Explaining how a radar operator can distinguish a woman from a man by watching the blips on his radar scope, an Army spokesman said a woman walks different than a man and produces a different wave on the radar.

"This latest development will provide the Army with the only ground-to-ground radar which can detect moving targets at such long range and which can operate in fog or darkness."

A rolling tank, truck or jeep can be seen ten miles away. While the average distance for spotting a soldier in typical battle terrain has been two miles, the Army said that in one test under ideal conditions a walking soldier was seen fifteen miles away. Each type of target seen by the new radar produces a different sound and an experienced radar man could distinguish these sounds: Sounds made by a walking soldier, the whistle of a tank, the whine of a truck or jeep, the beat produced by a patrol and the "pulsating rumble indicating soldiers in marching formation." The radar set consists of a simple portable shelter with controls and scopes and a remotely-placed antenna mounted inside a five-foot bubble on top of a twenty-five foot pole.

Job gave testimony to something more wonderful for mankind: "When his candle shined upon my head, and when by his light I walked through darkness" (Job 29:3). "Doth not he see my ways, and count all my steps?" (Job 31:4).

David, too:

"O Lord, thou hast searched me, and known me. Thou knowest my downsitting and mine uprising, thou understandest my thought afar off. Thou compassest my path and my lying down, and art acquainted with all my ways" (Psalm 139:1-3).

Service

In the Bible, we are told to serve the Lord with all the *heart*. "And now, Israel, what doth the Lord thy God require of thee, but to fear the Lord thy God, to walk in all his ways, and to love him, and to serve the Lord thy God with all thy heart and with all thy soul" (Deuteronomy 10:12).

Serve the Lord without *fear.* "As he spake by the mouth of his holy prophets, which have been since the world began . . . that he would grant unto us, that we being delivered out of the hand of our enemies might serve him without fear, in holiness and righteousness before him, all the days of our life" (Luke 1: 70, 74, 75).

Serve the Lord with *gladness.* "Serve the Lord with gladness: come before his presence with singing" (Psalm 100:2).

Serve the Lord with a willing *mind.* "And thou, Solomon my son, know thou the God of thy father, and serve him with a perfect heart and with a willing mind" (I Chronicles 28:9).

Serve the Lord with a pure *conscience.* "I thank God, whom I serve from my forefathers with pure conscience, that without ceasing I have remembrance of thee in my prayers night and day" (II Timothy 1:3).

Serve the Lord acceptably – with *reverence.* "Wherefore we receiving a kingdom which cannot be moved, let us have grace, whereby we may serve God acceptably with reverence and godly fear" (Hebrews 12:28).

Serve the Lord with *humility.* "Ye know . . . after what manner I have been with you at all seasons, serving the Lord with all humility of mind, and with many tears and temptations which befell me . . ." (Acts 20:18, 19).

Only One Defeat

ONLY once did Man O' War meet defeat in a race. That was in 1919 – when for the only time in his life he trailed another horse across the finish line. He was only two years old and had won six consecutive starts. Then, in one race, came a horse named Upset. Horsemen will tell you that bad racing luck beat Big Red that day. There was an assistant starter working at Saratoga that afternoon and the break from the barrier was delayed five minutes, with the champ, always nervous at the post, dancing and bobbing his head. And when the field broke away, Big Red was off sidewise, fifth in a seven-horse field.

Those who engage in horse racing tell us that he made a gallant try. When he hit the half way mark, he was fourth. He loomed up to third place at the three quarters. In the turn into the stretch, he moved into second. Ten lengths from home, he was "nodding at Upset's saddle girth." But Upset won by a whisker.

You like to think about this great horse that the upset by Upset never happened.

You like to think, too, that upsets some men have had never happened – as, for example, Noah. There is a page in his life we wish had never been written. Then there is Abraham – failing in an hour of emergency, prone in the mire down in Egypt. Then there is Jacob with his trickery. And Moses harassed in Egypt and trying to shake the sands in God's hour glass to make them run faster – as evidenced by his killing an Egyptian. And David, upset by the sight of a beautiful woman, tarnishes his name – and writes a black chapter. Elijah, too, was upset and prayed to die. But all of these, after upsets tragic, won great victories as did Man O' War, one year later, when he upset Upset and all backers of Upset.

Cripples

EDITOR ROBERT C. RUARK, writes that the United States has become a nation of cripples. Note these words:

"I do not expect very much to come of this experiment among the dry-dry martini fraternity. But I do think this is a very strong indication of a general softening process in America, which was commented on the other day by a heart specialist. This pump-expert allowed that too much coddling – too much actual protection – was being administered to the American public in terms of 'tension' crises, health fads and the avoidance of work. We have a fresh 'crises,' either of nerves or alleged actuality, every hour on the hour.

"The diet business, the pros and cons of smoking, the accent on fats, saturated and unsaturated; the strain of overwork – all are hurled at your head with sufficient staccato rapidity to build a tension or a crisis where none existed.

"It is quite possible that tensions and crises were not unknown to our forebears, a lot of whom lived to advanced senility on a diet of cornpone, sorghum and fried fatback. Butter and eggs were the signpost to security, and a slang phrase which still persists was 'living off the fat of the land.' I think we have become a nation of cripples, due to all the pampering and prescriptions and frets and fumes."

Ruark's words call to mind what Mildred M. North wrote:

Two cripples entered a church one day;
Crippled–but each in a different way:
One had a body strong and whole
But it sheltered a warped and twisted soul.
The other walked with a halting gait,
But his soul was "tall and fair and straight."
They shared a pew. They shared a book.
But on each face was a different look:
One was alight with hope and joy
And faith that nothing could destroy.
The other joined not in prayer or hymn,
No smile relaxed his features grim.
His neighbor had wronged him; his heart was sore.
He thought of himself and nothing more.

The words that were read from the Holy Book
Struck deafened ears and a forlorn look.
To one came comfort – his soul was fed;
The other gained nothing from what was said.
Two cripples left the church that day;
Crippled – but each in a different way:
A twisted foot did one body mar,
But the twisted soul was sadder far.

One Verse Survives

MRS. BARBAULD wrote voluminous poetry. But only one stanza of her written poetry survives.

Life! We have been long together,
Through pleasant and through cloudy weather;
'Tis hard to part when friends are dear.
Perhaps 'twill cause a smile, a tear;
Then steal away, give little warning,
Choose thine own time;
Say not "Goodnight," but in some brighter clime
Bid me "Good morning!"

Wordsworth used to repeat this verse. He wished they were his words – the highest praise that Wordsworth knew how to give.

Madame d' Arblay, in her old age, said these words over to herself as she went to bed.

Tennyson called them sweet words. Miss Thackeray said: "These words are almost sacred." They were written about 1813, but published posthumously.

We wonder if Mrs. Barbauld knew of Mr. and Mrs. Lamb – Scotch martyrs of the 16th century. Both were condemned by the authorities – he to be hanged, she to be tied in a sack and drowned in a pool. The wife on parting said to her husband: "Husband, be glad we have lived together many joyful days; and this day, on which we are to die, we ought to esteem the most joyful of all – because now we shall have joy forever. Therefore, I shall not bid you 'Goodnight,' for we shall meet in heaven."

Just here we are made to think of the last letter the sainted Dr. Meyer wrote, giving us written evidence of the peace which he had in Christ.

> I have just heard to my surprise that I have only a few days to live. It may be before this reaches you, I shall have entered the palace. Don't trouble to write. We shall meet you in the morning.

Powerful Pentolite

A SUPER explosive, called Pentolite, twenty per cent more powerful than TNT, is being used in rocket projectiles. Major General L. H. Campbell, chief of Army Ordinance, announcing this, said that a "small quantity of this explosive" would penetrate five feet of reinforced concrete. Beside providing "terrific punch" for bazooka ammunition and other rocket projectiles, the Army added, Pentolite also is employed in rifle grenades, antitank explosives, certain types of artillery shells, for demolition work and for clearing wrecked harbors such as that of Cherbourg, France.

Would it not be high praise for a man if we could say that he was a Pentolite Christian – not a puny Christian – providing terrific punch against evils that are as adamant against Christian truth as reinforced concrete? Powerful Pentolite projectiles! May such teach us not to be prissy and puny in our performances.

Which Death Choose You?

IN YEARS far gone, the position of Court Jester, as this position related itself to ancient sovereign, was an important post – and the Court Jester was a most important member of the king's household. By means of quips, he kept the king in good humor – and entertained the members of the royal household.

Some writer (I am sorry I forgot his name) tells us what he believes to be the best retort any Court Jester ever gave. It was the retort given his Sovereign, a dyspeptic dictator who had the ancient "power of life or death" over all his subjects, and it was supposed to be legally impossible for the king to change any sentence he set on a subject. Becoming irritated by his Court Jester, in a sudden rage of wrath, the King sentenced his Court Jester to death. Then, realizing too late his rash decree, the king said to the Court Jester: "In consideration of your faithful services, I will permit you to select the manner in which you prefer to die." The Court Jester instantly answered: "I select to die of *old age*."

That's good! But it holds not the wisdom we find in these words:

"A soft answer turneth away wrath: but grievous words stir up anger. The tongue of the wise useth knowledge aright: but the mouth of fools poureth out foolishness" (Proverbs 15:1, 2). Nor as much wisdom as we find in these words:

"He that is slow to anger is better than the mighty; and he that ruleth his spirit than he that taketh a city" (Proverbs 16:32).

Burned Out Bulb

WE READ in a town newspaper: Mrs. C. E. McLeroy is mighty proud of her refrigerator. The inside light bulb, which goes on when the door is opened, just burned out. But it had been in constant use since Mrs. McLeroy bought the appliance fourteen years ago. "I think that's pretty good service from a little old light bulb," she said.

Would that all Christians everywhere would be as that bulb in letting their light shine before men (Matthew 5:16) – in loving light rather than darkness because their deeds are righteous.

Poor Handwriting

Ruth Millett, who writes so many delightful and wise articles, asks people whose handwriting is poor not to apologize for such.

"Are you ashamed of your handwriting? You can stop apologizing for your illegible scratchings. A handwriting study made at one of our large universities has come up with the comforting discovery (comforting to all of us scribblers), that the smarter a person is, the worse his scrawl. It's thinking faster than you write that makes handwriting messy. The faster you think, naturally, the poorer your penmanship. The handwriting experts who made the study claim that anyone can improve his handwriting if he really tries. But who wants to, if an illegible scribbler indicates a high I. Q.?

"In case you doubt the findings, here's a clincher: In the same edition of the newspaper in which I read about the handwriting study was a little story about a Southern mayor who received a letter on White House stationery – but couldn't make out the signature. So he sent a photostat of the letter to Pierre Salinger, presidential press secretary, with the question: 'Maybe I am a prize boob, but whose signature is this?' Came back Salinger's one-line reply: 'That happens to be the signature of John F. Kennedy.' So now all of us who can't write a decent hand can quit apologizing. And all those who have been taking pride in their beautiful penmanship can just start forgetting to cross their T's, dot their I's and practice making O's look like U's."

We must never forget that we, as Christians, are living epistles read and known of all men (II Corinthians 3:2, 3). And such epistles must be legible. God expects such.

FACTS

Chicken-Feed

Farmers in the grasshopper-infested regions of the Northwest have devised a means of turning the destructive pests into chicken-feed. With troughs placed in front of the automobiles, the farmers drive through grain fields. The insects fall into clear water in the troughs. They are later poured into sacks to dry and will be fed to chickens next winter. One farmer "harvested" thirty bushels of grasshoppers to the acre by this method!

Pre-Mortem and Post-Mortem

When Victor Hugo was at what seemed to be the height of his power, and enjoying the emoluments of fame, he came into disfavor with Napoleon III. In fact, the ruler almost despised

Hugo. And, as a consequence, Hugo was exiled for nineteen long years that seemed a measure of eternity to him.

But we read that when those fateful years were over, and Victor Hugo died — when his heart could no longer feel hurts, when his hand could no longer write books that were strong and influential in many circles — famous were the funeral obsequies. The largest funeral of France was that of Victor Hugo. All the great institutions were represented. There were huge floral floats following detachments of soldiers. Ten thousand soldiers were needed to control the millions who gathered to watch the procession in the year 1883.

So, even today, some are cannonaded before they die and canonized when and after they are buried. 'Tis sad, 'tis true!

Paradoxical

In Los Angeles, Judge Yankwich had such a case as make judges want to scream — or, if they be foolish and evil enough to be profane, to do worse.

Luther Wright and Hermann Rongg appeared before Federal Judge Leon R. Yankwich, each claiming ownership of a patent. The judge attempted to moderate the dispute, declaring:

"Well, one of you must be wrong."

"That's right," declared Rongg, "I'm Rongg, and I'm right."

Then Wright interrupted:

"He's wrong, your honor. I'm right and Rongg is wrong."

The judge couldn't quite make it out, but he opined:

"Well, you both can't be right. After all, right is right and wrong is wrong."

But largely upon the strength of a letter Wright wrote Rongg, Judge Yankwich at length terminated the Wright-Rongg dispute by ruling:

"Paradoxical though it may appear, in this case Wright is wrong and Rongg is right, and I so enter judgment."

Hannibal Not First

An historian has discovered through research that the famed Hannibal of Carthage, who almost conquered Rome, was not the first to invade Italy using elephants as mighty machines of war, heavy-weight cavalry such as tanks became in modern times.

King Pyrrhus of Epirus brought twenty elephants into a series of great battles with the Romans. He won, but his losses were so heavy that he said, "One more such victory and I am lost." Hence the term "Pyrrhic Victory."

So, Hannibal was not the first to use elephants in war.

Next thing we know somebody will be telling us that P. T. Barnum and the Ringling brothers weren't the first to make money out of showing elephants off to the "suckers."

Stairs in Tomb

In Egypt, excavators have uncovered three more stone stairs in Seti I tomb's newly discovered corridor which they think lead to a secret chamber in which the pharaoh stored his treasures.

Kamal El Mallakh, Egyptian archaeological expert, said the newly discovered stairs now number twenty-eight and stretch two hundred and thirty-six yards. Mallakh said this is the longest rock-hewn tomb ever found in Egypt.

Seti's reign was known as the golden era because he devoted much time exploiting gold mines in Egyptian deserts. Egyptian archaeologists say his tomb may contain treasures many times greater than the wealth of Tut-Ankh-Amen.

Newspapers Wrong

WHEN Henry Ward Beecher was preaching in Brooklyn, he carried a handful of flowers into the pulpit one Lord's Day and placed them in a vase that they might adorn the stand from which he spoke. The newspapers, the next day, carried lengthy articles condemning Beecher for desecrating the pulpit with flowers.

And when Morse was trying to get money from Congress for a telegraph line from Baltimore to Washington, he had to endure the adverse criticisms of the press for eleven years.

And when, in 1845, Mr. Adam Thompson got up the first bathtub in America, the newspapers said he was "going to spoil the democratic simplicity of the republic."

And when Cyrus Field was trying to lay the Atlantic cable, the newspapers denounced his cable as "a mad freak of stubborn ignorance."

But what these newspapers said in the long ago about the matters just mentioned was not more foolish than what the newspapers say today in advocacy of the legal sale of whisky.

Judging!

JUDGING from the records of the divorce courts and from the domestic infelicity rampant today, we should say that some of those who set sail on the sea of matrimony wish they had missed the boat. We can judge that, too, from what some have written.

What a tragedy that so many orange blossoms have become frosted! What tragedy and sorrow abide in a home where matrimony milk turns to clabber! Nothing of this kind ever would be if only the Bible injunctions were obeyed by married people: "Giving thanks always for all things unto God and the Father in the name of our Lord Jesus Christ; Submitting yourselves one to another in the fear of God: Wives, submit yourselves unto your own husbands, as unto the Lord" (Ephesians 5:20-22). "Nevertheless let every one of you in particular so love his wife even as himself; and the wife see that she reverence her husband" (Ephesians 5:33).

Hunger

THE following proverbs on hunger we have read:

"Hunger fetches the wolf out of the woods."

"Hunger finds no fault with the cooking."

"Hunger is good kitchen meat."

"Hunger is the best sauce."

"Hunger makes raw beans a relish."

"Hungry horses make a clean manger."

"Hungry men think the cook lazy."

Petty Processions

FABRE tells us that he got a procession of caterpillars started around the rim of a big palm vase. Now, a caterpillar leaves a trail of silk behind it that acts as a lifeline to guide it back from the grazing grounds to the nest. But Fabre cut this line where it reached the rim, and the caterpillars, completing the circle of the rim of the vase, guided by the lifeline they had left unwittingly behind, started around again. All day long they marched around and around, a solid ring of caterpillars each with its head to the tail of the one who went before. Fabre says: "Far into the night they still journeyed on, slaves to their lifeline and bound to follow the one ahead." The next day they resumed their patient march. The third, the fourth, the fifth day and night they went on. The sixth night, the seventh day, the seventh night, and still the go-around that was far from merry, kept up, and with its marchers as footsore and weary as were ever members of Stonewall Jackson's foot cavalry or John J. Pershing's heroes of the Argonne drive.

"Slaves to their line." So we find it in the world of human beings. Round and round in a dizzy whirl of life – getting nowhere, gaining nothing worth while. What fools those caterpillars! What fools some mortals be! Petty processions plentiful there are today–people slaves to their line. And very poor lines many times.

Seneca said: "No slavery is more disgraceful than voluntary slavery." "Even under roofs of marble and of gold, slavery dwells." And Lowell declared: "They are slaves who dare not be in the right with two or three." And Sallust asked long ago a question that we can well ask ourselves and answer: "Romans, born to empire, will you endure slavery with equanimity?" Will you, let me ask, be "a slave to your line"?

Christmas Abolished

In 1659, according to *Enzyklopadie fur Theology und Kirche,* the General Court of Massachusetts enacted a law providing "a fine of five shillings for every offense if a body be found observing, by abstinence from work, by celebrating or attending a religious service . . . such a day as Christmas Day." England had enacted similar laws about the same time, which were repealed in 1662. The Massachusetts law, however, was not repealed until 1681.

This law is obsolete. The truth is never out of date. And the dateless Christ has bent the date lines of all the nations around His manger cradle.

Some Definition

Spencer thus defines evolution: "Evolution is a change from an indefinite, incoherent homogeneity to a definite, coherent heterogeneity through continuous differentiations and integrations."

News About Newspapers

Do you know that newspapers do not measure people – only exhibit them?

Do you know that newspapers are a sort of public confessional?

Do you know that the corrupter who needs darkness for his success dreads an honest newspaper?

Do you know that newspapers do not know–sometimes– what news is news?

Artificial Burdens

In Oakland, Calif., Peter Rizzo fell from a canoe into a lake. Weighted down by an artificial leg, he was drowned.

Some today are so weighted down with artificial things they are doing more drowning than swimming when it comes to the rescue of the perishing. By artificial things some are "drowned like pigs when they attempt to swim" – "drowned as by the flood of Egypt."

Spanking and Crying

A little lad was watching the male of the species among the flock of chickens. Suddenly the rooster flapped his wings and let forth a lusty crow. The little lad called excitedly, "Mother, Mother, the rooster spanked hisself and cried."

Maybe there are some things about us humans that ought to cause us to spank ourselves – and cry. But whether there is much spanking or not these days, there is much crying. Still there is, as Balzac says, the "cry of anguish which, like a pebble thrown over a precipice, reveals the depths of despair." Still there are cries which are like "the cry as wild as any coming of madness."

Still we feel a kindred experience with those who say:

My heart is crying like a tired child,
For one fond look, one gentle, loving word.

Quotations

"MONKEYS ought not to investigate buzz-saws."

"In my estimation there are more successes in failure than in those who win."

"Embalmed in the brief immortality of a success magazine."

The beating of mine own heart
Was all the sound I heard.

"A nation in its whole lifetime flowers with but few whose names remain upon the roll of the world in after generations." – *Ex-President Hoover*

"Too much attention is being given to the student and not enough to the teacher." – *I. L. Wandel, Professor of Education, Columbia University*

"Reno's system of divorce is that of a slot machine. You put in the papers and up pops a divorce." – *Judge Ben Lindsey*

"My loin cloth is an organic evolution of my life." – *Mahatma Gandhi*

"We were not crooked enough to forecast what the crooked liquor traffic would do." – *Dr. Robert E. Corradini, Executive Secretary of the Alcohol Information Committee of New York*

"The English language is a collection of noises which we make in order to communicate with each other." – *George Bernard Shaw*

"One doesn't mind hot weather if one expects it." – *Mrs. Dolly Gann*

"The dethronement of man as the undisputed head of the family is one of the factors in the breakdown of the familiar, old-style home."–*Rev. Harold Holt, Oak Park, Ill.*

"The inventor is the modern saint." – *Prof. Harry A. Overstreet, College of the City of New York*

"No matter how important or big the offender, history shows that he is eventually caught." – *Amos W. W. Woodcock, Prohibition Commissioner*

"Even under Socialism wages must be paid according to the work done and not according to the needs of the workers." – *Joseph Stalin*

Gentle Quotations

"A GENTLE heart is tied with easy thread."

"A gentle tongue is a tree of life."

"Blood with gentle manners breed."

"Let gentle blood show generous might."

"To others gentle, to himself severe."

"I do not like noise unless I make it myself."

"I gave the mouse a hole and she has become my heir."

"I had rather ride on an ass that carries me than on the horse that throws me."

"I never fared worse than when I wished for supper."

"I sucked not this out of my fingers' ends."

"I taught you to swim and now you drown me."

"I wasn't born in a wood to be scared by an owl."

The Curse of Comfort

I HAVE often said to my people that the curse of comfort is upon us – that our danger is spiritual diabetes, too much sugar – that the cushion and not the cross is the symbol that describes too many of us – that our boys were sometimes pampered and petted into failure. And I was glad when I ran upon this from Dr. Frank Crane: "We all want to 'help' boys. Yet that which makes a boy great is that which hinders him. Many a promising lad needs only to be kicked out, battered, discouraged, and opposed, to make a man of him!"

A Scorching Compliment

IT HAPPENED at Canal and St. Charles Streets, New Orleans, La. A woman automobile driver narrowly missed colliding with a motorist of the meeker sex.

Lifting his hat, the man said: "Madam, allow me to congratulate you on adding to the sport of driving. Never look where you are going. It would take all the fun out of operating an automobile." And the woman thought it was a compliment. Makes me think of what Hugo wrote: "A compliment is something like a kiss through a veil." That pedestrian's compliment was "a rosebud set with little willful thorns." How often much that passes for compliment is:

The barren verbiage, current among men,
Light coin, the tinsel clink of compliment.

A Doctor and Quacks

DR. RUDOLPH MATAS, internationally honored and of unquestionably high standing, once, in New Orleans where he lived, made a call. That was when as a more or less ordinary practitioner his medical duties took him out in the rain to the house of a friend whose wife was sick.

"Good night for ducks," remarked the patient's husband.

Dr. Matas drew himself up in mock seriousness. "Do you mean to insinuate," he said, "that I am a quack?"

"Quackery gives birth to nothing — gives death to all things."

I Deny and Affirm

I DENY that there is any such thing as luck. I have not forgotten the man who saw a horseshoe in the road and picked it up and, as he did so, was hit by a car that tumbled him with fourteen broken bones into a field of four-leaf clovers. So I affirm that this universe is managed by a God who is the great Designer behind all design, the great Law-maker behind all law.

I deny that circumstances and obstacles are stronger than I. I affirm that in any environment and in the face of any obstacles, I can make them my servants — not my masters.

Wool

WOOL has a "big four." Wool is composed of carbon, nitrogen, hydrogen, sulphur, and oxygen. Yet nobody has to know all that to be warmed in sleep by a wool blanket. And I don't have to know all the Bible to know how to be saved. And I don't have to know there are seven colors in every ray of light to recognize my mother's face.

Lightning and Thunder

"LIGHTNING danced a skeleton dance on the black, invisible peaks to the north, and the thunder rolled down their sides like demon laughter.

"The lightning was cracking its shining bones down the hillside and thunder was falling down the slopes like a lost shipload of brass drums."

—HELEN TOPPING MILLER

Overture and Rebuke

A CERTAIN husband who quarrelled frequently with his wife (may his tribe become extinct) made overtures after the quarrel:

"What little present shall I get for the one I love best?" he asked.

The wife, with rebuking sarcasm, said: "How about a box of cigars?"

Anyway, we all know that a man who is wrapped up in himself is wrapped up in a mighty little package.

Rough Treatment

ONCE I went in an art gallery – and I got "turribul rough" treatment, as the guide book said I would.

The guide book said that, on entering, I would be *struck* by a statue of Hercules.

Then I would be *stunned* by the splendor of the great staircase.

Then a certain picture would be *full of punch.*

Then another magnificent painting would *crush* me.

Then brilliant colors would *run riot* everywhere.

And the guide book told the truth – rough treatment for any visitor.

Strange Will Recorded

IN HOLLISTER, CALIF., once lived Dr. James V. Sommers. He died recently, leaving one of the strangest wills ever recorded in San Benito County. Sommers was known on the Pacific Coast for his poetical ability as well as his extraordinary knowledge of horses. Preceding his will was this verse:

In a horse-drawn rig take me out to where they dig
My last home, for better or worse;
For I'll sleep just as sound from a wagon, I'll be bound,
As I would from a nickel-plated hearse.

Coming Eclipses

ASTRONOMERS have listed for us the coming total eclipses of the sun in the United States. If the Lord Jesus tarry, the following total eclipses will come:

1970 – Crosses Florida from west to east.

1979 – Enters United States near the mouth of the Columbia river and crosses northern Montana into Canada.

2017 – Sweeps across entire United States on a route through Oregon, near Denver, Nashville, and Wilmington, N. C.

Further eclipses in the United States will fall in the years 2024, 2044, 2045, 2052, and 2073.

Things Geographical

THE shortest distance from the Atlantic to the Pacific across the United States is between points near Charleston, S.C., and San Diego, Calif.,–2152 miles.

The highest tide in the world is in the Bay of Fundy, Canada – a rise of fifty-three feet.

The swiftest river known is the Rhone – reaching a velocity of forty miles an hour in places.

The widest river known is the Amazon – nearly fifty miles at its main mouth.

Fifty Years Ago

WE HAVE this from the *Evangelical Press:*

Fifty years ago nobody wore a wrist watch. Nobody had appendicitis. Nobody knew about vitamins. Nobody had a radio or had seen television. Most young men lured the young ladies into a date with a shiny horse and buggy and had "livery bills." Most folks read by candle and kerosene light. None traveled on these manmade birds. The butcher "threw in" a chunk of liver. The merchant "threw in" a pair of suspenders with every suit. The baker "threw in" an extra doughnut to make it a "baker's dozen." Nobody listened in on the "party line." Nobody knew about iceless refrigerators and fireless cookers. Alcoholics were called "drunkards." Most folks blew out the light when retiring for the night. Young men "showed off" by jumping from a trolley before it stopped. We never heard of penicillin and chlorophyllin. How did we live? Times indeed have changed!

Persistence in a Task

WHEN you feel that being persistent in a task is drudgery, think of the bee. A red clover blossom contains less than one-eighth of a grain of sugar. Now seven thousand grains are required to make a pound of honey. A bee, flitting here and there among the flowers in many places for sweetness, must visit fifty-six thousand clover heads for a pound of honey – and there are about sixty flower tubes to each clover head. When a bee performs that operation sixty times fifty-six thousand, or three million, three hundred and sixty thousand times, it secures sweetness enough for only one pound of honey.

What wonders, looking at a pound of honey in the comb, we take as a mere commonplace.

But foolish are we if we take as a commonplace what Solomon wrote:

"My son, eat thou honey, because it is good; and the honeycomb, which is sweet to thy taste: so shall the knowledge of wisdom be unto thy soul: when thou hast found it, then there shall be a reward, and thy expectation shall not be cut off" (Proverbs 24:13, 14).

"It is not good to eat much honey: so for men to search their own glory is not glory" (Proverbs 25:27).

From Two Now Dead

THOMAS R. MARSHALL, one-time Vice-President, and Frank Crane whose pen was laid away by death, are gone from us. But, in rummaging recently among a mass and mess of clippings, I ran upon these words from them.

Listen to Marshall: "Gentlemen may cry 'Peace! Peace!' but there will be no peace until the church resumes its functions, renews its faith and proves its faith by works. It is vain to enact laws punishing murder if the elders are to continue working little children to death. It is useless to forbid larceny if deacons make large church contributions out of excess profits wrung jointly from labor and the ultimate consumer. The church, with a complacent smile, has turned over to the state the enforcement of the moral law, and the state has failed, as it always will, to enforce it."

Give ear to Crane: "Happiness is not something handed down to you from heaven nor something you can couzen yourself into by some fanciful cult, making yourself happy as the Irishman who tried to lift himself over the fence by his boot straps; you can't get it by taking a pill or a drink; you can't crawl into it through the convolutions of a syllogism, nor buy it with money, nor capture it by violence of the will. It is simpler than all that. Hence so many miss it. For you get so you can be happy precisely as you get so you can play the violin – by practice."

Looking Glass and Fool

AN OLD conundrum asks: "What is the difference between a looking glass and a fool?"

The answer is: "The looking glass

reflects without speaking and the fool speaks without reflecting."

To which may be added what Plautus said: "*Praeter speciem stultus es*," which being translated is, "You are a bigger fool than you look." But 'tis true that "the fool who speaks without reflecting always finds a greater fool to admire him" – and "he is a fool who expects sense from a fool."

Rolling Wheel

I walked along the broad highway,
And passed where a child was hard
at play;
Pushing his wheel that was shiny new,
It left a track as it followed through.

Years later I walked the same highway,
Another lad pushed the wheel this
day,
And through the years the wheel
had worn,
And it left no track as it rolled along.

The conscience is a wheel, I thought,
That leaves its track upon the heart,
Till, left unchecked to roll and wear,
It one day leaves no imprint there.

–S/SGT. JARVIS D. ANDERSON

Cancer Cause

SO MANY *dread* cancer.

So many have cancer.

So many have died of cancer.

From Dallas, Texas, comes the report that a nationally recognized surgeon says the tar in tobacco has been proved beyond question to be cancer-causing.

Dr. Alton Ochsner of New Orleans, Louisiana, was there to address the Texas Academy of General Practices opening a three-day meeting. He said he hopes to convince every family doctor in Texas to become highly suspicious of lung cancer in every smoker past forty who has a respiratory ailment.

Dr. Ochsner suggested cigarette companies could spend some of their money to find out the relationship between smoking and lung cancer.

"It is logical that, once the cancer-causing agent in tar has been isolated, it could be removed without hurting the taste of the cigarettes."

He suggested a chest X-ray every three months for smokers past forty to save lives if lung cancer develops.

The surgeon cited statistics which he said show a close parallel between an increase in smoking and lung cancer. Dr. Ochsner said the figures probably would not cause many persons to quit smoking.

He told about a laboratory experiment with a large group of animals. Tar from tobacco was applied to the skin and mucous membranes of the animals for a long time. At the end of two years 44 per cent of the animals had developed cancer.

Dr. Ochsner said, "The man of fifty who has smoked a pack of cigarettes a day for twenty years is fifty times more likely to develop lung cancer than a man of fifty who has never smoked."

The more cigarettes smoked, he said, the greater the danger. Three packs daily are a bigger threat than two.

The surgeon said the once-rare cancer of the lung is now by far the most common type of cancer in men.

Four Kinds of Readers

DR. JOHN SNAPE, quoting Coleridge, gives us this delightful bit of delicious wisdom and wise comment:

"Coleridge has said that there are four classes of readers. The first he compares to an hour-glass whose reading is like the sand that runs out, and leaves not a trace behind. The second class is like a sponge, which takes in everything, retains everything, returns nothing, except under pressure, and then returns it in exactly the same condition in which it was received. A third class is like a jelly-bag which strains away all that is valuable, and retains within itself only dregs and refuse. The fourth class is like the slave of Golconda, who cast aside all that is worthless, and kept only the pure gems. All students of the Bible ought to be like the slave of Golconda in their search for the pure gems of truth."

Declarations and Death

On November 29, 1953, Dr. Ernest William Barnes, former Anglican bishop of Birmingham, England, and a frequent storm center of religious controversy, died.

He rejected belief in miracles—"The Bible is wrong," he once said.

He campaigned for euthanasia – mercy killing – or sterilization of unfit persons.

He urged church leaders to cut out from the Bible its story of creation as related in the book of Genesis. "Science had proved it could not be accepted as fact," he said.

He doubted validity of the virgin birth and Christ's physical resurrection.

"The time has come," he said, "when the mistaken assumptions of the prescientific, precritical era must be repudiated."

These views – expressed with brilliant oratory and incisive pen – were planted in the minds of many as pernicious and poisonous weeds planted in a garden, as the tares of Satan sown among the fields of Biblical wheat. I wish his evil views were as dead as his once well-fed and well-clothed body. But – alas! – evil teaching of falsehood continues to agitate the currents of life long after the false teacher is dead and turned to dust.

Quickness

Quickness is shown in the time it takes a baseball to travel from the pitcher's hand to the plate. Bob Feller's pitching was clocked at 98.6 mph. This means that his ball traveled 145 feet a second and took about 1/3 second to move from Feller's hand until it covered the plate.

Quickness is shown in how a cat falls. Like the magician's hand, a falling feline moves quicker than the human eye, so nobody has ever actually seen how a cat always manages to land on its feet. A *Houston Post* photographer, Chester O'Donnell, recently attached a new gadget known as an electronic flash to his camera and shot a series of pictures of a tumbling tabby. The shutter speed was 1/100 of a second, the flash time, 1/5000 of a second. The cat was held all feet together and all feet up at a height of three and one-half feet. Even the camera could not catch the cat falling with its feet up.

But more wonderful than this quickness of the cat is the quickness with which Jesus shall appear a second time upon this earth. He said: "He which testifieth these things said, Surely I come quickly" (Revelation 22:20).

Geographical Clock

Millard L. Beyer of Hempstead, N. Y., has patented a geographical clock with eight "faces" to tell the corresponding time in any selected time zone in the world. The time "faces" consist of transparent tape bands with hour and minute calibrations. They are set with one band beneath another, down the surface of a vertical, clock activated drum. The drum is translucent and lighted from within. The bands can be changed for any desired location.

But no matter how often this clock tells the time in any zone in the world, it cannot stay the swift flight of time – nor annul these Bible statements:

"Go to now, ye that say, To day or to morrow we will go into such a city, and continue there a year, and buy and sell, and get gain: whereas ye know not what shall be on the morrow. For what is your life? It is even a vapour, that appeareth for a little time, and then vanisheth away" (James 4:13, 14).

Tiny Tim

TINY TIM is terrible. What mean I by that statement? I mean that from Dover, Delaware, comes the announcement that the War Department has removed the veil of secrecy around "Tiny Tim," a powerful rocket which an army spokesman said is "by far the deadliest thing ever fired from an airplane."

Col. Donald B. Diehl, commanding officer of the 414th Army Air Force base unit at the Dover army air field, said the rocket "can sink almost anything that floats."

"It has driven holes all the way through a light cruiser from side to side," the colonel reported. "It goes through a destroyer as if it were a piece of paper."

The new weapon, which can be fired from any present type American fighter plane or medium bomber, was described by Col. Diehl as a "huge rocket 11.75 inches in diameter and 12 feet long."

"Several Tiny Tims were used against Japanese shipping and reinforced pillboxes before the end of the war," he added, "and it was found that few targets could withstand a direct hit from the rocket, traveling in excess of 1,500 miles an hour."

But as great as the terror created by Tiny Tim, that terror of the nowadays does not go beyond the terror the people had at Mount Sinai:

"For they could not endure that which was commanded, And if so much as a beast touch the mountain, it shall be stoned, or thrust through with a dart. And so terrible was the sight, that Moses said, I exceedingly fear and quake" (Hebrews 12:20, 21).

Mechanical Man

AFTER seven years of work, Andrew Baber, a watchmaker, perfected a mechanical man that could talk, walk and shoot a pistol with Baber's aid.

This mechanical man is just as accomplished as some real "flesh-and-blood" folks who believe in the freedom of speech, yet have nothing worth listening to, who have as many brains in their heads as in their heels, and who hit no target of definite goals.

Same Tag

FROM Chicago – Associated Press – comes the news that Charles H. Sobel, once he finds a good number, likes to keep it. It was back in 1913 that Sobel purchased his first car for $450.00, and requested a license number under ten thousand for the car. He was given the number eight thousand. Now in 1963 – fifty years later – and twenty-four cars later – he still receives plate number eight thousand. The same tag!

But let us think of some other realities that are the *same:*

"The *same* was the first altar that he built" (I Samuel 14:35).

"Asahel . . . fell down there and died in the *same* place" (II Samuel 2:23).

"Zion . . . the *same* is the city of David" (II Samuel 5:7).

"But thou art the *same,* and thy years shall have no end" (Psalm 102:27).

"The *same* wicked man shall die in his iniquity" (Ezekiel 3:18).

"The *same* shall be called great in the kingdom of heaven" (Matthew 5:19).

"Jesus Christ the *same* yesterday, and today, and forever" (Hebrews 13:8).

"The *same* shall be clothed in white" (Revelation 3:5).

Accidents

AMERICA is a nation of records. Many of them are good ones; others are quite the contrary. In the latter class belongs the record relating to accidents, released by the National Safety Council.

The unenviable total of the hundred and ten thousand accidental deaths represents the toll for 1962 according to the Safety Council's figures. And to this frightful sacrifice must be added ten million injuries. Classified as to causes, it is discovered that the automobile as an instrument of death has increased its power, setting a new high mark of forty-one thousand lives.

However, it doubtless will be surprising to most people to learn that four million injuries occurred, as the Safety Council says, "with alarming frequency – in the kitchen, in the bathroom, in the bedroom, in the attic, in the garage – everywhere."

Excerpts From Ethridge

LIKE salt for unpalatable foods are these words from the columnist, Tom Ethridge:

"The weapons in Cuba may not be offensive, but Cuba is. Some men battle their way to the top, and some bottle their way to the bottom. In economic geography, almost all countries touch the United States. Today's underprivileged child is the one who has to share the family car with parents. Among the big worries of today's businessmen are the large numbers of unemployed still on the payroll. Blessed are the young, for they shall inherit our public debt. Elvis Presley, the Tupelo Tune-Twister, is living the good life and eating high on the hog. Hollywood reports that Elvis owns fifteen automobiles, including an all-pink Cadillac with built-in television and hi-fi."

The Forgotten War

CONTINUED centennial commemorations of the Civil War tend to obscure the fact that 1962 was also the sesquicentennial of another war, the War of 1812. This is not surprising, for it was a minor war compared to the great conflict between the states. It was an unpopular war (we still call it by its date rather than a name), and a strange war. Ironically, it nearly led to secession by the New England states which, forty years later, were to oppose secession by the South.

It was a war that did not begin until its major causes had ceased to exist – the impressment of American seamen and blockade of United States shipping by the British. It was a war in which the major battle was fought a week after the peace treaty had been signed. Yet for all that, it enriched our history with more than its share of memorable episodes:

The brilliant naval feats of the Constitution and Essex, the Wasp and Enterprise;

Capt. James Lawrence's dying words on the deck of the Chesapeake – "Don't give up the ship!"

Perry's victory on Lake Erie – "We have met the enemy and they are ours."

The capture of Washington and the burning of the White House.

The bombardment of Fort McHenry and the birth of the "Star Spangled Banner."

Andy Jackson and the Battle of New Orleans.

Historians have begun to take a second look at this neglected war. In spite of the fact that it could have been averted, it did result in certain benefits, such as a new feeling of national unity. It put the final seal on the American Revolution, convincing Britain that America was indeed bent upon following her own destiny.

For that reason, some call it "The Second War of Independence."

But shell-shocked men in our hospitals, crippled men on crutches, one-legged and one-armed men, and some blind men who find every sunlit day as dark as blackest midnight, and white crosses as numerous as trees in the king's forest testify that there are millions who remember ever and forget never certain wars – with all their crimson horrors – wondering if ever nations will learn wars no more.

A Sugar Source

Sugar cane waste has been turned by the agriculture department into a new source of rayon – a silky dress material for women. Department chemists, using lowpriced nitric acid, succeeded in developing a process by which highgrade cellulose, base material for rayon, is produced from bagasse, the waste from sugar cane after the sugar has been extracted. The discovery is regarded as important as most rayon manufacturers depend upon wood pulp for cellulose and the American forests and wood supplies are gradually diminishing.

Sugar cane mills accumulate between 250,000 and 500,000 tons of bagasse annually. Much of this material has been used in manufacturing insulating building material. Other quantities have been used as fuel in the mills.

It is a good thing when things and people are good for more than you think they are.

Three Obituaries

1. Joshua

"Joshua, the son of Nun, the servant of the Lord, died, being an hundred and ten years old" (Judges 2:8).

In obituary notices, the highest honors attained by the deceased are mentioned. It was not so in Joshua's case. He is not described as "the late Commander-in-Chief" or "this general of outstanding ability," but as "the servant of the Lord." Such honor have all God's saints – from the humblest saint to the greatest.

2. Miss Wheat

In the Buck Branch Cemetery, Pearl River County, Mississippi, is this on a tombstone:

Take heed, dear friend, in passing by,
As you are now, so once was I;
As I am now, you soon will be,
Prepare for death and follow me.

3. Robert Louis Stevenson

Sculptors, paid out of the pocket of the governor-general of New Zealand, had to correct a poetic quotation on the tombstone of Robert Louis Stevenson. Governor-General Lord

Cobham discovered the error in lines from Stevenson's "Requiem," while visiting the grave at Vailima in Samoa.

The inscription read, "Home is the sailor, home from the sea and the hunter home from the hill." The Governor-General left $150 to have a "the" chiseled out to make it read, correctly: "Home is the sailor, home from sea, and the hunter home from the hill."

Troublesome Twins

We sometimes think of inferiority complexes and suppressions. Eccentricity is not mental weakness. If so, many of the greatest men in the world would have been locked up. Eccentricity has been called "ballooning the ego," a natural outcome of an inferiority complex or suppression in youth.

Beethoven waved his arms about and shouted. He was also a member of the no-hat brigade, most eccentric in those days.

Cardinal Richeleiu often imagined he was a horse, pretending to trot, jump and neigh like one.

Dr. Johnson had an obsessional neurosis which made him touch every post he passed.

Milton always wrote with his head hanging over the arm of his high chair.

The Duke of Wellington always carried six watches and incessantly boasted that he had never been late in his life.

World Water Shortage

"Water, water everywhere, nor any drop to drink. . . ."

Although three-fourths of the planet is covered by water, many areas are plagued by shortages of fresh water. In some areas the shortages are critical. In view of the anticipated sharp increase in water consumption over the next two decades, many experts are urging stepped up efforts to find an economical method for turning salt water into fresh water.

President Eisenhower said the U. S. has made genuine and exciting progress in developing an economic method for de-salting sea water and purifying brackish inland water.

Atomic Activities, published by the National Securities and Research Corp., said since conservation methods are not enough to assure future water needs "man must turn on the oceans, the only limitless source of the water so necessary to guarantee civilization's continued growth."

There are many known methods of de-salting sea water, but none of them are economical. Experts estimate that conversion costs must be reduced to about fifty cents per one thousand gallons to make any process economically feasible. Present costs run as much as four and a half times that amount. Atomic Activities said shortages exist in many areas of the world, including the United States. Water consumption in this country has jumped from 110 billion gallons a day in 1930 to 290 billion gallons daily in 1957. By 1975 consumption is expected to hit five hundred billions a day, three times the amount of water thundering over Niagara Falls each day.

Industry is the biggest user of water. It takes an estimated 50,000 gallons of processing water to produce a ton of paper, 65,000 gallons for a ton of steel, and 20,000 gallons for a ton of rayon.

While nations and states are in dispute about water rights, while millions use water in various ways, while drought-smitten fields cry for rain, while in some nations many have to buy water, we wonder how many ever thank God daily for water? It is God who, for His peoples' welfare, "turned the waters of Egypt into blood," who "opened the rock, and the waters gushed out" (Psalm 105: 29, 41), who "turned the flint into a fountain of waters" (Psalm 114:8).

Water shortage makes us rejoice over Radinner Springs – bubbling up from a bowl thirty feet deep at the rate of seventy thousand gallons a minute – maintaining a year-round temperature of sixty-eight degrees.

Findings in Mail

ONE newspaper editor said there are many things a columnist would never know if he did not open his mail – namely: That ancient Rome had a record breadline. During the height of the empire as many as one third of the city's inhabitants were fed at public expense.

That, except for the intervention of his mother, George Washington might have become a British admiral. She dissuaded him from accepting a commission in the navy and taking up a career before the mast.

That, according to the Fisherman magazine, the snail is a natural born pedestrian. Its eyes, mounted on periscope-like stalks, enable it to see around corners.

That, singer Lisa Kirk wants to know if you heard about the Texan who just ordered four small foreign sport cars. He's having them made into cuff-links.

That a frog breathes through its skin both on land and in the water.

That police estimate forty per cent of America's dope addicts live in New York City, and fourteen per cent of those who take narcotics are less than twenty years old.

That one alcoholic beverage has a specific disease named after it. This is absinthe. Imbibe too much of it and you get "absinthism."

That the Cafe St. Denis posts this gentle reminder to noisy patrons: "The whale gets caught only when it comes to the surface to blow."

That five of the sixty known types of anopheles mosquitoes which carry malaria have acquired resistance to today's most widely used insecticides.

That if you tend to be an eager beaver, you might heed this cautionary advice of Benjamin Disraeli: "Next to knowing when to seize an opportunity, the next most important thing in life is to know when to forego an opportunity."

That women's feet grow smaller as they grow older. Well, that's what they try to tell shoe clerks anyway.

That among some Gypsy tribes it is customary at the wedding feast to provide a small cake made of flour mixed with a little blood from the wrists of the bride and groom. The cake is eaten by the happy couple.

That the world record for non-stop talking – 133 hours – was set in 1955, by an Irishman, Kevin Sheenham of Limerick.

That the most dangerous periods for home accidents are between the hours of 10 A.M. and 1 P.M. – and 4 to 7 P.M.

That the earth's climate is expected to get hotter until A.D. 20,000. A new Ice Age is to begin around A.D. 50,000.

That TNT, the explosive, is so stable you can ordinarily hit it with a hammer or touch a match to it in safety.

That it is possible for some people to sleep with both eyes open. This has been going on in our office for years!

That Joe Garcia of Melbourne, Australia, once ate 480 oysters in 60 minutes and didn't find a single pearl.

That it was George Bernard Shaw

who observed, "We have no more right to consume happiness without producing it than to consume wealth without producing it."

Airlines Use Ocean of Oil

The domestic scheduled airlines are major customers of the U. S. oil industry. To keep America's fleet of scheduled airlines flying, millions of gallons of gasoline are purchased each year. Figures for a recent year show that domestic scheduled lines used 685,534,977 gallons of gasoline and 7,145,093 gallons of oil. That amounts to an hourly consumption, day and night, for the entire twelve months, of more than seventy-nine thousand gallons of gas and oil.

Many uses of *oil* are set forth in the Bible:

At Bethel, Jacob "took the stone he had put for his pillow and poured oil on the top of it" (Genesis 28:18).

"Oil for the light, spices for anointing oil" (Exodus 25:6).

"Cakes unleavened, tempered with oil" (Exodus 29:2).

"He made the holy anointing oil." (Exodus .37:29).

"Cakes of fine flour mingled with oil" (Leviticus 2:4).

"The rock poured out for me rivers of oil" (Job 29:6).

"Thou anointest my head with oil" (Psalm 23:5).

"Oil of gladness" (Psalm 45:7).

1859 — OIL — 1963

Only one hundred and four years ago, "Colonel" Edwin L. Drake, formerly of New Haven, Conn., brought in at Titusville, Penn., the world's first commercially successful oil well. Only a few years later, ill health forced him out of the business. The $15,000 to $20,000 he had accumulated was lost on the stock market and he, like many a run-of-the-mill oil prospector, died penniless.

That is only one small part of a fabulous story. The oil industry, in one of the massive public relations programs of the decade, has done the nation a service this year in reminding it of its youth; as well as of the gigantic things it has wrought in ours and other nations. All too soon, as is well recorded at least in the economic ledgers, oil became the "elixir of war," fueling the engines of aggression and tyranny, defense and holy crusade.

Assuredly it has worked, too, in billions after billions of barrels, as the instrument of man's constructive desires, as well as for his material profit. Atomic, solar, and all the other "new" energies only seem to stimulate the productive uses for oil.

Other oil millions have found their way into the great philanthropic foundations and into countless other progressive works. And today, the industry stands militant and alert as before. It merits a salute, and a nation's challenge to a broadly beneficial future.

After So Long

Four instances.

1. In St. Louis – a medal after seventeen years. Dist. Judge Roy Harper finally has the evidence that he was a hero seventeen years ago during World War II. Judge Harper, then a captain in the 35th Fighter Group, was awarded the medal for meritorious service in New Guinea. He received the orders but never the medal. An officer from Scott Air Force Base near St. Louis heard about the situation, pulled some strings and arranged a presentation in the judge's chambers of a medal more than seventeen years late in coming.

2. In Pittsburgh – damages paid.

Yes, and high time! Mrs. Harper H. Smith, eighty, recently received twenty-four dollars restitution for damages to her car. The vehicle was broken into by four youths in 1937. Explaining the delay in payment, Clerk of Courts Thomas E. Barrett said that about five thousand restitution cases were recently transferred to his office from the county probation office.

3. In New York – a book worm turns. A bookworm – apparently a very slow reader – has returned thirty-two books borrowed from the Brooklyn Public Library in 1935. The books, which had run up fines totaling $5,521 were left on the library steps in a box. "Better late than never."

4. Mrs. Nellie Clark of the Reid Community has U. S. mail service after a sixty-eight-year wait. The Vardaman Route #2 was extended two-tenths of a mile to include Mrs. Clark's home. Her mail had been delivered to a neighbor's box.

But now, "Isn't it wonderful?" Mrs. Clark said, "I just can't believe I have my own mail box!"

Eye-Size Telescope

THE development of a telescope so tiny it can fit on the eye like a contact lens and double the vision of the partially blind has been announced. Its inventor, Dr. William Feinblood of New York City, said more than half a million persons with only partial sight may benefit from his "miniscope."

He said he will publish all data necessary for manufacturing the device so doctors and laboratories everywhere can produce them. "It is not a commercial thing at all," he said. He predicted that many persons now legally classed as blind could be restored to useful vision and normal activities through his device. It increases the vision of the partially blind by two hundred per cent and provides a field of vision eighty per cent of normal, he said.

But this cannot help the eye that is "dim by reason of sorrow" (Job 17:7), or "consumed with grief" (Psalm 31:9) – nor make righteous "the eye that mocketh at his father" (Proverbs 30:17).

Small X-ray Machine

AN X-RAY machine smaller than a match stick has been developed by a physicist at Armour Research Foundation. Coupled with an image intensifier, the small radiation generator could conceivably be carried in a physician's bag for on the spot pictures of a fracture or of an open safety pin hidden in a child's throat.

The conventional X-ray tube is a bulky, complex and expensive vacuum lamp that sends out a stream of electrons from a hot filament under high voltage. As the fast-moving electrons slam against a tungsten target, X-rays are created.

The miniature X-ray device, a tenth of an inch in diameter and three-tenths of an inch long, uses a radioactive isotope as a power supply and tungsten or lead as a target.

Most isotopes are not suitable because of their short duration of life. But one that has been found very satisfactory by Reiffel is strontium-90, the bad acting element in atomic bomb fallout. When kept under control by shielding, the beta rays spontaneously emitted by the strontium can be adapted to provide a revealing glimpse into dense tissue or metal.

One possible application is in cancer treatment. The radiation device could be fastened to the end of a gastroscope, which would then be lowered into the interior of the stomach to irradiate a malignancy. Reiffel has assigned his patent rights to the Armour Foundation.

Of this we could say it is evidence of the strength of the small, the might of a mite.

Fifty-Eighth Anniversary

Sixteen military jet planes streaked through the skies at near supersonic speeds over the sand flats of North Carolina's Outer Banks, where man's first powered flight was made fifty-eight years ago.

The flyover signaled the start of ceremonies at the Wright Brothers National Memorial commemorating Wilbur and Orville Wright's achievement of December 17, 1903. The Wright brothers failed in their first attempt to fly their rickety plane. That was on December 14, 1903. Then on the morning of December 17th, Orville climbed abroad the plane, which was on a wooden track that stretched sixty feet across the sand. They had invited people living in the area to watch, but only three men from a life station, a fisherman and a boy were on hand.

Wilbur ran alongside the plane, steadying a wing as the craft moved along the track, its two large fan blades powered by a twelve-horse-power engine. After moving forty feet down the track, the craft lifted, and Wilbur stopped running and stood watching. The plane rose about eight feet above the earth, dipped, rose again to about ten feet, then settled to the sand. The flight had lasted twelve seconds. The plane had flown one hundred and twenty feet.

The brothers from Dayton, Ohio, made two more flights of two hundred feet, alternating at the controls. Then, on the fourth flight, with Wilbur at the controls, the plane nosed to the ground fifty nine seconds and eight hundred and fifty-two feet from the takeoff point. It was damaged, and the brothers made no more flights that winter.

In 1907, the Wrights won an Army contract and built a plane to the Army's specifications. The Army said the plane would have to stay in the air at least an hour and average forty miles an hour over a ten-mile course.

Chemists Milk Bees

Chemists of Montana State College have rigged up an electric chair to take the sting out of bees, wasps and hornets. The device is not designed to kill, but to "milk" them for their venom for analytical and immunologic study. Previous techniques to obtain such venom in its pure state, they said, have been less productive.

To protect the insects – and the scientists – the captive bee, wasp or hornet is anesthetized with a whiff of gas (carbon dioxide). This knocks it out long enough for the handling that follows. The insensible insect is bound with a quarter inch strip of aluminum foil to his chair, a half-cylinder of brass wire mesh mounted on a rigid wire. The wire is affixed to a rubber stopper to insulate the handler. Another wire runs to a key switch and a spark coil with six-volt direct current power supply.

As the insect begins to revive, the operator turns the switch, and the electrically excited insect lets loose its venom through its sting lancet into the collecting well of a microscope. Two or three insects can be "milked" each minute in this manner. Its only apparent other effect, they said, is that it makes the insects very hungry and thirsty.

Vehicles and Bridges

FROM Pascagoula, Mississippi, comes the report that a staggering total of almost thirty-five million vehicles have used the busy U. S. Highway 99 toll bridges there and at Bay St. Louis.

In a report covering June operations and to-date totals, the State Highway Department said 245,488 vehicles crossed the Bay St. Louis span during June, with 269,064 moving over the Pascagoula bridge in the same period.

Although the Bay St. Louis unit was opened August 2, 1953, and the Pascagoula bridge on Oct. 15, 1954 – fourteen months later – the report clearly indicates a greatly heavier volume of traffic at Pascagoula. Toll collections also reflect the narrowing gap between the spans.

We are all beneficiaries of those who made vehicles, and toll bridges and coins possible.

Radio Breaks Stare

NATCHEZ, MISSISSIPPI, policemen, Willie Stroud and Grady Leverett, chanced upon a chance in a lifetime – seeing a velvet-tail rattlesnake and a jet black cat charming one another. In a routine tour of Natchez-Under-The-Hill about 12:30 A.M., Officer Stroud noticed a cat staring at something near the foot of Silver Street. After turning around, the officers stopped at the spot and put the spotlight on the cat and then on a coiled snake about one yard away. Both were spell-binding and spellbound.

The snake was perfectly still except for its weaving tail with ten rattles and a button. The cat was perfectly still, perked ears and all, except for its tail, also weaving back and forth.

Neither the car nor the spotlight broke the spell. Then the officers radioed for Lt. Pete Haley to witness the strange contest. The return radio call broke the spell. The cat started easing away backward, still charming the snake. The snake then started to break its pose, easing away, when officer Stroud shot and killed it with a service revolver. The snake measured four and one-half feet long. The cat is long gone. The debate is just begun: Who would have won the charming contest if the snake and cat were not interrupted?

Potency and Promises

WE THINK of these when we read that cobalt potency has been hiked one hundred-fold. Radio-active cobalt, one hundred times more potent a gram than it was possible to produce in the past, is being prepared by the Atomic Energy Commission. A gram of the material now being supplied is three times as powerful as a gram of radium, for which it is proposed as a substitute.

This greatly increased activity is due to new methods of preparation adopted in the commission's uranium piles at Oak Ridge and Chicago.

The exploding form of cobalt is one of the most promising of the new isotopes in the field of medicine. It behaves much like radium, is less poisonous and is vastly cheaper. Promising results in treatment of cancers have been reported, but more investigation is considered necessary. The material can be produced in almost limitless quantities by the new method.

The potency of a gram of some other isotope preparations which have no immediate medical application has been increased in the same ratio. At the same time, there has been an enormous increase in the production, although not in the potency, of radioactive iodine which has much promise in the treatment of various thyroid disorders. Prepared by a different method which involves transmutation of the element tellurium, the new iodine samples are much purer than the old.

I wish my power in preaching and the power of people in prayer could be "hiked one hundred fold" – increased in reach and power as when a rill becomes a river.

The Costliest Epic

THE average dub at financial matters can take considerable heart from the movie called "Cleopatra." The forty million dollars poured out to achieve this epic makes it the most expensive motion picture in history.

The record of waste and false starts and illogical decisions that went into this film is one to make a man feel that he may not be such a clumsy steward of his worldly goods after all. Before the picture was in the can, the budget had grown from two million to the awesome figure mentioned above. There may be a happy ending a la Hollywood. The studio is said to have taken in fifteen millions in advance bookings already. But the stereotype of cold-eyed motion picture executives combining art with shrewd money-saving moves falls apart completely. The movie tycoons will never again look quite the same.

Eighty More Every Minute

A SCIENTIST has predicted that, if the world's population grows at the current rate for seventy centuries, the mass of humanity will equal the total mass of the earth.

Marston Bates of the University of Michigan estimated that the number of people in the world grows by at least eighty every minute, about the equivalent of the 3,500,000 population of Chicago every month and by about forty-eight million a year. He theorized, too, that there will be shifts in the relative sizes of races and nationalities by the year two thousand.

The ecologist—he studies organisms in relation to their environment – said it is absurd to think of the earth completely covered by people. For one thing, he added, much of the land is unsuitable for human habitation. For another thing, he said, to maintain present living standards, there would have to be an economic growth rate of three per cent a year —"a figure difficult for any nation to attain."

The human population of the world was about three billion in 1960. If trends persist, Bates figured, it will be more than six billion by the year two thousand. "China will account for about one billion, five hundred million of these," he wrote, "and India, if it can find means of support, another billion. The proportions of different races and nationalities will generally be quite different from those prevailing now – if nationality continues to have meaning."

Bates said the most densely populated nations, in many cases, are growing at the fastest rates. He said China and India are growing at the rate of 2.3 per cent or so a year while the United States and the Soviet Union have an annual growth of 1.7 per cent each.

$100,000 Violin

BENNO RABINOFF, the concert violinist, recently was invited to dinner at a restaurant by a violin enthusiast. The violin fan arrived carrying a violin case. After dinner he opened it. There was an exquisite instrument of red-brown, still glowing with the varnish applied by the master violin maker, Antonio Stradivari. It was made in 1734. Rabinoff's companion said he was tendering the violin to the concert artist as a gift. "Why are you giving this to me?" Rabinoff in an interview said he asked the man. "The man said, 'I want to hear it sing again. It has been silent too long.'"

The donor then made one stipulation — his name never was to be revealed. Rabinoff said the violin once was owned by Fritz Kreisler and was last played by him in Carnegie Hall more than a decade ago. In 1946, it came into the possession of a Jacques Gordon, first violinist of the Gordon Quartet. Two years later, Gordon died. Then it came into the possession of the man who does not want to be known. Rabinoff said the violin was one of the three greatest in the world and that it was worth $100,000.

But what would the violin be worth were there no musician to use it — to make it "sing again"?

Men in Space

HERE is a comparison of the manned space shots of Russians Yuri Gagarin, Gherman Titov, Andrian Nikolayev and Pavel Popovich and U. S. astronauts Alan B. Shepherd, Jr., Virgil I. Grissom, John H. Glenn, Jr., Malcom Scott Carpenter, Walter M. Schirra, Jr. and Gordon Cooper.

	Date	*Orbits*	*Altitude (miles)*	*Flight Time*	*Distance Traveled (miles)*
Gagarin	4/12/61	1	110-187	1 hr. 48 min.	26,000
Shephard	5/5/61	suborbit	116	15 min.	302
Grissom	7/21/61	suborbit	118	16 min.	303
Titov	8/6/61	17	100-159	25 hrs. 18 min.	435,000
Glenn	2/20/62	3	100-162	4 hrs. 56 min.	81,000
Carpenter	5/24/62	3	99-167	4 hrs. 56 min.	81,250
Nikolayev	8/11/62	64	114-156	94 hrs. 35 min.	1,612,000
Popovich	8/12/62	48	112-158	70 hrs. 57 min.	1,247,000
Shirra	10/3/62	6	100-176	9 hrs. 13 min.	170,000
Cooper	5/15/63	22	100-166	34 hrs. 19 min.	600,000

All orbital spacecraft traveled approximately 17,500 miles an hour. The suborbital flights reached about 5,200 m.p.h. The U. S. Mercury capsules each weighed about 4,000 pounds and the Russian Vostoks each about 10,400 pounds. Thrust of the Russian booster rockets was estimated at 1.3 million pounds. The Atlas used on U. S. Orbital flights has 362,000 pounds.

Microwave Oven

A COMPACT oven that utilizes microwave energy to cook a meal in a matter of seconds is demonstrated at the American Pavilion. Known as the "Kwik Kooker," the high-speed oven cooks pastries in seven seconds, a hamburger in twenty-four seconds and casseroles are ready in forty seconds. The "Kwik Kooker" is used to demonstrate speedy and nutritious preparation of cold and frozen foods dispensed from vending machines. The microwave oven is a product of the Rudd-Melikian, Inc. of Hatboro, Pennsylvania.

Microwave energy cooks fast because when it strikes any food surface, it penetrates, producing instant heat – not only on the surface, but deep within the food as well. Compared to this, conventional ovens depend upon heat conduction from outside the food to the inside. Therefore, the heating process is slow. High oven temperatures will speed the process, but will burn the surface before the inside is cooked. Besides cooking the food more quickly and evenly, the microwave oven will not heat the container because air and most glass, china and paper containers transmit the energy without absorption.

Ketosis Killed

An "ugly duckling" of the chemical world which became a "swan" with the help of the Oklahoma State University researchers, today is saving farmers and ranchers throughout the world millions of dollars in treatment of the dairy cattle disease, Ketosis.

It is the powerful synthetic hormone fluoroprednisolone, long disregarded as a possible treatment of Ketosis because it is toxic to man and some other species.

Hydrocortisone had been used successfully but its cost was prohibitive at about seven dollars per head, Dr. Dennis Goetsch, of the OSU physiology and pharmacology department, said.

Ketosis, quite common in dairy cattle, results in extreme loss in milk production.

"OSU entered the picture a few years ago and became interested in hydrocortisone molecules which had been altered to enhance their potency," Goetsch said. "We found that fluoroprednisolone was especially potent." "We had reason to believe it was different enough that the hormone would not be toxic to the cow."

In brief, this proved to be the case, and the OSU researchers were in business. Another break came when the compound, unlike many orally administered substances, was not digested in the cow's system and retained its effectiveness. Consequently, oral administration as follow-up treatment is possible.

Fluoroprednisolone, tremendously powerful compared to hydrocortisone, costs less than one dollar per day per cow in Ketosis treatment.

In use of hydrocortisone, one thousand milligrams per day for three days is required, while it takes only twenty to forty milligrams of fluoroprednisolone per day for three days. "It is thirty times more potent," Goetsch said, "and this is where the great savings are possible."

Fifteen-Hundred-Mile Trip

From Landen, Wyoming, through the Associated Press, comes this news of interest: Lou Holt retired and moved to Jasper, Arkansas. The moving company was instructed to take along the Holt's family cat but the movers couldn't catch it. Holt's wife, Mary, arrived back at Landen, after a trip of nearly fifteen hundred miles, to round up her pet. It took her five minutes and fifteen cents worth of liver to trap the cat.

Jewish Migration

In Tel Aviv, Israel, Dr. Israel Goldstein, former president of the Zionist Organization of America, told American Zionist delegates that since the establishment of Israel fifteen years ago, 1,150,000 Jews have come to Israel at a cost of $1,750,000 or $1,400 each.

Goldstein, now president of the Jewish national fund Heren Hayessod, addressed an afternoon session of the 68th ZOA convention. He said fifty-five per cent of the required transportation and resettlement amounts have come from Jewish contributors outside Israel, mostly from the United States. Giving the present Israel population (including non-Jewish minorities) as 2,035,000, Goldstein declared it was realistic to envisage for 1970 a total population of three million – five hundred thousand of them newcomers.

GOD
His Love and Power

Pecans Plentiful

PECANS plenteous.

Pralines plenteous.

Pies plenteous.

All this for man's physical welfare – because the 1953 pecan crop smashed all records. But how much more to be desired than plentiful pecans for plentiful pralines, and plentiful pies for plentiful people is the plenteous grace of God for the spiritual welfare of people. "Plenteous grace with Thee is found–grace to cover all my sin." How great is God's grace–God's unlimited and unmerited favor to the utterly undeserving. How much better it is to say that "great grace was upon them all" (Acts 4:33) than that they were plentifully fed physically. How much more to be valued for the lessening of the sum of human anguish than the report of great crops is the statement: "Where sin abounded, grace did much more abound" (Romans 5:20).

Mice Plague

SOME years ago, Australia suffered from a plague of mice. In some parts of South Australia traffic on the highways was hampered. Some farmers, finding it hopeless to try to protect their property, abandoned it to mice.

If the Bible had told of this happening in the days of Abraham or Lot, there would be some rising up to say and sitting down to declare and running around to make assertions that such could not be. How untenanted of wisdom is such unbelief. It makes us think of what Ben Johnson wrote:

As untenanted of man
As a castle under ban
By a doom.

When we think of those who believe that the mice overran Australia and who do not believe that the frogs encamped abundantly in Egypt, we say that their position, mental and spiritual, is "as unbearable to a believer as a five-act, unactable, intractable tragedy" – as unthinkable as a tree without roots – as unwelcome as Banquo's ghost, or "wallowish potions to a nice stomach."

Great Ingenuity

THE humble creatures of earth and air and sea show forth God's thought. Insects are ingenious. The firefly that plays hide-and-seek on a summer night shows us that insects had a flashlight before we did.

God made it so.

The ichneumon fly has a drill with which she can bore a hole four inches deep in a tree and deposit her eggs.

God made it so.

Beetles and carpenter bees have drills. The carpenter bee can drill a hole fourteen inches deep.

God made it so.

There is a certain ant that makes a tunnel through a foot of solid stone.

God made it so.

The sawfly, which worked before man had a saw, has two tiny saws, working alternately back and forth, side by side, to produce grooves in trees.

God made it so.

Spiders are real engineers, surpassing the architects of the Brooklyn bridge in many ways.

God made it so.

The oak tortrix draws the edges of a leaf together with thread until he has made a comfortable shelter for himself.

God made it so.

A Terrific Note

THE most terrific note I have ever heard was the fierce, shrill, titanic shriek of a cyclone not two hundred yards away from me. All the evening thereafter, the clouds dashed hither and thither without aim or drift. In gusts from every quarter, the wind came and went. All the night long I heard it, moaning and groaning, as if it were some human being crying for the harm he had done. That day I got a better conception of what the Book says: "They are like the chaff which the wind driveth away." I also got comfort in recalling the truth: "A man shall be as a hiding-place from the wind." And amid the babbling of "wild tongues that hold not God in awe," "noisy as burial-howlders at full cry," how sweet to sing:

Boisterous waves obey Thy will,
When Thou sayest to them, "Be still."

The Sea and Things Pertaining

THE English woman, the Hon. Eleanour Norton, has given us this lovely bit of meditation:

Exquisite is the sea
 In the moonlight night,
And exquisite the foam,
 Like lines of light.

Far from the coast of France
 A light wind blows,
As delicate and soft
 As a summer rose.

Far, far overhead,
 Like a myriad eyes,
The solemn, exquisite stars
 Enrich the skies.

The dreaming earth is still,
 And for an hour,
Beauty is captive bound,
 Like a bird or flower.

A Child's Letter

PERHAPS the quaintest letter in the White House collection is one which came from a child to President Cleveland, written in September, 1895. This is what it says: "To His Majesty, President Cleveland; Dear President: I'm in a dreadful state of mind; and I thought I would write and tell you all. About two years ago — as near as I can remember, it is two years — I used two postage stamps that had been used before on letters, perhaps more than two, but I can only remember of doing it twice. I did not realize what I had done until lately. My mind is constantly turning on that subject, and I think of it night and day. Now, dear President, will you please forgive me? and I promise you I will never do it again; Enclosed find cost of three stamps, and please forgive me, for I was then but thirteen years old, for I am heartily sorry for what I have done. From one of your subjects."

If a child asks of a President forgiveness for taking so little – how much more should many more ask forgiveness of God and man for stealing much more – and, asking forgiveness, to make restitution.

Depths Desired

ON SEPTEMBER 30, 1953, the world learned that Prof. Auguste Piccard and his son, Jacques, dived two miles beneath the surface of the sea off the Island of Ponza, Italy. Down in those depths, Piccard reported, there is a gravelike calm and Stygian blackness broken only by ghostly flickers of phosphorescence hinting at unknown forms of life.

"There was nothing else to see," the frail, 69-year-old professor said when he returned to the surface in the steel diving boat he calls a bathyscaphe. "Even our powerful searchlight grayed away in the silent, sunless darkness of the abyss."

The wispy scientist, who twenty years ago invaded the stratosphere by flying up ten miles in a balloon, bobbed back to the rain-swept surface of the Tyrrhenian Sea too excited and too tired to tell of his experiences immediately. He cupped his oil-stained hands and howled gleefully across one hundred feet of sea to correspondents in an Italian corvette: "Three thousand, one hundred and fifty meters!" That's 10,339 feet – only a bit under two miles. Later, rested, Piccard talked eagerly. "We are so happy," he said. "So happy – and so tired."

Excitedly, Piccard told newsmen and Italian navy officers: "At 3,150 meters the blackness is absolute. It is broken only occasionally by numerous tiny phosphorescent flickers."

Soon Jacques added: "The blackness was incredible. There was little or nothing to see, even with the full force of our searchlight."

Piccard's diving boat is named *Trieste.* It is a stubby craft, about thirteen feet wide amidships. The *Trieste* is lowered by cable, sinking with the help of two steel balls held in place magnetically. The Piccards ride in a compartment, about six feet in diameter, beneath the boat. Two small electric motors permit navigation. The craft is raised by cutting the magnetic field, which allows the steel balls to drop off. Compressed within tanks aboardship are about 22,000 gallons of buoyant gas, which help to lift the craft to the surface.

But as wonderful as all this is, more wonderful is the work of the Creator in making the sea which men call the Mediterranean. And still more wonderful is the truth that the prophet Micah wrote: "Thou wilt cast all their sins into the depths of the sea" (Micah 7:19).

99.1 Per Cent Pure

THE Long Island Railroad reported in October, 1953, that 686 of its 17,031 trains ran late during September, giving the railroad an on-time efficiency index for the month of 99.1 per cent.

The total scheduled running time of the trains was 1,049,872 minutes, and the delays totaled 9,501 minutes. Two switch failures in Pennsylvania Station, on September 9 and September 29, affected 106 trains and resulted in delays of 1,293 minutes. Equipment trouble on a train September

8 interfered with 58 trains and delayed them 1,191 minutes.

The railroad's September record was better than that of August by .08 per cent, when the one-time efficiency rating was 99.02 per cent. In August, 18,317 trains were operated with scheduled running time of 1,130, 017 minutes. Of these, 767 were delayed a total of 11,901 minutes.

But more to be valued than this near-perfect record are the words of our Lord:

"As for God, his way is perfect; the word of the Lord is tried; he is a buckler to all them that trust in him" (II Samuel 22:31).

"The law of the Lord is perfect, converting the soul: the testimony of the Lord is sure, making wise the simple" (Psalm 19:7).

"Be ye therefore perfect, even as your Father which is in heaven is perfect" (Matthew 5:48).

"But we know that, when he shall appear, we shall be like him; for we shall see him as he is. And every man that hath this hope in him purifieth himself, even as he is pure" (I John 3:2, 3).

"I thank God, whom I serve from my forefathers with pure conscience, that without ceasing I have remembrance of thee in my prayers night and day" (II Timothy 1:3).

Rice Remarks

Dr. Merton S. Rice writes of the vast and the minute in these words:

"I looked with amazement through a great telescope. The vastness of creation crushed my tiny soul. I went careening across inestimable distances. I had to abandon even the words I had learned as expressions of distance for they were so small they were meaningless in the vast spaces of the heavens. God is a word for the vast.

"The scientist who stood beside me, and spoke easily of light-years as measures of distance, invited me to turn squarely about and front just as confounding a fact of divine workmanship in the opposite direction.

"I put my wondering eye to the microscope. It seemed a reverse telescope. He directed my marvel as we careened farther and farther into the mystery of the minute. He told me the ever-increasingly wonderful story of the littles. What I had seen in the solar systems in the heavens, he paralleled with the story of atoms and electrons, and then astounded me by declaring that the very same mathematics that computed the spaces of the heavens, likewise laid the formulas for the conduct of the minute.

The God of the vast is likewise the God of the minute.

"O Lord our Lord, how excellent is thy name in all the earth" (Psalm 8:9).

The God of the *big* is also the God of the *little*. The atomic universe that lies at man's feet is as vast and perplexing as that which stretches out over his head. Each atom with its infinitesimal suns and revolving worlds is a miniature solar system—fashioned after the order of the heavens. Yet a million atoms stacked on top of each other would not measure the distance of a hair's breadth. Thus the microscope and telescope balance—giving credence to God's Word.

Judges and Justices

Zulcucus, lawgiver of the Locrians, made a law that adultery should be punished with the loss of both the offender's eyes; and it turned out so unhappily that his own son was the first to commit that crime, and, that he might at once express the tenderness of a father and the uprightness of a judge, he caused one of his son's eyes to be put out and one of his own.

Philip of Macedon, being urged to interpose his credit and authority with the judges, in behalf of one of his attendants, whose reputation, it was said, would be totally ruined by a regular course of justice, replied: "Very probably, but of the two, I had rather he should ruin his reputation than I mine."

One of the most remarkable instances of impartial justice, on record, was exhibited by Brutus, the Roman Consul. Rome at that time being a Republic, was governed by consuls. A conspiracy was formed by Tarquin, among the young nobility, to destroy the government and to make him king. This plot was discovered, and the brave and patriotic Brutus had the mortification and unhappiness to discover that two of his sons were ringleaders. His office was such that he was compelled to sit in judgment upon them; but he, nevertheless, amid the tears of all the spectators, condemned them to be beheaded in his presence. The most powerful feelings of natural affection were overruled by a sense of his duty as an impartial judge. "He ceased to be a father," says an ancient author, "that he might execute the duties of a consul, and chose to live childless rather than to neglect the public punishment of a crime."

No matter what judgments men have made, we are glad for the Psalmist's words:

"The judgments of the Lord are true and righteous altogether. More to be desired are they than gold, yea, than much fine gold: sweeter also than honey and the honeycomb. Moreover by them is thy servant warned: and in keeping of them there is great reward" (Psalm 19:9-11).

Paul exclaimed:

"O the depth of the riches both of the wisdom and knowledge of God! how unsearchable are his judgments, and his ways past finding out! For who hath known the mind of the Lord? or who hath been his counsellor?" (Romans 11:33, 34).

Electric Bloodhound

Scientists in San Antonio are working with an electronic bloodhound so sensitive it can detect alcohol in a man's saliva from a bottle of beer he drank the day before. They plan on using the blood-hound to sniff out possible signs of life on the sun-seared desert of Mars. It is called the gas chromatograph.

Dr. Thomas B. Weber of the School of Areospace Medicine at Brooks Air Force Base, holds a patent on a miniaturized version of the gas chromatograph that has a supersensitive detection apparatus no larger than the end of a man's thumb. No longer do the scientists have to talk about traces in a mixture of chemicals in terms of parts in a hundred or thousand. With gas chromatography, chemists at the school can detect a few parts in a million or even a billion.

"Here for the first time is a method that appears to be unlimited in its possibilities for identifying trace materials in minute quantities," Dr. Weber said.

How does it work? A small tube of plastic or metal is stuffed with something such as activated charcoal. A mixture of gases is forced into it. The molecules constituting each of the gases will have different physical characteristics – such as size and shape. This means some of them will slip through the little holes in the charcoal faster than others. As the gases come out of the other end of the tube they are measured with a super-sensitive thermometer called a thermistor. A pen makes a line on a moving piece of graph paper. The position of the humps on the graph paper tells the scientists what kind of gas molecule came through the tube and in what order. The size of the hump tells just what percentage of the gas molecule is present in the mixture.

But more of a bloodhound is sin than man's electronic bloodhounds, for 'tis written: "Be sure your sin will find you out" (Numbers 32:23).

More so are God's eyes: ". . . the Lord's . . . . eyes behold, his eyelids try, the children of men" (Psalm 11:4). "For the ways of man are before the eyes of the Lord, and he pondereth all his goings. His own iniquities shall take the wicked himself, and he shall be holden with the cords of his sins" (Proverbs 5:21, 22). "The eyes of the Lord are in every place, beholding the evil and the good" (Proverbs 15:3).

Wolfe's Words

THOMAS WOLFE wrote these words in an attempt to define man:

"For what are we, brother? We are a phantom flare of grieved desire, the ghostling and phosphoric flicker of immortal time, a brevity of days haunted by the eternity of the earth. We are an unspeakable utterance, an insatiable hunger, and unquenchable thirst, a lust that bursts our sinews, explodes our brains, sickens and rots our guts, and rips our hearts asunder. We are a twist of passion, a moment's flame of love and ecstasy, a sinew of bright blood and agony, a lost cry, a music of pain and joy, a haunting of brief sharp hours, an almost captured beauty, a demon's whisper of unbodied memory. We are the dupes of time."

If Satan ever wrote a review of books, he could read statements like that and say something about a "black leopard" transforming himself into an angel of light.

Just here we should note what King David wrote centuries ago:

"When I consider thy heavens, the work of thy fingers, the moon and the stars, which thou hast ordained; what is man, that thou art mindful of him? and the son of man, that thou visitest him? For thou hast made him a little lower than the angels, and hast crowned him with glory and honour. Thou madest him to have dominion over the works of thy hands; thou hast put all things under his feet: All sheep and oxen, yea, and the beasts of the field; the fowl of the air, and the fish of the sea, and whatsoever passeth through the paths of the seas" (Psalm 8:3-8).

"So we thy people and sheep of thy pasture will give thee thanks for ever: we will shew forth thy praise to all generations (Psalm 79:13).

And Jesus said:

"And he said unto them, What man shall there be among you, that shall have one sheep, and if it fall into a pit on the sabbath day, will he not lay hold on it, and lift it out? How much then is a man better than a sheep?" (Matthew 12:11).

Facts About the Moon

AGE – probably about the same as the earth, but specifically unknown.

Diameter – 2,160 miles, compared to 7,967 for the earth.

Temperature – in sunlight, it reaches 250 degrees (F). In the dark it drops to 215 degrees below zero (F).

Speed – 2,287 miles per hour. Period of revolution around the earth – twenty seven days, seven hours, forty-three minutes and eleven and five tenths seconds. Period of rotation on its axis – about the same.

Light – the moon gives about 1-465,000 as much light as the sun. It is about a quarter as bright as a candle at the distance of one yard.

Craters – there are some thirty thousand craters on the visible side of the moon, ranging from one to eighteen miles in diameter. The deepest is Newman's crater, 23,800 feet from rim to bottom.

Plains – there are walled plains with diameters from sixty to one hundred fifty miles. There are ringed plains with diameters ten to sixty miles. The floors of the ringed plains seem to be lower than the outside.

Seas – there are fourteen large, smooth, dark areas, covering about half of the visible area of the moon. They are erroneously called seas. There apparently is no water on the moon.

Rills – there are narrow crevices, usually less than two miles wide, but ranging as far as three hundred miles along the moon's surface.

Rays – there are bright streaks of unknown origin five to ten miles wide and up to fifteen hundred miles in length on the surface of the moon.

Distance from earth – 252,710 miles at the farthest; 221,900 miles at the least – measured from the center of the earth to the center of the moon. Surface measurements are, of course, shorter.

Some facts, too, we find in the Bible – about the moon. God created it – "When I consider thy heavens, the work of thy fingers, the moon and the stars, which thou hast ordained" (Psalm 8:3). "He appointed the moon for seasons" (Psalm 104:19). Joseph spoke of the moon – "And he dreamed yet another dream, and told it his brethren, and said, Behold, I have dreamed a dream more; and, behold, the sun and the moon and the eleven stars made obeisance to me" (Genesis 37:9).

The moon belongs to the Lord of heaven – ". . . man or woman, that hath wrought wickedness in the sight of the Lord thy God . . . . And hath gone and served other gods, and worshipped them, either the sun, or moon, or any of the host of heaven, which I have not commanded" (Deuteronomy 17:23).

Joshua gave a command to the moon: "Stand thou still . . . ; and thou, Moon, in the valley of Ajalon . . . . and the moon stayed" (Joshua 10:12, 13). Job speaks of "the moon walking in brightness" (Job 31:26). David says: "Praise ye him, sun and moon" (Psalm 148:3). Paul says: "One glory of the sun, and another glory of the moon" (I Corinthians 15:41).

Springtime Comes to Corkscrew

I READ this in a newspaper:
"Spring has sprung at a South Florida beauty spot with a delightful name, Corkscrew Swamp. It's not far from Immokalee, about one hundred and fifty miles from Miami. The giant cypress in Corkscrew Swamp "play dead" all winter. Their towering heads are now plumed with feathery, bright green foliage. Early rains also have brought varying shades of green to the lichens, fungus, ferns, vines and flowers amid the gray tree trunks. This bower of greenery is the nursery of some seventy-five hundred baby storks in three thousand nests. When groups of their parents rise in a flock, sunlight glints from their chalk-white feathers and black-bor-

dered wings. This handsome bird is the wood ibis, the American stork.

"There were no stork nests in Corkscrew Swamp a year ago. Drought had parched the pools from which the parent birds get their food. Nature's wisdom forbade them to produce offspring for starvation. Although water is more plentiful now, Corkscrew Swamp has yet to be assured of a permanent supply. Nearby drainage projects will keep the storks perched on the edge of uncertainty unless dams can be built to store water among their cypress trees.

"The storks, however, have no monopoly on Corkscrew Swamp. It is a veritable babel of bird voices. Much of the chatter comes from the young storks. Sweeter tones are added by visiting warblers and vireos. Other small birds flit and twitter through the greenwood. Among them are cardinals, mocking birds, cat birds, sparrows, black birds, red-starts, wrens, flycatchers and painted buntings.

"The scene at Corkscrew Swamp makes it hard to believe that the sanctuary was in danger of being wiped out by wild fires a year ago. Water levels make the difference."

Whaler and Whales

The 19,308-ton Tonan Maru, mothership of the Tonan Maru whaling fleet which went to the Antarctic Ocean, returned with a cargo of 1,029 tons of whale meat and 1,233 tons of whale oil. The fleet, owned by the Nippon Suisan Kaisha, Ltd., competed with eighteen whaling fleets from five countries including Japan, Norway, Britain, the Netherlands and the Soviet Union in what is called the Whaling Olympics. The fleet caught 898 whales and produced 21,197 tons of whale meat, 12,302 tons of whale oil and 8,826 kilograms of liver oil.

I wonder how many thoughts those whalers had of "the Lord who has dominion from sea to sea, and from the river unto the ends of the earth" (Psalm 72:8) – and who "gave to the sea his decree, that the waters should not pass his commandment, when he appointed the foundations of the earth" (Proverbs 8:29)?

Power

"Behold, the nations are as a drop of a bucket, and are counted as the small dust of the balance (less than a pinch): he taketh up the isles as a very little thing. All nations before him are as nothing; and they are counted to him less than nothing, and vanity" (Isaiah 40:15, 17).

A volcanic eruption is more powerful than an H-Bomb; an earthquake is one hundred thousand times more powerful than an Atom bomb; a hurricane lifts sixty million, or more, tons of water and generates more power every ten seconds than *all* the electric power used in the United States in a year! *One flash* of lightning would keep any home lit for thirty-five years. Two years ago, Hurricane Carla, three hundred and fifty miles in diameter, one of the most violent hurricanes in recorded weather history, whirled in from the Gulf of Mexico onto the coast of Texas. She had ninety times as much energy as Russia's fifty megaton bomb and pushed forty-six *million* tons of water before her.

"Cease ye from man, whose breath is in his nostrils: for wherein is he to be accounted of?" (Isaiah 2:22). What Isaiah is saying is this: why trust man, he can only hold one noseful of air at a time. *Man is a one-lunger*. We go around wheezing, fighting for one nose-full of breath. My, how proud man is of what he does between wheezes. We are frail and sinful and have nothing to brag about. Even our good works, so called, are tainted with wrong motives. Let us realize that in ourselves we are nothing, but *in Christ* can become "something" for Him.

So writes William M. Jones, pastor of the First Baptist Church, Clinton, North Carolina.

GRATITUDE

Water Wells Welcomed

FROM Taipeh, Formosa, in February, 1960, came the news that an estimated $22 million project to dig 1750 water wells on Formosa is expected to increase the island's rice production by almost three hundred thousand tons a year. So the Government gladly announces.

In Formosa doubtless the Chinese there will have as much joy and gratitude as when – in the centuries long ago – Isaac dwelt in Gerar and "digged again the wells of water which they had digged in the days of Abraham his father" (Genesis 26:18). Yes, as much gratitude as when "it came to pass . . . that Isaac's servants came and told him concerning the well which they had digged and said unto him, We have found water" (Genesis 26:32).

Yet, we wonder how many in Isaac's day thanked God for water? And how many in Formosa will thank God for water? And how many of us have ever, in all the years of our lives, praised God for water – and the various uses thereof, such as the making of ice when water is frozen and the production of steam when water is heated to 212 degrees and the cleansing mankind receives from water and the slaking of thirst for human bodies and the members of the animal and bird kingdoms and for the extinguishing of destructive fires with the use of water? And how many of us show gratitude to God for the drinkings we have in many realms from wells we ourselves did not dig, but which our forefathers digged?

Thanksgiving

IT IS good for us to emphasize the blessings we receive. When we approach the day which has been set aside as a national day of thanks by our President, millions of Americans remind themselves of this special day. All of us should thank God in our hearts for the many blessings we have received and gather in groups to praise God for His many benedictions. America has much for which to thank God. Most of our freedoms are intact after having been severely threatened through the last two decades. Unsurpassed material prosperity has come to all of us. People are turning back to God in great numbers and our churches are better supported in every way. Man is more prone to ask God for something than he is to thank Him for things received. This is prominently emphasized in the fact that we set aside a day to thank Him for His blessings. This teaches us two things: we do not have to be nudged to ask God for something and we are so procrastinating in giving Him thanks for the things we do receive. Since this seems to be the pattern human nature follows, we should all exercise our powers of choice and choose to thank God daily for what He has done for us. It is blessing enough just to be here, and then to receive the many benefits we do makes life doubly worthwhile. (Editorial by Leon Macon, Editor of *The Alabama Baptist*).

Lasting Gratitude

In 1918 Sgt. Maj. Robert S. MacCormack saved the life of his commanding officer, Maj. Harry D. Parkin, on a battlefield in France. He has just received his twenty-fifth annual letter of thanks from Parkin, now a real estate dealer in Los Angeles.

"Dear Bob," Parkin wrote, "I want to thank you for the twenty-five years of life which ordinarily I would not have had were it not for you. I am grateful to you."

For our salvation through trust in Christ we should give thanks not 25 times but 25,000 times. We should be found "giving thanks always for all things" (Ephesians 5:20). And "offer a sacrifice of thanksgiving" (Amos 4:5). And say with Paul, "I thank Jesus Christ our Lord" (I Timothy 1:12). With David we should say:

"O give thanks unto the Lord, for he is good: for his mercy endureth for ever.

"Oh that men would praise the Lord for his goodness, and for his wonderful works to the children of men!" (Psalm 107:1, 8)

Six Million to Stanford

Stanford University will receive more than six million dollars under the will of Margaret Jacks. Miss Jacks, last surviving child of pioneer landowner David Jacks, died at the age of eighty-seven on April 4th, 1962. Superior Judge Stanley K. Lawson signed the final decree distributing the major portion of Miss Jacks' $7,100,000 estate to the university. Judge Lawson said this was the largest gift to Stanford since those made by Senator and Mrs. Leland Stanford to found the University in 1891.

The distribution of cash, securities and land was made to Wells Fargo Bank, as trustee. The principal will be turned over to Stanford in 1966. Income from the estate will go to the University.

We hope that God will be glorified in the use of this money as the sun is glorified in rare and beautiful flowers.

HOLINESS

A Questionnaire

Doctor Sheldon prepared a questionnaire for his own use — and each question was quite personal.

Now, here we are — we preachers, we teachers, we deacons, we older ones who are expected to give spiritually proper precept and example to the young folks of our day — and we are to stand an examination. This examination consists of twelve questions from Sheldon's questionnaire. And the young people are to examine our answers in the light of their knowledge of us. What mark will we make?

How shall we grade ourselves? But here are the questions. Honest now – no cheating – what is your grade?

1. What is the best thing you have done since you were born?
2. If you had to write your own obituary, what could you truthfully put on the tombstone?
3. Do you give as much to the church as you spend for amusements?
4. If you put as many dollars into the church collection as you did mean things during the week, how much would you have to add?
5. Do little children and old people like to meet you?
6. Do you smoke, and if so, do you urge your boys and girls to smoke for the reasons your radio ads give?
7. Have you ever started a talk about Christianity in a Club Car?
8. When you die, how many people will be sorry, and will any of them drive the car slowly home from the cemetery?
9. What are you most enthusiastic about, and why?
10. How many friends have you to whom you would feel free to go for financial help, if you were in great need?
11. Do you love your wife as much now as you did when you married her?
12. As you grow older, do you grow better?

Not Ink but Blood Laws

Plutarch tells us that Draco, the Athenian legislator, who flourished 600 B.C., made the least theft punishable by death, because, as he said, small offenses deserved it – and he could find not a great punishment for the most heinous. His laws were repealed by Solon.

But if we would deal more severely in our lives with "the little foxes that spoil the vines," we would be better off – morally and spiritually. And others, too.

Years Ago

Back in 1850, persons could not ride on the Boston and Maine railroad on Sunday unless they satisfied the railroad officials they were making the trip to attend church services.

When New York elevated lines began operating, many citizens boycotted it because trains were run on Sundays.

But now "even Sunday shines no Sabbath day to me." I can't help but believe that that was better for folks than it is now – when a Sabbath day's journey is twice around the golf course. And the Lord's day has been disparaged and disregarded in graver ways than when one wrote:

> To Banbury came I, O profane one,
> Where I saw a Puritan one
> Hanging of his cat on Monday,
> For killing of a mouse on Sunday.

The Tongue Loosed

"And the string of his tongue was loosed, and he spake plain" (Mark 7:35).

Recalling this miracle wrought by Jesus, a Christian friend – "Sister Ida" – on the other side the Atlantic has written the following prayer:

> Loose Thou my tongue, so silent have I been, Lord,
> In telling others of Thy love divine;
> Loose Thou my tongue, and use it for Thy glory,
> That straying lambs, back to Thy fold may come.
>
> Loose Thou my tongue, that Thou canst always help me
> To strengthen those by storm and tempest tossed;

Loose Thou my tongue, to guide the sad and lonely
To find in Thee, their refuge and their rock.

Loose Thou my tongue, for Thee, O blessed Master,
That I may speak Thy words of truth divine;
Loose Thou my tongue, that I may tell the story
Of all the wondrous things that Thou hast done.

Loose Thou my tongue, baptize with love and fire, Lord,
To teach Thy Cross and resurrection power;
Loose Thou my tongue, and fill me with Thy fullness
Till others, too, shall crown Thee Lord of all.

This prayer, if prayed from clean hearts and lives submissive to God's will, would put tongues of fire where there are now tongues draped in icicles – would melt the frozen fountains of testimony and start refreshing streams in dry gardens – would give us the plain language of truth where there is now evasive stammering and beclouding bombast.

Linguists

CARDINAL MEZZOFANTI, born at Bologna, Italy, and died at Rome in 1849, could speak one hundred and fourteen languages and dialects.

Mithridates, King of Pontus, famous linguist of ancient times, was thoroughly conversant with the languages of the twenty-five nations over which he ruled.

And Plutarch testifies in his writings that Cleopatra, Queen of Egypt, spoke most langauges.

"Blind Tom" could repeat speeches in many languages that he had heard, but he made his own thoughts known in grunts.

Yet – no matter how many languages one speaks if his life does not speak in love to God, the best language is left unspoken!

A Complicated Sting

A BEE's sting is painful. Complicated, too. So R. E. Snodgrass, Smithsonian Institute, informs us. In order for a bee to sting, twenty-two muscles are brought into action, the number of muscles being greater for a queen than for a worker. The art of stinging, we are informed, involves three separate sets of movements in the sting mechanism – the outward thrust of the stinging shaft, the depression of the shaft, the movements of the lancets on the stylet of the sting. The extension and restriction of the stinging shaft are brought about by a contraction and expansion of the abdomen, the abdomen acting like a bulb.

But most interesting and significant to me, is that Mr. Snodgrass says that the bringing into play of all this highly complicated mechanism does not call for any particular skill on the part of the bee, the stinging being largely an automatic act. The bee never takes aim. And now – listen! It takes not much skill to shoot out the arrows of the tongue and breed adder's poison under the lips. The folks we know who have tongues that would clip a hedge do not have to be skillful to be painful. Don't forget, King Ahab was killed by a bowman who did not take aim.

How Hard to Kill!

IN A newspaper report of the capture of Mrs. Muriel Pawley and Charles Cockran, British subjects, we have a strange statement! After almost six weeks in the hands of a gang of brigands, these two good people were released – through the efforts of British and Japanese diplomatic and military officials. The newspapers said:

"The bandits demanded heavy ransom for their release, threatening to cut off their heads and THEN PUT THEM TO DEATH, if the money was not forthcoming!"

But you can cut off the head and tail and then try to put to death a false tale – and it will not die! Indeed, adder's poison is under the tongue!

Large Watermelons

WATERMELONS grown in Turkestan along the Tigris River have under special conditions reached the weight of two hundred and seventy-five pounds. So says the Department of Agriculture. A watermelon grown near Hope, Ark., and weighing one hundred and thirty-six pounds was, one year, sent to President Coolidge.

But melons smaller than these are just as sweet and good. So, in spiritual things, are "little melon" folks who live big lives in little places, greatly to be praised.

40-Year-Old Debt

AN ANONYMOUS person has repaid a 40-year-old $3 debt to *The Philadelphia Inquirer*. The *Inquirer* received three old crumpled one-dollar bills enclosed in a letter postmarked Binghamton, N. Y. "When I was a boy living on Vine Street, one night I peddled a hundred papers about 40 years ago," it read. "I never came down and paid for them. So now I am enclosing $3 for them. I hope you will pardon me for not acting promptly."

The interest at 6% on that $3 for forty years would amount to $7.20. I hope this anonymous restitutioner did not go forty years before believing what all men should believe and practice so as to "provide things honest in the sight of all men" (Roman 12:17).

Palm Tree Lessons

IN A scrap book twenty-five years old, I found this: "The Arabs have a saying about the palm tree, that it stands with its feet in salt water and its head in the sun. They often cannot drink the brackish water found in the oasis where the palm tree grows; but they tap the tree and drink the sweet palm wine. The palm tree, by the magic of its inner life, can so change the elements found in the unkindly soil around it that they minister to its growth and strength and fruit-bearing. So you and I, in our earthly life, must often have our feet in the mire and bitterness of sin around us; and upon our heads will often beat the fierce heat of temptation. But in spite of these things we shall be able to grow and grow strong, rejecting the evil and assimilating the good, if within us there is the making of a new life through Jesus Christ."

Honesty

IN BALTIMORE, a man lost $3,278. He got it back. This is how it was:

George Gerczak, who put all his cash in one basket and then sold the basket, has his $3,278 back, thanks to the honesty of a farmer. The 63-year-old Gerczak had reported the money was in a bag on a pile of bushel baskets in his produce store and apparently was left in one of thirty-three baskets he sold to a stranger. Fred Schlaile, Randallstown, Md., farmer, showed up at a police station with the bag of money shortly after reading of Gerczak's plight. He said the cash was among the baskets when he unloaded them and he figured the man who lost the money would tell the newspapers. So he watched the papers – and Gerczak got his money back.

I wish I could as easily get money back from some to whom I have made loans.

Would that I could get all people to give heed to God's words: "Provide things honest in the sight of all men" (Romans 12:17). "Providing for honest things, not only in the sight of the Lord, but also in the sight of men" (II Corinthians 8:21). "Let us walk honestly, as in the day; not in rioting and drunkenness, not in chambering and wantonness, not in strife and envying" (Romans 13:13).

Gossip

The tongue a tiny member is,
Which starts a mighty flame;
The jungle beasts can man control,
The tongue he cannot tame.

Gossip is a mopping cloth,
Dragged across a dirty floor;
And though the excess is pressed off,
Always there is one drop more.

Gossip is but sodden driftwood,
Tossed upon a rocky beach;
And though it's separate from the
flood,
It is never out of reach.

The tongue a tiny member is,
Which starts a mighty flame;
The jungle beasts can man control,
The tongue he cannot tame.

—S./Sgt. Jarvis D. Anderson

Ask This Question

The pastor of a fashionable congregation startled his members one Sunday morning by flinging this question at them: "What have you done today that nobody but a Christian would do?"

Ask this question of yourself. What would be your answer?

Comments on Character

From a ninety-year-old scrap book, I found these words concerning character:

"Life, good influence, works, are each and all the expression of character.

"Character, or else lack of character, always tells. Character is variable.

"Character is cumulative. Character is not confined to education, for good, or for bad.

"Character soon opens a way for itself. Character tells even when money and everything else is wanting.

"Character will give you standing when family name and clothing will not.

"Character is innate principle.

"Character does, and must show itself in face, carriage, spirit, words and business. It is a real entity, and full of life.

"Character calls to itself, like character.

"Character can only fellowship with character that is like itself.

"Christian character, in its last analysis, is Jesus Christ in the heart and life, or else the lack of Christ.

"Christ in you, the hope of glory."

Golden Ignorance

Mr. Moody tells of a steamboat that got stranded on a sand bar on the Mississippi River, and the Captain could not get her off.

Eventually, a hard-looking man stepped on board, and said: "I am told that you are in need of a pilot to help you out of this difficulty."

"Yes, we are," said the Captain, "Are you a pilot?"

"Well, that's what they call me," answered the man.

"Do you know where the snags and sandbars are?"

"No, sir."

"Then how do you expect to run this steamboat if you do not know where the snags and the sandbars are? – if you are not familiar with the places of danger?"

"Easy enough; I know where they ain't."

That is better knowledge for our young people today.

Not only the body but the soul must throw out its protective powers.

Character must be defended. The great defender of the soul is modesty. Immodesty is the gateway through which the conquerors of the soul march. What feathers are to a bird, what bark is to the tree, so modesty is to the human heart. Modesty is being threatened by this radio, movie, television, airplane age. It is a dangerous thing to be ignorant of life's great mysteries, but it is more dangerous to the young to be blase about morals. The swaggering youth who has lost his power to blush is a poor companion for a young woman.

Nothing can so damage a young person as unholy knowledge of life's holiest things!

Penny Runs Up a Bill

In Boone, Iowa, one April day, a motorist went after a penny. Then things happened. Mrs. Sam Saddoris moved her car to get a penny that rolled beneath it. The car lurched, hit a parking meter, broke a window as it bounced against a building, rolled half a block down the sidewalk and stopped.

Damage to the car was $102. Damage to the window and parking meter was not estimated. Police said they weren't even sure whether Mrs. Saddoris found the penny.

That makes us think of what Solomon said: "Take us the foxes, the little foxes that spoil the vines: for our vines have tender grapes" (Song of Solomon 2:15).

And of what James wrote, too: "Even so the tongue is a little member, and boasteth great things. Behold, how great a matter a little fire kindleth!" (James 3:5).

Conversation for Christ

I read the other day of a German scholar who gave his entire attention for years to Greek nouns and expressed regret on his death bed that he had not specialized more strictly by devoting his whole life to the study of the dative case. His eye held nothing but the fine thread of this Greek study. He had no taste for music, for philosophy, for art – for many things that are so supremely worthwhile.

Oft we see the same tragic thing existing in the lives of people as to their making their conversation count for Christ and the kingdom. Somehow it seems we have taken Christ out of our conversations entirely too often – even with a perpetuity of frequency.

When the heart is full, it is easy to talk. How better could the memory of God be whetted than by frequently making Him the subject of conversation – in the home, on the street, the last thought at night, the first in the morning?

Encouragement to Keep On

Mr. Moody said: "I visited Mr. Prang's chromo establishment in Boston, and saw the process of printing a picture of some public man. The first stone made hardly any impression on the paper. The second stone showed no sign of change. The third, no sign. The fifth and sixth showed only outlines of a man's head. The tenth, the man's face, chin, nose, and forehead appeared. The fifteenth and twentieth looked like a dim picture. The twenty-eighth impression stood forth as natural as life. It looked as though it would speak to you." So, carefully and prayerfully read the Word of God – read the same chapters again and again – and the twenty-eighth time Christ Jesus will shine forth. And something of the beauty of being "transformed into the same image from glory unto glory will possess your life."

So Cold

Last winter it was so cold that the sea froze along the British shore, trapping fish in the ice, their heads jutting out. Starving seabirds swooped down to peck at them. Swans froze in a river at Christchurch, Hampshire, in England, their legs trapped in the ice. Foxes glided over to devour them. Lean mixture anti-freeze in Britishers' cars turned to ice, and truck drivers lighted fires under their trucks to thaw them out. A policeman said it looked like a barbeque.

In Chicago, Michael Reese Hospital reported admission of a new case of frostbite every fifteen minutes. A nineteen-year-old Chicago girl waited for a Loop bus for thirty-five minutes, then collapsed from the cold.

An Englewood, Colorado, woman suffered frostbite after she got her finger stuck in a gatepost and had to spend two hours in six-below weather.

People were riding bicycles across the ice on the Oresund, the strait between Sweden and Denmark.

Moreover, it was so cold in Hamilton, Ontario, that this took place: Linda Revill, 9, was on her way to school in sub-freezing weather when she decided to put her tongue on a metal cross outside a church. A policeman warmed the cross with towels soaked in warm water to release Linda. It might be good for many households, many churches, many communities, yea, for whole nations, if some tongues that "setteth on fire the course of nature, and are set on fire of hell, and are worlds of iniquity" (James 3:6), could be frozen and not loosened – not for a long time!

Ironic Gifts

When in India, I saw the King Koti Palace. And I saw cartoons deriding Nizam of Hyderabad – once reckoned the richest man in the world. He accepted a money order for one piasa sent by a Bombay girl to assist him in his "current financial distress." The piasa is worth about one-fifth of a United States cent. It was reported from Hyderabad that the Nizam's office had begun to accept such remittances from all over India after returning many to senders earlier.

Token and ironic remittances by several help-the-Nizam-clubs began pouring into the King Koti Palace of the Nizam after a newspaper report said he had informed the Indian government he could not contribute much to its defense effort in the China border conflict. The Nizam contributed two hundred thousand rupees (about $40,000) but when asked for more pleaded poverty.

But I dare to say that the ironic gifts sent in derision to the Nizam were not more evil than the small gifts made out of men's abundance to

Christ's cause – and in the spirit often of a miser paying taxes. If some gifts can be ironic – can not some gifts, far short of sacrifice, be iniquitous? Yea – verily.

Tampa Without Power

In Tampa, Florida, something went wrong one day – and the entire city was without electrical power for more than two and one-half hours. Hospitals, the police department and several radio stations went on emergency power.

"We were testing some of our equipment when something went wrong," said a spokesman for the Tampa Electric Company. "We're not sure just what happened." He said the mishap knocked out the three main generators that feed the city. They were repaired, and service was resumed in the early afternoon.

Sadder than for Tampa to be without electrical power for two and one-half hours is the fact that many who profess to be Christians have gone for years without spiritual power. Homes, churches, individuals there are that for years have been without spiritual power. Yet there are those who have had spiritual power. "But ye shall receive power, after that the Holy Ghost is come upon you" (Acts 1:8). "Stephen, full of faith and power, did great wonders and miracles among the people" (Acts 6:8). "God anointed Jesus of Nazareth with the Holy Ghost and with power: who went about doing good, and healing all that were oppressed of the devil; for God was with him" (Acts 10:38).

Paul said: "Most gladly therefore will I rather glory in my infirmities, that the power of Christ may rest upon me" (II Corinthians 12:9). "He called the twelve and . . . . gave them power over unclean spirits" (Mark 6:7). "And the power of the Lord was present to heal them" (Luke 5:17).

Life a Pen

Folks say that life is a journey, a song, a sob, the flight of an arrow, a burst of music down a busy street – and so on. But Lillian Wright who spoke of life as a pen, put a library of wisdom in four lines:

Write well, my pen; be sure and true;
Make no mis-statement, and no lies;
This is a manuscript that you
May not revise.

And Governor Pilate said: "What I have written, I have written."

The Human Body

The average human body within its flesh-and-bone area has enough fat to make seven bars of soap, ten gallons of water, thirty to forty teaspoonfuls of salt, sulphur enough to kill the fleas on a medium-size dog, one-fourth pound of sugar, phosphorous enough to make twenty-two hundred match heads, lime enough to whitewash a small chicken coop, carbon enough to make nine thousand lead pencils—all worth 98¢ at the drug store.

How far short these enumerations fall of setting forth the worth of the human body when yielded to God as an instrument of righteousness. Note:

"Now the body is not for fornication, but for the Lord; and the Lord for the body" (I Corinthians 6:13).

"Know ye not that your bodies are the members of Christ?" (I Corinthians 6:15).

"What? know ye not that your body is the temple of the Holy Ghost which is in you, which ye have of God, and ye are not your own? For ye are bought with a price: therefore glorify God in your body, and in your spirit, which are God's" (I Corinthians 6:19, 20).

"Always bearing about in the body the dying of the Lord Jesus, that the life also of Jesus might be made manifest in our body. For we which live are alway delivered unto death for Jesus' sake, that the life also of Jesus might be made manifest in our mortal flesh" (II Corinthians 4:10, 11).

Try It

IT MAY be hard to believe, but it is true that

$$
\begin{aligned}
1 \times 9 + 2 &= 11\\
12 \times 9 + 3 &= 111\\
123 \times 9 + 4 &= 1111\\
1234 \times 9 + 5 &= 11111\\
12345 \times 9 + 6 &= 111111\\
123456 \times 9 + 7 &= 1111111\\
1234567 \times 9 + 8 &= 11111111\\
12345678 \times 9 + 9 &= 111111111\\
123456789 \times 9 + 10 &= 1111111111
\end{aligned}
$$

It may be hard for some to believe these words:

"And we know that all things work together for good to them that love God, to them who are the called according to his purpose" (Romans 8: 28).

But just try loving God – by day, by night, in all places.

"For the Lord God is a sun and shield: the Lord will give grace and glory: No good thing will he withhold from them that walk uprightly" (Psalm 84:11).

But just try walking uprightly – always and everywhere.

Incendiary Bullet

IN SAN JUAN CAPISTRANO, California, a young rifleman has admitted firing an incendiary bullet which touched off California's worst brush fire of the year. Investigators said that Jerry Stewart was target practicing on his father's ranch and failed to note that one of the bullets was incendiary. The shell set dry grass ablaze. Stewart said he tried to beat out the fire but it spread quickly in the rolling hills near the historic mission village.

The fire blackened more than sixty thousand acres and destroyed seventeen cabins and homes. More than two thousand firefighters battled it. The fire moved south onto the Camp Pendleton Marine reservation, but caused no damage as firemen and Marines rushed to halt its advance. Marine Corps helicopters were used to fly firemen to the hot spots.

We think of some words from the Bible: "Behold, how great a matter a little fire kindleth!" (James 3:5). "Dead flies cause the ointment of the apothecary to send forth a stinking savour; so doth a little folly him that is in reputation for wisdom and honour" (Ecclesiastes 10:1). "Take us the foxes, the little foxes, that spoil the vines" (Song of Solomon 2:15).

Swine and Men

"AND when he was come to the other side into the country of the Gergesenes, there met him two possessed with devils, coming out of the tombs, exceeding fierce, so that no man might pass by that way. And, behold, they cried out, saying, What have we to do with thee, Jesus, thou Son of God? art thou come hither to torment us before the time? And there was a good way off from them an herd of many swine feeding. So the devils besought him, saying, If thou cast us out, suffer us to go away into the herd of swine. And he said unto them, Go. And when they were come out, they went into the herd of swine: and, behold, the whole herd of swine ran violently down a steep place into the sea, and perished in the waters. And they that kept them fled, and went their ways into the city, and told everything, and what was befallen to the possessed of the devils. And,. behold, the whole city came out to meet Jesus: and when they saw him, they besought him that he would depart out of their coasts" (Matthew 8:28-34).

Some poet wrote this about Jesus being asked to leave the country:

Rabbi be gone! The powers
Bring loss to us and ours;
Our ways are not Thine.
Thou lovest men; We love swine.
Oh, get thee hence, Omnipotence,
And take this fool of Thine;
His soul, what care we for his soul?
What good to us that Thou hast made him whole,
Since we have lost our swine?
And Christ went sadly,
He had wrought for them a sign,
Of love and hope and tenderness divine,
They only wanted swine.
Christ stands outside your door,
And gently knocks,
But if your gold or swine
The entrance blocks,
He forces no man's hold; He will depart,
And leave you to the pleasures of your heart.

Victory Over Barnacles

Interesting to those who know their boats — and their barnacles — is a special article which declares that the old bugaboo of seagoing vessels, the barnacle, has been licked. By using a special paint with a heavy mercury content, the United States Navy has banished the troublesome ectozoa.

Since man put ships on salt water, the barnacle family has been a primary and important enemy of shipping. Specifically, the barnacle is an animal about the size of a dime, consisting of flesh without a heart, equipped with six pairs of legs, and possessing the greatest tenacity known in history, since once firmly attached, it holds on indefinitely, chucking its shell, losing its eyes and growing new armor in which it will be a life-long prisoner. Its ravages cost ship owners millions of dollars annually. A year-old growth on a ship of 10,000 tons deadweight may amount to as much as thirty tons. It causes a slowdown of natural ship speed, increases fuel consumption, and stimulates excessive vibration which may render fire control apparatus useless.

Regular routines exist in ship repair yards for barnacle removals. If the ship is a large one, it is drydocked and the hull hosed down with fresh water. Then the sides are scraped and wire-brushed, following which paint is applied. Taking about eight hours, the cost ranges from five hundred to seven hundred dollars.

The Navy's riddance of barnacles is accomplished by spraying the special paint smoking hot, once the hull is clean and dry, and providing a surface to which the barnacle can not attach itself, a matter certainly most pleasing and soul-satisfying to every man who ever had anything to do with a ship.

How wonderfully beneficial it would be if human beings would get rid of the undesirable barnacles of bad habits which militate against health and happiness.

Tiny Rocket and Satellite

A thumb-sized rocket engine, fueled with a hypodermic needle but powerful enough to change a satellite's orbit in space, was announced by Areojet-General Corp.

The engine, called microrocket, develops between a tenth and a hundredth of a pound of thrust, compared with 430,000 pounds of thrust for the Aerojet first stage of the Titan II intercontinental missile. The engine, which weighs half an ounce, was test fired for thirty minutes in a vacuum chamber at the firm's plant. It is designed primarily to operate in space where, the company said, it would be powerful enough to make a satellite rotate or even change its orbit. The firm said it would operate all day on a gallon of fuel.

Makes us think of what James wrote: "Behold, we put bits in the horses' mouths, that they may obey us; and we turn about their whole body. Behold also the ships, which though they be so great, and are driven of fierce winds, yet are they turned about with a very small helm, whithersoever the governor listeth" (James 3:3, 4).

Tongue Tragedies

AT CATANIA, SICILY, on Tuesday, July 19th, 1960, Mt. Etna, a giant long asleep, awoke in violent eruption and added twenty-five feet to its height since being racked by the first of a continuing series of explosions. In the past two thousand years, the volcano has erupted five hundred times – taking the lives of one million people.

A worse record has the human tongue – with all its spitting venom and violent expressions of Satanic tempers.

Solomon wrote:

"Put away from thee a froward mouth, and perverse lips put far from thee" (Proverbs 4:24).

"In all labour there is profit: but the talk of the lips tendeth only to penury" (Proverbs 14:23).

"A fool's mouth is his destruction, and his lips are the snare of his soul. The words of a talebearer are as wounds, and they go down into the innermost parts of the belly" (Proverbs 18:7, 8).

". . . but the lips of a fool will swallow up himself" (Ecclesiastes 10:12).

"They have sharpened their tongues like a serpent; adders' poison is under their lips" (Psalm 140:3).

". . . the poison of asps is under their lips" (Romans 3:13).

"But the tongue can no man tame; it is an unruly evil, full of deadly poison" (James 3:8).

Pipe Puffers Seek Crown

THERE'S a reason for that smoke-filled room at a down town hotel in Richmond, Virginia – but it has nothing to do with politics. It's the scene of the annual world's championship of the International Association of Pipe Smokers Clubs. More than fifty starters were expected.

The contestants, armed with 3.3 grams of special contest tobacco and two kitchen matches, have sixty seconds to get their pipes lit. The winner is the gentleman – or woman – who emits the last puff of smoke.

"That person will be the one who smokes slowly, casually and relaxed," said the convention chairman. The record is two hours, five minutes, seven seconds set by the late Max Igree of Flint, Michigan, in 1954.

Champion of the cheap!

Hurt of a Hyphen

THE space ship Mariner II made big headlines when it completed its thirty-six-million-mile trip toward Venus. Until then, we did not know very much about our closest neighbor.

Most of us have forgotten that Mariner II had a forerunner, Mariner I, which attempted the same journey through space about two years ago. What happened that time?

Well, there was nothing wrong with Mariner I. It was just as close to perfect as the scientists could make it. But when it was launched, it went off course and missed Venus by tens of thousands of miles. Why?

It seems that in typing out the electronic instructions to the missile, someone left out a hyphen. That meant that the signals were off by one electronic impulse. And, of course, the missile behaved – or misbehaved – in accordance with the faulty instructions.

Damage? The project was held up for two years – and eighteen *million* taxpayer's dollars were wasted. That's what a hyphen can cost!

So one wrong word we speak, one evil deed, one foolish decision can hurt *much* – and many.

Riches from a Rug

OVER in Columbus, Georgia, riches from a rug are apt to come to Emil Garrett. From an investment of $250 he hopes to make a profit of $149,750. Garrett paid a Chinese general $250 for the rug while serving in Tientsin with the Marine Corps. Upon his return to the United States, Garrett took it to the Smithsonian Institute for appraisal. The Smithsonian director couldn't appraise it because there was only one other like it in the world and it belonged to an Indian potentate. But Smithsonian records did show that the rug once adorned a Chinese palace. It hadn't been heard of since 1923, when the palace was abandoned.

Garrett set an arbitrary price of $150,000 on the rug and until he can get it, the rug is being stored in a bank. Inlaid with five to seven pounds of solid gold, the rug measures 7½ by 9 feet.

Can you imagine a man walking with boots foul with filth and heavy with mud upon such a rug – without receiving censure for such walking? Such a thought makes us think of these words:

"Of how much sorer punishment, suppose ye, shall he be thought worthy, who hath trodden under foot the Son of God, and hath counted the blood of the Covenant, wherewith he was sanctified, an unholy thing, and hath done despite unto the Spirit of grace?" (Hebrews 10:29).

Tons of Talladega Turkey Tainted

DECEMBER 6th, 1949, in Birmingham, Alabama, recorder Ralph Parker talked a lot of turkey in court and condemned – more than seven tons of it. The seven tons of Thanksgiving Day fowl, all dressed, was condemned after county health officers charged that the meat was spoiled. Two turkey salesmen from Talladega county brought the birds to Birmingham before the Thanksgiving Day. The packing house for which they were intended refused to accept them.

I wonder how many tons of books would be condemned if all that are tainted with mental sewerage and spoiled with that which is not truth were condemned?

Massee's Mouth

THE eloquent mouth of Dr. J. C. Massee, once the renowned pastor of Tremont Temple in Boston, Massachusetts, uttered many wise things. But he never said anything more applicable to many church members than this:

"Men join the church. They take that Holy Name upon themselves.

They enter into covenant with each other in the name of the Father and of the Son and of the Holy Spirit, inviting Holy Trinity to witness and support their purpose of faithfulness, purity, love, co-operation, liberality, of personal effort to win a lost world to Christ. Yet American churches are filled with men and women who flagrantly and frivolously and constantly ignore the obligations of their voluntary covenants. Thousands of church members have changed residence without changing church membership. They stand aloof from the local church. They take no local responsibility for Christ. They settle into becoming church drifters and sermon tasters. God will not hold such guiltless. He has declared it in His Word."

1700-Degree Heat

A NEWS item from Chicago gives us the information that heavy timber buildings are safer from fire damage than structures built with so-called "non-combustible" materials, reports the National Lumber Manufacturers Association. Temperatures inside a burning building can reach 1700 degrees often within ten minutes. But wood beams char to a depth of only one and one-half inches after a full hour of that temperature, the organization says, and charring is usually not sufficient to cause collapse.

I would that against temptations and in the midst of fiery afflictions, we would show such spiritual resistance — and be, though charred, never brought to collapse.

Tongue Dial

A PHOENIX, ARIZONA, restaurant owner dialed police with his tongue one Saturday night after three men robbed and bound him at his home.

Jack Durante told police the three jumped him when he answered his doorbell. After knocking Durante out and binding his hands and feet with tape, the trio fled with six hundred dollars and a ring he valued at ten thousand. Durante said he crawled to his living room, knocked a telephone off a table, and dialed the phone with his tongue to report the crime.

Would that tongues were as skilled in speaking truths human ears should hear and human hearts should harbor.

HUMAN NATURE

Fashions

DR. LOUIS ALBERT BANKS, in his book, *The Sinner and His Friends,* says: "The havoc wrought by fashions even in this matter of adornment has made many a page of tragedy. In the fifteenth century the historian tells us the head-dresses of women in Flanders rose to a height so enormous that those of a later date were dwarfs in comparison. One writer declares that so high and broad were these hair ornaments, with their huge artificial ears, that women could not go through an ordinary door. Thomas Conecte, a Carmelite friar, preached with great earnestness against these absurdities, and so angered the society people of his time that he was burned to death in Rome in the year 1434 on account of his attack on the follies of fashion."

About this, I say what some politicians say: "No comment."

Strange People

PEOPLE who talk about prayer, but never pray.

People who say tithing is right, but never tithe.

People who wish to belong to the church, but never attend or support the church program.

People who say the Bible is God's Word to man, but never read it.

People who say eternity is more important than time, but who live for the present life.

People who criticize others for things they do themselves.

People who stay from church for trivial reasons, and then sing, "O How I Love Jesus."

People who follow the devil all their lives, but expect to go to heaven.

All of which makes us think of what Solomon wrote: "The way of man is froward and strange" (Proverbs 21:8).

Never an Auto

IN LONDON ENGLAND, lived Walter Lavender for eighty-five years. In all those eighty-five years, he never forgave the internal combustion engine for replacing the horse. He never rode in an automobile.

His granddaughter, Mrs. Jill Cavanagh, told the newsmen: "He once pointed to a motor hearse and said, 'I don't want to go to my grave in one of them. It isn't fit and proper.' When he knew he was dying, he made my grandmother and me promise that we would get him a horse-drawn hearse."

At first the family had no success. "There isn't an undertaker in the country who still uses horses," they were told. But Walter got his wish. A film studio provided four bays and a splendid black carriage to carry the horse lover to his grave.

Walter, in life, traveled in his own horse cart. "We had thought," Mrs. Cavanagh said, "that if we couldn't get this hearse we might take him to the cemetery in his own cart, behind his old mare, Brenda. But I'm afraid she might have been too frisky."

Just as strange as this long-manifested attitude of Lavender as to the automobile is the action of many who hear the words of Jesus for years and never become doers of the Word.

Words Concerning Wills

1. FRANKLIN'S 1790 will.

Massachusetts Supreme Judicial Court refused to terminate the trust fund established in 1790 by Benjamin Franklin for the benefit of Boston and Massachusetts. The court, in an eleven-page decision, said the fund should continue until 1991, the date set by Franklin in his will. According to the will, Boston and Massachusetts as well as Philadelphia and Pennsylvania, were to divide the balance of funds left in trust.

In later years, the Franklin funds were devoted to investments. The Supreme Court said the market value of the Boston fund on February 28, 1959, was $1,578,098. By an act of the 1958 Legislature, both Boston and the state were authorized to pay over their share of the fund for the use of the Franklin Technical Institute if the Supreme Court should order the fund ended now.

2. Alfred Clark's will.

Polish-born Alieja Purdom Clark will receive the bulk of an estimated ten-million-dollar estate left by Alfred Clark, who died thirteen days after their wedding. According to Clark's will, the thirty-two-year-old former actress will receive a lifetime income from two trust funds. Mrs. Clark also can have up to $100,000 a year from the principal of one of the funds, if she desires, according to the will. Clark, heir to Singer sewing machine millions, died of natural causes.

3. Foulke's will.

Roland R. Foulke, an attorney for more than sixty years, left a two-and-a-half-line one-sentence will to dispose of his estate. Foulke, who lived in a hotel, died at the age of eighty-five.

4. Wayne Morris' will.

Unusual this one. Actor Wayne Morris wrote his own final script in his own handwriting — a will in which he asked that $300 be spent for booze and canapes instead of a funeral so his friends wouldn't go away sober.

Morris died of a heart attack while on a Navy carrier in San Francisco Bay. He was an ace in World War II. "One hundred dollars shall be expended at the discretion of my closest surviving relatives for the purpose of buying booze and canapes for my friends," he wrote in his 1955 will. "On second thought, make it $300 because I don't want my friends to go away sober or serious. This is to take the place of a funeral or memorial service."

5. In Newton, Massachusetts, for fifty years lived Charles W. Abbott — and for fifty years was employed as a personal secretary for Mrs. Maude Kimball, an elderly widow.

He retired two years ago — on a social security pension. Mrs. Kimball died recently. Her will when allowed in probate court bequeathed Abbott $1,296,500.

6. In Lafayette, Indiana, a retired farmer considered a miser by his neighbors has provided for a new elementary school in Lafayette, according to his will. The will of Thomas Miller, eighty-five, who died recently calls for a grade school to be named after him. Attorneys said Miller's estate amounts to more than $500,000. School officials said a new school could cost between $450,000 and $500,000.

Miller had no close relatives. He retired from farming in 1947, moving to Lafayette. Neighbors said he never owned a car, ate corn flakes to save money when his bank account dipped below a certain amount, and gave apples to children, then charged their parents ten cents apiece for them.

Bottle and 4,650-Mile Trip

A NAVY man who for years has been throwing bottles containing notes into oceans has finally had an answer. Chief Quartermaster William W. Doller, stationed at U. S. Pacific Fleet Headquarters, said a bottle he tossed into the Pacific off the Galapagos Islands, January 15, 1960, was recovered on Saipan — nineteen months and 4,650 miles later.

The note in the bottle promised the finder five dollars if he contacted Doller. Doller said he received notification of the recovery from Manuel Blaz Sablan, who lives at Saipan's Talafofo beach. "I've been throwing bottles into the sea for many years because I get a kick out of it," Doller said, "and this is even a bigger kick. It's the first one that's been answered."

Another Bequeathment

IN MANITOWAC, WISCONSIN, John Cooper Smith, retired Chicago produce dealer, died. He left his widow an estate of fifty thousand dollars, his will showed. He also made this bequest: "To my remaining relatives I give the sunshine, the birds and the bees, wherever the above mentioned sunshine, birds and bees may be found."

A Duel

THE man who said that there is always a duel in our dual natures would enjoy this exquisite poem by Elias Lieberman:

Life is a land of sunlit domes,
Death is King of the catacombs.

You and I — in a parting breath —
Tremble as life flings a glove at death.

Life is a youth with a glittering shield
Death is a swordsman who bids him yield.

You and I — and a taunt like a knife —
Pause while death makes a thrust at life.

Death is a bleached and barren plain;
Life is the silver, slanting rain.

Mocking the waste land — you and I
Watch a duel of earth and sky.

Concerning Cigarettes

T. M. JONES, Secretary-Treasurer, Alabama State Chiropractic Association, wrote the following to the editor of the Montgomery Advertiser:

"Americans will continue to poison their bodies with tobacco, disregarding warnings which have been scientifically proved. Americans are funny people. They sprang into action recently when word was received that smallpox carriers might have infected people in a crowded city. An all-out search was launched for everyone who might have come into contact with the infected youth. Yet, presented every day with graphic evidence that smoking not only causes many ailments, but also shortens the life span appreciably, people go right on smoking at a constant rate. The warning from expert sources the world over seems to fall on deaf ears, regardless of the fact that smoking is harmful to their well being.

"Studies of 187,000 men showed that the death rate from heart disease was twice as high among smokers as it was for non-smokers. Another experiment showed that smoking thickens the blood. Another study of 15,000 smokers and non-smokers showed that smokers accounted for ten per cent more organic disease and fifteen per cent more over-rapid pulse.

"Naturally, the adverse effects of smoking are not confined to the heart. They would include the throat, mouth and lung cancer, in addition to other disorders. Many experts feel it is even worse for women to smoke than men, due to the effect smoking has upon their offspring.

"True, it takes real will power to quit smoking, but it shouldn't be hard when one considers the health benefits to be gained and the hazards to be avoided. A recent study showed that about two-thirds of the adult population of the United States are smokers. This is ample proof that the warnings of tobacco's hazards to health haven't been heeded. If you are a smoker, this is an appeal to you in the interest of your health, quit smoking and live longer."

And from a London, England, newspaper these words:

"Every twenty minutes a person in Britain dies from lung cancer, a government peer told the House of Lords. He pledged the official poster campaign against cigarettes smoking will go on, 'however long the process may be.'

"The Lord Newton, partiamentary

secretary of the Ministry of Health, said deaths from lung cancer had risen from 592 in 1920 to 26,383 in 1962. During the same period, he said, cigarette sales rocketed from thirty-six billion to one hundred ten billion. Some peers, however, challenged the validity of Newton's statistics, and Earl Alexander of Hillsborough, a Laborite, asked: 'Where is the medical proof that each particular person, dying from lung cancer, dies because he smoked cigarettes?' "

Is it not strange that human beings spend money for and find pleasure in that which hogs hate, which dogs despise, which goats hold in scorn, which buzzards seek not?

Long to Melt

"ICEBERGS have been known to take as long as two hundred years to melt." This statement from science urges us to say that, judging from the warmth some humans possess as to spiritual realities, they will still be icebergs if they live to be two hundred!

Critical Caricature

I HAD the great joy recently of spending half a day with the Hon. Wm. H. Townshend, who wrote "Lincoln's Home Town" – thirty thousand copies of which were sold in a few months at five dollars per copy. Mr. Townshend is the greatest living authority on Lincoln since Dr. Barton's death. A certain university offered him fifty thousand dollars for his Lincoln collection, among which is a glove Lincoln wore and a piece of crepe from his coffin. But what interests me greatly was a critical caricature of Lincoln which was written after Lincoln was nominated for the Presidency. One statement in that book I give:

> When Lincoln walks down the street, he is composed mostly of bones and looks like the offspring of a happy marriage between a derrick and a windmill.

Poison pens and tattling tongues dripping adder's poison are instruments of Satan. It would be good for many if those who wield poison pens would have paralyzed hands. What a blessing it would be to many if tattling, gossiping, slanderous and lying tongues would be smitten with dumbness.

Epitaphs

CENTURIES ago, the Egyptians, Greeks and Romans put epitaphs on tombs and monuments. They furnished the germ idea of most of the mortuary inscriptions of modern times. Many different kinds we have. For example:

Henry II's: "To me, who thought the earth's extent too small; Now eight poor feet, a narrow space, are all."

Meleager's: "Hail, universal mother! Lightly rest on that dead form, which when with life invested n'er oppressed its fellow-worm."

Saon's: "Beneath this stone Acanthian Saon lies, in holy sleep; the good man never dies."

Shakespeare's:

> Good friend, for Jesus' sake forbeare
> To digg the dust enclosed heare;
> Bleste be the man that spares these stones,
> And curst be he that moves my bones.

This is but a mild echo of the terrible denunciation which Roman epitaphs frequently pronounced upon those who violated the sanctity of the tomb – e.g.:

"I give to the Gods below this tomb to keep – to Pluto – to Demeter, to Persephone, and the Erinnyes, and all the Gods below. If any one shall disfigure this sepulchre, or shall open it, or shall move anything from it, to him let there be no earth to walk, no sea to sail, but may he be rooted out with all his race. May he feel all diseases, shuddering, and fever, and madness, and whatsoever ills exists for beasts or men. May these light on him who dares move aught from this tomb."

Sir Henry Wotton's on Sir Albertus Moreton and his wife: "He first deceased: she for a little tried to live without him—liked it not—and died."

Garrick's on Quin:

The tongue which set the table in a roar,
And charmed the public ear is heard no more;
Closed are those eyes, the harbinger of wit,
Which spake before the tongue, what Shakespeare writ.
Cold is that hand which ever was stretched forth,
To friendship's call, to succor modest worth;
Here lies James Quin! Deign, reader, to be taught,
Whate'er thy strength of body, force of thought,
In Nature's happiest mould however cast,
To this complexion thou must come at last.

Epitaphs

In the First Baptist Church of Malden, Mass., is a bronze tablet to the memory of Adoniram Judson, which reads:

Rev. Adoniram Judson,
Born August 9th, 1788,
Died April 12th, 1850.

Malden his birthplace,
The ocean his sepulchre,
Converted Burmans and
The Burman Bible
His Monument,
His record is on high.

On Tom Paine's tombstone: "I hope for happiness beyond the grave."

On Moody's tombstone: "He that doeth the will of God abideth forever."

On William Jennings Bryan's tombstone in Arlington Cemetery:

Statesman, yet friend of truth,
A soul sincere,
In action faithful and in honor clear.

On Dame Dorothy Selby's tomb:

In heart a Lydia, and in tongue a Hanna,
In zeal a Ruth, in wedlock a Susanna,
Prudently simple, providentially wary.
To the world a Martha, and to heaven a Mary.

On John Keat's tomb – 1820: "Here lies one whose name was written in water."

On a bishop's tomb: "Here rests a man who never rested here."

HUMOR

Twin Worries

A little weekly, not weakly, brings a good laugh.

From the bedroom of the twin boys came the mingled sounds of loud weeping and hearty laughter, so father went upstairs to investigate.

"What's the matter up here?" he inquired.

The joyous twin indicated his weeping brother.

"Nothing," he chuckled. "Only nurse has given Alexander two baths and hasn't given me one."

Catching a Man

A MAN tried to catch another man. The pursuer failed to catch the man pursued. A bystander said: "Why didn't you catch that man?" "Because the closer I got to him, the farther he was away, and the last I saw of him he was clean out of sight."

A Lost Hat

OCTOBER 19, 1931, on a bulletin board at the University of Minnesota, the following notice was posted: "Lost, in Anatomy Building, a new style feather with a small black hat on it. Finder please return feather. You may keep the hat!"

Make your own comment! Well, here goes: "Such a pot must have such a lid." And: "Who hath no head needs no hat."

Topeka Kan

IN THE scrapbook of a dead friend, I found this:

How much did Philadelphia Pa?
How much does Columbus O?
How many eggs did Louisiana La?
What grass did Joplin Mo?
We call Minneapolis Minn,
Why not Annapolis Ann?
If you can't tell the reason why,.
Perhaps Topeka Kan.

—THE LOG

A Little Help

MY FATHER was fond of fun. He liked also to read the *Yorkville Enquirer.* I won't wonder, when the *Enquirer* contains such delicious humor as the following: A man was charged with kissing a girl against her will. During the court proceeding the girl went into the witness box to give her evidence.

"Now," said the counsel for the defense, "you say the defendant took you by surprise, and that you gave him no encouragement whatsoever?"

"That is perfectly correct," replied the girl.

"Very well, then," went on the counsel, "but doesn't it strike you as strange that he should have managed to kiss you when you say you were unwilling and considering that you are almost two feet taller than the defendant?"

The girl returned a very indignant stare.

"Well, what of it?" she retorted, "I can stoop, can't I?"

A Cow for Sale

BILL NYE, the humorist, had a cow to sell, the story goes, and advertized her as follows: "Owing to my ill health I will sell at my residence, in township 19, range 18, according to the government survey, one plush raspberry cow, aged eight years. She is of undoubted courage and gives milk frequently. To one who does not fear death in any form she would be a great boon. She is very much attached to her present home with a stay chain, but she will be sold to anyone who will agree to treat her right. She is one-fourth short horn and three-fourths hyena. I will also throw in a double-barrel shotgun, which goes with her. Her name is Rose. I would rather sell her to a non-resident."

Eating and Music

"EATING is too frequently irksome. What we need is a union of mush and melody. The day is not far distant when music and mastication will march down through the dim vista of years together.

"The Baked Bean Chant, the Vermicelli Waltz, the Mush and Milk

March, the sad and touchful Pumpkin Pie Refrain, the gay and rollicking Oxtail Soup Gallop, and the melting Ice Cream Serenade, will yet be common musical names!"

—Bill Nye

Flying Feathers

A certain rather exclusive club had replaced its familiar black-coated male staff with young, and in some cases, pretty waitresses. One day a member who had been strongly opposed to the change arrived at the club for lunch.

"How's the duck?" he asked an attractive waitress rather gruffly.

"Oh, I'm fine!" she replied pertly, "and how's the old pelican feeling himself?"

Summing Up Cases

A Pennsylvania judge recently summed up a case before him in this fashion: "The ham was there, the prisoner was there. The ham was gone, the prisoner was gone."

Which leads the Manchester *Guardian* to remark that the American love of wisecracks extends even to the judicial bench. This was no more of a wisecrack than Lord St. Helier's summing up of a divorce case:

"If the husband were the brute to his wife she says he was, she was well rid of him. If he is the saint he makes himself out to be, he is far too good for any woman."

A Sedalia Sign

Walter Winchell tells us that a depression victim in Sedalia, Mo., displayed the following sign in his cigar store window:

"John is closing this shop on the first. The following services we have rendered for the past twenty years will be found at these places: Stamps at the post office. Free ice water at the soda fountain next door. Telephone at the hotel. Baseball scores at Western Union. Road information at the Chamber of Commerce. Railroad information at the depot. Magazines at drug stores. And loafing on the court house lawn – Poor John."

A Short Story

The Texas oil man was getting married and was nervous about it. He told the minister that the fee would be in proportion to the brevity of the service, and that if he used a long service, he wouldn't receive a cent. When the wedding day came, the couple stood before the minister, in the bride's home, and the minister said to the man, "Take her?" – to the woman, "Take him?" and then closed the ceremony by pronouncing, "Took . . ." a whole ceremony in five words.

P.S. He got a $500.00 fee – or to be brief – $100 a word.

Plain Flu

We've often wondered how a guy felt on the receiving end of a hook scissors, and

What pain went with a back body drop,

What sensations came with an airplane spin, plus having a couple toes twisted out by the roots,

Then to have a big hulk drop his 230 pounds on the tummy and bounce a head against a hard, hard mat;

Just how a runner must feel when eleven or so tacklers snatch his props from under him and drape nineteen hundred pounds of flesh on him like a roof,

What the reaction was when a linesman rammed his head into one's midsection at about thirty-eight miles an hour,

Or what the sensation was when one stepped from a street car back-'ards and did a sprawl so the public could laugh,

How a young father walking a crying babe felt when his unprotected shin bounced off a chair rocker,

To say nothing of having a base-runner ram his spikes deep into one's leg,

We've tried to picture the misery of a cinder in each eye, cutting wisdom teeth, wearing shoes too tight and having water blisters on each hoof,

We've even dreamed of falling over cliffs and dashing on the rocks a million feet below and wondered how much it would hurt when we made a landing;

Even stepped on tacks and had stone bruises on our heels along with having a bumble bee select our neck for a landing field,

And once we remember a guy putting chewing gum on our hat band and how we did jump when we tried to tip our kelly to a lady friend,

But now all mystery has passed away. We know all these pains and aches and bumps and shocks by their first name,

We know, too, the jar of trying to navigate our icy streets and going a-boom and how thankful we were that he had no glass in our systems,

Because we've had the flu!

Aging Early

I READ this the other day, which made me think of why and how preachers are oft hindered in doing what God meant them to do – by things just as foolish and just as time-taking.

One morning the parcel post carrier had a package for a Mrs. Goldstein, who lives in the outskirts of Brooklyn. He blew his whistle several times and yelled the name Goldstein before a voice from the top floor answered. "Yaas?"

"Package for Mrs. Goldstein," he said. "Will you please come down and sign for it?"

"Wot kinda package?" the voice asked.

"A large one," replied the postman.

"From who comes it?"

"From a Mr. Stein."

"From where?" persisted the lady.

"From California," he told her, in resigned accents. "Will you please come down and sign for it?"

"Wot's in der package?" she asked.

"I can't tell you, madam," the postman hollered. "I don't know."

"You don't know and ken't tell me wot's in der package?" she repeated in surprised tones.

"No, madam," he answered, losing all that was left of his temper. "I can not."

There was a pause. "Vell," she finally said, "you'll hev to come back tomorrow. Mrs. Goldstein ain't home."

Teeth Talk

IN DARWIN, AUSTRALIA, a captured burglar, George Dean, demonstrated for police how he broke into buildings by prying apart metal louvers with his teeth. Policemen say Dean, 22, developed his jaw power as a cattleman chewing on bones and partly-cooked meat.

The patriarch, Job, said this about teeth:

"His teeth are terrible round about" (Job 41:14).

David said: "Thou hast broken the teeth of the ungodly" (Psalm 3:7).

"The sons of men, whose teeth are spears and arrows" (Psalm 57:4).

Solomon said: "There is a generation, whose teeth are as swords, and their jaw teeth as knives, to devour the poor from off the earth, and the needy from among men" (Proverbs 30:14).

Jeremiah said: "He has also broken my teeth with gravel stones" (Lamentations 3:16).

Daniel said: "After this I saw in the night visions, and behold a fourth beast, dreadful and terrible, and strong exceedingly; and it had great iron teeth" (Daniel 7:7).

The murderers of Stephen "gnashed on him with their teeth" (Acts 7:54).

To turn from wise words to silly words that cheer us I give a boy's "Essay on Teeth":

"My teacher asked me to write an assay.

Teeth is my subject.

Teeth is a noble animal.

Teeth is hatched in the mouth.

Most every man has teeth 'cepting a hen, she ain't got any – she swallows her vittles whole and chews them with her gizzard.

My grandmother has false teeth; she puts them in a glass of water. I told her she ought to buy her a gizzard.

A man has one mouth, one nose, and two ears and two eyes.

His mouth is to hatch teeth in; his nose is to sniffle air with; his eyes are to catch dust in and his ears is to keep his hat from falling down over his face.

Man has one skeleton.

A skeleton is what's left when the insides are taken out and the outsides are taken off.

Man has one spinal column. His head sits on one end and he sits on the other end.

Man has one skull. His brains are on the inside if'n he's got any. His hair is on the outside if'n he's got any.

Woman's has ankles. Ankles are to keep the calves from coming down and eating up the corns.

And that's all I know about teeth."

Tickled at Tombs

We surely find it not hard to be tickled and smile when we read the following written or carved above the buried dead:

About *General Wolfe:*

He marched without dread or fears
At the head of his bold grenadiers;
But what was remarkable – nay, very particular –
He climbed up rocks that were perpendicular.

About *Mr. Foote:*

Here lies one Foote, whose death may thousands save,
For Death hath now one foot within the grave.

About a *Mr. Box:*

Here lies one Box within another.
The one of wood was very good,
We can not say so much for t'other.

Swift about *Earl of Kildare:*

Who killed Kildare? Who dared Kildare to kill?
Death killed Kildare—who dare kill whom he will.

About physician *Chard:*

Here lies the corpse of Chard,
Who filled the half of this church yard.

About *Arabella:*

Here rests in silent clay
Miss Arabella Young,
Who on the 21st of May
Began to hold her tongue.

In New Hampshire churchyard:

To all my friends I bid adieu,
A more sudden death you never knew.
As I was leading the old mare to drink
She kicked, and killed me quicker than a wink.

No name:

Here I lies, and no wonder I'm dead,
For the wheel of a wagon went over my
head.

On tombstone in Scotland:

John Carnegie lies here,
Descended from Adam and Eve;
If any can boast of a pedigree higher,
He will willingly give them leave.

Two Smile Producers

If a smile is worth one hundred frowns in any market, then the following ought to be a frown dispenser:

Dr. Earle Williams, a Dallas oral surgeon, has an example of how quick Baylor's Dr. W. R. White is at repartee. Dr. Williams says a fun-loving emcee once introduced Dr. White in this manner: "We have all types of doctors – doctors of medicine, doctors of theology, doctors of psychology and so forth. But tonight we have a doctor of veterinary medicine, Dr. White."

Doctor White rose and responded: "Yes, I am a doctor of veterinary medicine – and this is the first time I've ever been introduced by a former patient."

Lane is an honest speaker who will start out with a joke – and admit that it hasn't an earthly thing to do with his talk. There was, he said, a gorilla that dropped into a neighboring bistro, asked for a scotch and soda and put a ten dollar bill on the bar. The bartender didn't have anything in the way of change but fifty cents, so he stepped into the manager's office for help out of his predicament.

"Just give him the fifty cents," said the manager, "these gorillas are pretty dumb – he won't do anything."

So the bartender came back, gave the gorilla the fifty cents and said, conversationally, "You know, we don't get many gorillas in here these days." "No wonder," said the gorilla, "at $9.50 a drink."

Smile a Bit

A dear fellow who has a merry heart that doeth good like a medicine handed me the following. Maybe you will smile. Then 'tis worth while,

Shortest man – Nehemiah (Knee-High-Miah)

Bildad, the Shuhite (Shoe-Height)

Smallest man – Peter. He slept upon his watch.

Straightest man – Joseph. Pharaoh made him a ruler.

First electrician – Noah who in unloading the ark made the ark-light.

First woman – Genesis (Jenny's Sis).

First cannery – Noah, who filled a boat with preserved pears.

One who used bad words at the earliest age – Job, who cursed the day he was born.

Noah was the first man to become like a hungry cat – he went one hundred fifty days without finding Ararat (Ary rat or E'er a rat).

Transcription of part of a sermon:

As delivered: "Moses was an austere man who made atonement for the sins of his people."

Transcription: "Moses was an oysterman who made ointment for the shins of his people."

Another part of another sermon:

As delivered: "The Lord smote Job with sore boils."

As transcribed: "The Lord shot Job with four balls."

Light Words with Heavy Meaning

There was the wife who complained to her husband, "Look at these old clothes I have to wear; if anyone came to visit, they would think I was the cook." The husband replied, "Well, they'd change their minds if they stayed for dinner."

Judge: "What possible excuse can you give for acquitting that murderer?"

Jury Foreman: "Insanity, your honor."

Judge: "What, all twelve of you!"

"He who thinketh by the inch and talketh by the yard, deserveth to be kicked by the foot."

Frank Markey Speaks

"Dear! Dear! The British always have a different word for it. Do you know what the 'hire-purchase' plan is? Well, that's their term for our installment plan . . . . Today's favorite gag: Young Housewife – 'Are these eggs strictly fresh?' Grocer (to his clerk) – 'Feel those eggs, Joe, and see if they're cool enough to sell yet.'

"Country editor speaking: 'When I was a young boy I walked eight miles to school. Now they send a ten thousand dollar bus to haul the kids a few miles and then build a one hundred thousand dollar gymnasium for exercise.' . . . During the past few years scores of skyscrapers were erected in New York City and practically all the steel girders were swung into place and joined by two hundred and fifty Mohawk Indians who have their own residential section in Brooklyn. They walk about and jump from beam to beam with great ease and seem to be as surefooted as mules. These Mohawks are never idle and are paid premium wages for their dangerous work . . . .

A London travel bureau advertises this leisurely fourteen-day vacation trip: 'Five days in Morocco with optional excursion to Leningrad. Coach and air to Ostend; night journey to Potsdam. Proceed via Posnan, Warsaw and Smolensk to Moscow.' Now, who said American tourists travel too fast to see the sights?"

Specs O' Spice

Bobby Pickett, bright young comic of Somerville, Mass., gives, in these words, some of his favorite jokes – clean spice:

A first-grade teacher asked her young pupils to draw a picture of John Glenn's space flight. The children worked hard on the project for about fifteen minutes, then submitted their results to the teacher for her comments. In the corner of one youngster's drawing was the outline of a woman. This puzzled the teacher and she asked: "Janie, who is this woman in your picture?" "Oh," replied the first-grader, "that is Kate Canaveral."

"I see," commented the cynic, "by the number of divorces that this is still the land of the free." "Yes," added the optimist, "but by the number of marriages, I would judge it is still the home of the brave."

Did you hear about the new Mafia car – two hoods up front?

A Texan went into a bar and said, "Give me the tallest glass you've got and one lemon." The bartender obliged. The Texan squeezed the lemon and got almost a pint of juice. Tossing aside the lemon rind, he said, "I'd like to see anyone else get that much juice from just one lemon." A little fellow standing near-by said: "Let me have a tall glass and the lemon rind you just threw away." He then took the lemon rind and squeezed another full glass of juice from the already used rind. "Man!" exclaimed the Texan, "I never saw anything like that. How did you do it?" "Well, you see," replied the man quietly, "I'm with the Internal Revenue Service."

Did you ever hear about the real estate man's girl friend who sued him for breach of promise? She expected a lot!

My neighbor stays up every night, he says, to get the late news . . . . that's when his wife comes home from work!

Definition of a hypocrite: A man who hands his pay check to his wife with a smile on his face.

INFORMATION

Color Indications

HERE are the colors that indicate academic specialties on the university or professional level:

Agriculture, maize.
Theology, scarlet.
Laws, purple.
Philosophy, philosophy blue.
Medicine, green.
Music, pink.
Nursing, apricot.
Pharmacy, olive.
Dentistry, lilac.
Optometry, orchid.
Education, light blue.
Public health, salmon.
Forestry, russet.

Suicide Statements

DR. WALTER C. ALVAREZ, Emeritus Consultant in Medicine, Mayo Clinic, makes known the following truths concerning suicides.

In the United States among persons between the ages of fifteen and fifty years suicide today is the fifth leading cause of death. It is surprising how many youngsters commit suicide.

In 1960, 19,450 persons committed suicide. This figure, which is bad enough, does not include the 100,000 or more people who die each year from complications caused by an attempt at suicide which did not immediately kill, but later did. Also, not listed are the many hidden suicides whose certificates of death are not accurate because their physician did not care to outrage the person's family. Naturally, the family much prefers that their loved one's death read accident and not suicide.

We all know of cases in which a man fell out of a window. In such a case the family may know perfectly well that for some time the person had been much depressed and had been talking of suicide and perhaps threatening it: but the official record made is that of an accidental death.

Many a person also who took enough capsules of some barbiturate to cause death is put down as having taken a few extra by mistake.

I look forward to the day when all people will realize that a person who commits suicide was not bad, but ill or very unhappy. Usually he was badly depressed, and sometimes I happen to know that he had one or two depressed relatives who committed suicide.

Some elderly people commit suicide because they are dying of disease, or they feel that life no longer holds for them any usefulness of satisfaction or joy.

Fortunately, in some countries in which suicide used to be looked on as a serious crime, it is no longer so considered.

Chinese Feet Binding

Dr. Theo van Dellen tells us that the practice of binding the feet of Chinese women existed more than a thousand years. The fashion has become obsolete• and it would be difficult to find this type of deformity in any woman under thirty years of age. No one knows how the custom started except that the Ancient Chinese considered small and lotus-shaped feet the acme of beauty. Parents realized that girls with normal feet would be hard to marry off.

The deforming process was begun when the children were between two and six years old; after it was completed these women could hardly walk. This was not the reason for binding but it did keep the women indoors and out of temptation and mischief.

It is difficult to describe the appearance of these poor feet. Molding and tight bandages raised the arches upward like a tent and shortened the feet. The big toe was turned outward and the other four toes were bent under the soles. When the mutilation was complete the heels and four smaller toes bore the weight of the body.

The Canadian Journal of Surgery carried an article on the subject by two Chinese physicians living in Hong Kong. These men say the gait had no resilience or spring and the women walked "with a stamping gait like wearing wooden stilts." It was almost impossible to go up and down stairs, walk on a slope or run. Special shoes with a raised heel had to be worn because of the misshapen front part of the foot.

Binding the feet in this way is extremely painful and not harmless. Pressure sores often developed during the process, especially when it was done by inexperienced persons. The bandages may have been put on so tightly that circulation was impaired and the ensuing gangrene required amputation. Fungi infections of the toes and nails were common because of the poor hygienic state of the feet.

Tuberculosis of the bones of the feet occurred also and osteomalicia (loss of calcium) was encouraged because these house-bound women never got any sunlight or out of door exercise.

I'm happy foot-binding is out of style and I'm sure the Chinese women are, too.

Spiders

Black widow spiders are spinning webs for the United States Army, and saving the government thousands of dollars each year. Kept in jars and fed on flies, the notoriously venomous spiders docilely produce nets of dark strands for use as cross hairs in telescopes, microscopes, gunsights and other instruments.

My brother, T. K. ("Tackhole") Lee for years the world's champion marksman, milked spiders to get the cross hair for his famous "Lee Dot" rifle sight.

The black widow was selected for military service over other species because of the strength and elasticity of her web, which has been found capable of withstanding compressed-air blasts of up to ninety pounds.

Spider webs, made largely by the dominant female, come in all shapes and textures. The threads range from invisible single fibers to combined lines woven into snares heavy enough to entangle a snake or a mouse.

In all, there are some twenty-five thousand known species of spiders, each with its own style of web.

The black widow's weaving is coarse and irregular, with a central tunnel where she lies in wait for victims. A member of the poisonous world-wide genus Latrodectus, she is fond of setting up housekeeping in dark, protected spots in and around human dwellings. Though she attacks man only on accidental contact, her bite is excruciatingly painful and occasionally has proved fatal.

Naturalists call the symmetrical orb web the spider's masterpiece. Spun in many forms, it is distinguished by dry radiating spokes that intersect and support sticky encircling lines.

One handsome creation of a tropical orb spider is a circular golden net more than three feet across. It sometimes ensnares small birds.

Other web types include tangled mazes, closely woven sheets, funnels, hammocks, triangles and "lamp shades." The bowl and doily spider spins a double design, a horizontal sheet below an inverted bowl.

Even stranger is the way of the bolas spider. Swinging from a loose trapeze line, she draws from her abdominal spinnerets short lengths of thread that she finishes off with a sticky ball of silk. With these she lassoes passing insects, and draws in her prey.

Three times the Bible mentions the spider:

"The spider taketh hold with her hands, and is in kings' palaces" (Proverbs 30:28).

"So are the paths of all that forget God; and the hypocrite's hope shall perish: whose hope shall be cut off, and whose trust shall be a spider s web" (Job 8:13, 14).

"They . . . bring forth iniquity . . . . and weave the spider's web . . . . Their webs shall not become garments . . ." (Isaiah 59:4-6).

Druggist's Code

It is a sort of short hand. The scribble your doctor puts down on a slip of paper for you to take to your pharmacist may appear to be medical hocus-pocus. But prescription symbols aim at clarity, not mystery. The hieroglyphics are a shorthand used between druggists and physicians. The symbols are usually abbreviations for Latin words. The practice dates back to the time when Latin was the common language of the science.

Your doctor isn't trying to keep anything from you. In fact you can learn some of the more common prescription symbols yourself.

The familiar RX is an instruction to the druggest. It means "take thou of" and compound the medicine.

q.i.d.=Four times a day, and t.i.d. =three times a day.

a.a.=of each.

q.s.=in the amount of.

q.l.=as much as pleases.

c. with a line over it=with, and s with a line over it=without.

q.h.=every hour.

q.t.=drop, and qtt=drops.

p.c.=after meals, and a.m.=before meals.

Prescription language is getting simpler as more specific chemicals and drugs are used.

One-Half Dollar Worth $10,000

On July 15, 1959, in Marietta, Ohio, Probate Court officials wondered if anyone would respond to an unusual provision in the will of a Marietta dentist.

The will, filed Tuesday of that July week, is that of Dr. Braden E. Nida, who died July 5, 1959, at 62. Although there was no estimate of the estate, officials said his wife, a former wife and three children, are principal beneficiaries. But there was no immediate explanation of a provision which states that a $10,000 United States Treasury note will go to the person who, within a year, supplies the other half of a dollar bill attached to the will.

On July 21st, the half of the bill was reported found. Former Governor C. William O'Neil, now a Marietta and Columbus attorney, said that he had a client who had the other half of the torn bill which Dr. Braden E. Nida mentioned in his will. The serial number of the attached bill was P18975127H.

O'Neil said he planned to meet with the attorney for Nida's estate, Charles K. Heckles. The search for the missing half of the bill began July 14, 1959 – when the sixty-two-year-old dentist's will was probated.

Real riches for one man from a half of a dollar bill. But greater riches for all are found in the Bible, for we read:

"The fear of the Lord is clean, enduring for ever: the judgments of the Lord are true and righteous altogether. More to be desired are they than gold, yea, than much fine gold: sweeter also than honey and the honeycomb. Moreover by them is thy servant warned: and in keeping of them there is great reward" (Psalm 19:9-11).

Degrees

FROM the *Philippino American Herald,* we learn the following:

"Dr. Edward Francis Green, headmaster of Pennington School for Boys, a school which does not confer degrees upon graduates, says he will not be happy unless all of his boys have, before they leave the school, won the five following degrees:

"A.B. – Ardent Believer. Doubt does not accomplish things, belief accomplishes.

"M.D. – Magnificent Dreamer. Dream true, high ideals and move toward them.

"Litt.D. – Devotee of Literature. Become a lover of the best literature and remember that at the forefront of all books stands the Book – the Bible.

"F.R.S. – Fellow of Regular Supplication. Present yourself daily before the throne of God.

"D.D. – Doer of Deeds. By their fruits ye shall know them."

MISSIONS

Rejected by Missionary Board

THE following letter was printed by *The Western Voice,* June, 1953:

Rev. Saul Paul
Independent Missionary
Corinth, Greece
Dear Paul:

"We recently received an application from you for service under our Board. It is our policy to be as frank and open-minded as possible with all our applicants. We have made an exhaustive survey of your case. To be plain, we are surprised that you have been able to "pass" as a bona-fide missionary. We are told that you are afflicted with a severe eye-trouble. This is certain to be an insuperable handicap to an effective ministry. Our Board requires 20-20 vision.

"At Antioch, we learn you opposed Dr. Simon Peter, an esteemed denominational secretary and actually rebuked him publicly. You stirred up so much trouble at Antioch that a special Board meeting had to be convened in Jerusalem. We can not condone such actions.

"Do you think it seemly for a missionary to do part-time secular work? We hear that you are making tents on the side. In a letter to the church at Philippi you admitted that they were the only church supporting you. We wonder why?

"Furthermore, you have not graduated from our seminary, and you know we can not have our mission board represented by one who is not a graduate from a recognized university. We can not recognize the three years you spent in Arabia and Damascus because the schools are unknown. Our Board does not recognize private tutors such as you claim you have had.

"Is it true that you have a jail record? Certain brethren report that you did two years time at Caesarea and were imprisoned at Rome. You made so much trouble for the business men at Ephesus that they refer to you as 'the man who turned the world upside down.' Sensationalism, in missions, is uncalled for. We also deplore the lurid over-the-wall-in-a-basket-episode at Damascus.

"We are appalled at your obvious lack of conciliatory behavior. Have you ever suspected that gentler words might gain you more friends?

"Again you have disclosed sordid personal affairs of your past life, such as punishing the saints. This borders on sensationalism. I enclose a copy of Darius Carnegus' book, *How to Win Jews and Influence Greeks.*

"In one of your letters you refer to yourself as 'Paul the aged.' Our new mission policies do not envision a surplus of super-annunated recipients.

"We understand you are given to fantasies and dreams. First you said a 'bright light from heaven' caused you to fall to the earth, then you heard a voice calling *your* name. And at Troas, you say 'a man of Macedonia' called you and at another time you were caught up to the 'third heaven,' and even claimed 'the Lord stood by you.' We reckon that more realistic and practical minds are needed in the task of world evangelization.

"You have caused much trouble everywhere you have gone. You opposed the honorable Greek women at Berea and the leaders of your own nationality in Jerusalem. If a man can not get along with his own people, how can he serve foreigners?

"We learn that you are snake handler. At Malta, you picked up a poisonous serpent which is said to have bitten you, but you did not suffer harm.

"You admit that while you were serving time at Rome, that 'all forsook' you. Good men are not left friendless. Three fine brothers, Diotrephes, Demas, and Alexander the coppersmith, have notarized affidavits to the effect that it is impossible for them to cooperate with either you or your program.

"We know you had a bitter quarrel with a fellow missionary, Barnabas. Harsh words do not further God's work.

"You have written many letters to churches where you have formerly been pastor. In one of these letters, you accused a church member of living with his father's wife, and you caused the whole church to feel badly; and the poor fellow was expelled.

"You spent too much time talking

about 'the Second Coming of Christ.' Your letters to the people at Thessalonica were almost entirely devoted to this theme. Put first things first from now on.

"Your ministry has been far too flighty to be successful. First Asia Minor, then Macedonia, then Greece, then Italy and now you are talking about a wild goose chase to Spain. Concentration is more important than dissipation of one's powers. You cannot win the whole world by yourself. You are just one little Paul.

"Another episode of yours we do not approve of is that forced diet you placed upon all those soldiers and the ship's crew. You called it a fast, but you should know that doctors say that total abstinence from food is very harmful to the body.

"In a recent sermon, you said, 'God forbid that I should glory in anything save the cross of Christ.' It seems to us that you also ought to glory in heritage, our denominational program, the unified budget and the World Federation of Churches.

"Your sermons are much too long at times. At one place, you talked until after midnight, and a young man was so asleep that he fell out the window from the third story and was taken up dead, but you were reported to have restored his life by falling on him and embracing him. Do you expect us to believe that? We want practical men. You should have called a physician and had a rigid physical examination made and not been so inhuman. 'Stand up, speak up, and shut up' is our theme.

"Dr. Luke reports that you are a thin little man, bald, frequently sick and always so agitated over your churches that you sleep very poorly. He reports that you pad around the house praying half the night. A healthy mind in a robust body is our ideal for all applicants. A good night's sleep will give you zest, a zip, that you wake up full of zing.

"We find it best to send only married men into foreign service. We deplore your policy of persistent celibacy. Simon Magus has set up a matrimonial bureau at Samaria where the names of some very fine widows are available.

"You wrote recently to Timothy that 'you fought a good fight.' Fighting is hardly a recommendation for a missionary. No fight is a good fight. Jesus came, not to bring a sword, but peace. You boast that 'I fought wild beasts at Ephesus.' What on earth do you mean?

"It hurts me to tell you this, Brother Paul, but in all of my twenty-five years of experience, I have never met a man so opposite to the requirements of our Foreign Mission Board. If we accept you, we would break every rule of modern missionary practice."

Most sincerely yours,
J. Flavius Fluffyhead
Foreign Mission Board
Secretary

Great Missionary Sayings

"The world has many religions; it has but one Gospel" – George Owen.

"All the world is my parish" – John Wesley.

"I see no business in life but the work of Christ" – Henry Martyn.

"Fear God and work hard" – David Livingstone.

"We can do it if we will" – The Men of the Haystack.

"We can do it *and* we will" – Samuel B. Capen.

"The bigger the work, the greater the joy in doing it" – Henry M. Stanley.

"The lesson of the missionary is the enchanter's wand" – Charles Darwin.

"The work of winning the world to Christ is the most honorable and blessed service in which any human being can be employed" – C. F. Schwartz.

"I am in the best of services for the best of Masters and upon the best terms" – John Williams.

"Nothing earthly will make me give up my work in despair" – David Livingstone.

"The greatest hindrances to the evangelization of the world are those within the church" – John R. Mott.

"Prayer and pains, through faith in Jesus Christ, will do anything" – John Eliot (on last page of his Indian Grammar).

"What are Christians put into the world for except to do the impossible in the strength of God?" – General S. C. Armstrong.

"Let us advance upon our knees" – John Hardy Neesima.

"Tell the king that I purchase the road to Uganda with my life" – James Hannington.

"I am not here on a furlough; I am here for orders" – Hiram Bingham, Brooklyn, October, 1908.

"The medical missionary is a missionary and a half" – Robert Moffat.

"Every church should support two pastors – one for the thousands at home, the other for the millions abroad" – Jacob Chamberlain.

"I will place no value on anything I have or may possess except in relation to the kingdom of Christ" – Livingstone's resolution made in young manhood.

"Win China to Christ and the most powerful stronghold of Satan upon earth will have fallen" – Mr. Wong.

"The word 'discouragement' is not to be found in the dictionary of the kingdom of heaven" – Melinda Rankin.

"We are the children of the converts of foreign missionaries; and fairness means that I must do to others as men once did to me" – Malthie D. Babcock.

"We cannot serve God and mammon; but we can serve God *with* mammon" – Robert E. Speer.

"The prospects are as bright as the promises of God" – Adoniram Judson.

"Your love has a broken wing if it cannot fly across the sea" – Malthie D. Babcock.

To these statements I would like to add one statement of mine own – namely, "Unless our arms are twenty-five thousand miles in circumference-reach, they are too short."

REWARDS AND PUNISHMENTS

Lying Money

AFTER Jefferson Davis fled from Richmond, three wagons loaded with Confederate paper money, were captured on the edge of the mountains. With amazement, the handful of Union soldiers gazed at bills – bills piled up like bales of cotton. Being cold and cheerless, they pitched quoits that night for stakes. They played for one hundred thousand dollars a game – Confederate money. The next morning, one soldier bought a gray mule for three hundred thousand dollars and paid another hundred thousand to put one shoe on it. Meanwhile, the soldiers were cold and hungry and houseless. Lying money!

So Satan pays those who work for him in lying money — counterfeit money — and then jeers at their anguish and laughs at their heartbreak and soul sorrow.

Not a Friend

In *Memoirs of Talleyrand* we read how the great Frenchman, hearing that there was an American general stopping at a little inn, sought him out with a request for letters of introduction to prominent Americans. The story relates that upon Talleyrand's request, a look of utter despair came into the face of Benedict Arnold as he replied, "I am perhaps the only living American who can honestly lift his hand to God and say, 'I have not a friend, no not one, in all America.'"

Such a desert as traitorhood brought does sin bring to men and women who yield to it.

What Then?

The following verses were written by a young soldier — S/Sgt. Jarvis D. Anderson — who attended services at our church during the Korean War.

If you reach your goal of riches
    What then?
If you dress in pin-stripe britches,
    What then?

When your glory has diminished,
    What then?
And the doctor says you're finished,
    What then?

When each fading moment tells,
Like the echoes from a bell,
That you're headed straight for hell,
    What then?

—S./Sgt. Jarvis D. Anderson

Mysterious Tomb in Westminster Abbey

One Sunday in London — in October, 1953 — a mysterious tomb baffled the experts when Westminster Abbey opened its doors to the public for the first time in months.

The ancient abbey where British sovereigns are crowned had been closed for repairs since shortly after the coronation of Queen Elizabeth. During the repair work, laborers found a tomb believed to be more than five centuries old under the floor of Edward the Confessor's chapel. The discovery was kept secret by abbey officials. They still refused to give details, but reports said the tomb contained a wooden coffin. Inside were a skeleton and a crozier, the pastoral staff of a bishop.

Archeologists were trying to decide who was buried there. "I don't want to say anything yet about the finding of this tomb," Alan C. Don, dean of Westminster, said. "Our inquiries are not complete."

The abbey is the great royal mausoleum of Britain, with tombs dating back one thousand years. It also is the final resting place for many poets and statesmen. Queen Elizabeth I lies there. So does her cousin, Mary Queen of Scots. Henry VII has a marble tomb in the middle of the chapel he built, now used as the chapel of the Order of the Bath. A host of poets and authors are buried there. Britain's Unknown Soldier of World War I lies beneath a simple slab set into the floor of the central nave. But the greater mystery is that of which the Apostle wrote to the church at Corinth:

"Behold, I shew you a mystery; We shall not all sleep, but we shall all be changed, in a moment, in the twinkling of an eye, at the last trump:

for the trumpet shall sound, and the dead shall be raised incorruptible, and we shall be changed. For this corruptible must put on incorruption, and this mortal must put on immortality" (I Corinthians 15:51-53).

A greater mystery also did Paul mention when he wrote to Timothy, saying:

"And without controversy great is the mystery of godliness: God was manifest in the flesh, justified in the Spirit, seen of angels, preached unto the Gentiles, believed on in the world, received up into glory" (I Timothy 3:16).

And more to be wondered at than the inhabitant of a tomb over five hundred years old will be the wonder that the Apostle John wrote about:

"And I saw the dead, small and great, stand before God; and the books were opened: and another book was opened, which is the book of life: and the dead were judged out of those things which were written in the books, according to their works. And the sea gave up the dead which were in it; and death and hell delivered up the dead which were in them: and they were judged every man according to their works" (Revelation 20:12, 13).

Virtues of Venezuela

This news comes from a newspaper reporter who visited Caracas, Venezuela:

The Gran Sabana, a 5,000-foot high plateau in eastern Venezuela – the inspiration for the late Sir Conan Doyle's "The Lost World" – is now prepared to receive settlers.

A Caracas explorer, Capt. Charles C. Baughan, is prepared to fly in weekenders over the impenetrable jungle for a look at a region where gold and diamonds abound and where the world's highest waterfall, Angel Falls, can be found.

Venezuela last year produced $10,000,000 worth of diamonds and most of them came from the virgin Gran Sabana fields. Large quantities of gold nuggets were also yielded by the plateau's rivers.

The Gran Sabana is said to be the only place in the world where diamonds are found with alluvial gold. Vast quantities of iron, nickel, manganese, and other minerals have been discovered.

The wide prairies, dominated by lofty mountains, are a cattleman's paradise. The climate is pleasant and the rivers abound in fish.

Long closed to exploration and settlement because of the surrounding jungle, this "Land of Tomorrow" as Baughan calls it, is now being prepared to receive qualified settlers. No discrimination against foreigners exists in Venezuela. The underpopulated country wants both settlers and investors.

How entrancing!

But how much more alluring is the heavenly land Christians shall see some day!

Reward for Radar

Sir Robert Watson-Watt, the Scotsman who invented radar, was rewarded $140,000, the highest award ever made for a wartime invention. Watson-Watt, on a business trip to the United States, was one of twenty-one inventors who will receive a total of $264,880 for their work on radar.

What a fine reward!

But how much more wonderful the realities revealed in these words: "But love ye your enemies, and do good, and lend, hoping for nothing again; and your reward shall be great, and ye shall be the children of the Highest: for he is kind unto the unthankful and to the evil" (Luke 6:35).

Beyond

WHEN folk get discouraged amid earthly trials, let them think of what shall be theirs amid heavenly glories "some sweet day" and let them be faithful, remembering the day of rewards.

Spain inscribed on her coins the picture of the pillars of Hercules, which stood on either side of the straits of Gibralter, the extreme boundary of her empire, with only an unexplored ocean beyond; and on the scroll over the pillars was written *ne plus ultra,* nothing beyond. But afterward, when Columbus discovered America, Spain struck out the negative, and left the inscription *plus ultra,* more beyond.

On every life, on every soul, is this inscription, but what shall be beyond depends on our faithfulness here.

Notable Napoleonic Gift

THE Wide World Photo service published in December, 1953, the picture of a young woman wearing a gorgeous tiara. This tiara, now owned by a New York jewelry firm was given by Emperor Napoleon I of France to his first wife, Empress Josephine, in 1805. Set in gold and silver, it contains about 880 diamonds with a total weight of 260 carats.

Long ago the lovely eyes of the beautiful Josephine sparkled with delight to see these diamonds. Long since, too, were those eyes closed in death.

Long ago – over 150 years ago – did the hands of Napoleon place the tiara upon the brow of his Empress. But those hands long ago turned to dust by the strange alchemy of death. But the 880 diamonds are as bright with a luster which centuries and death cannot dim as ever they were.

It makes us think of the Bible truth which, though we all do fade as a leaf (Isaiah 64:6), though the rich man fades away in his ways as the grass withereth under the burning heat of the sun (James 1:11), though the earth mourneth and fadeth away (Isaiah 24:4), though the world languisheth and fadeth away (Isaiah 24:4), there is "an inheritance incorruptible and undefiled, and that fadeth not away, reserved in heaven for you" (I Peter. 1:4). How grateful we should ever be that "when the chief Shepherd shall appear, we [children of God by faith in Jesus Christ] shall receive a crown of glory that fadeth not away" (I Peter 5:4).

Revised Edition

ARTHUR was helping Bill pack for college. Bill's room was littered with the college miscellany of a young law student. Arthur picked up a frayed and tattered book from a corner shelf.

"Here's an old-timer," he said, reading the title. "*The Ideal Life.* Sounds like some my folks used to have." He thumbed through the yellowed pages.

"Yes," Bill agreed. "I must take that with me. My parents had that when they were first married. And I'm the youngest of a large family. We cut our religious teeth on the Bible and that book."

"Needs re-binding, doesn't it?" Arthur observed, handing it to his friend, who looked at it affectionately. "You know that old book reminds me of something that Benjamin Franklin wrote when he was a young fellow of twenty-two, and had just set up a printing business in Philadelphia."

"Go ahead," Bill encouraged. "Most every word Franklin wrote or said weighed a pound."

Arthur sat down in a chair and put his hands behind his head reflectively. "Young Franklin set up the type, just for practice, for what he jokingly called his own obituary, or, I should say, epitaph. He wrote these words:

> The body of Benjamin Franklin, Printer, (like the cover of an old book, its contents torn out, and stripped of its lettering and gilding), lies here, food for worms. But the work shall not be lost, for it will appear once more in a new and more elegant edition, revised and corrected by the Author."

"What a beautiful epitaph," Bill observed softly.

"Yes, and when he died, an old man, nothing more appropriate could be found to inscribe on his memorial stone," Arthur added.

Bill tucked the worn volume into his trunk, beside his Bible. "Sort of gives a fellow something to look forward to, doesn't it?" he concluded thoughtfully.

And we hear Paul saying: "And the dead shall be raised incorruptible, and we shall be changed. For this corruptible must put on incorruption, and this mortal must put on immortality" (I Corinthians 15:52, 53). And John: "But we know that, when he shall appear, we shall be like him; for we shall see him as he is" (I John 3:2).

No Avenging

"Thou shalt not avenge" (Leviticus 19:18).

In the East Indies are monkeys called avenging monkeys. Natives revere these animals and seldom destroy them. Their mode of revenge is to sprinkle rice or corn on the roof of an enemy's house or granary just as the rainy season begins. The monkeys will congregate on the roof, eat all they can find outside, and then rip off the tiles to get at what has fallen through crevices. Thus the home or granary is exposed to the weather and the contents ruined.

"Dearly beloved, avenge not yourselves, but rather give place unto wrath; for it is written, Vengeance is mine; I will repay, saith the Lord" (Romans 12:19).

$372 for a Mud Pie

In Memphis, Tennessee, four members of one family – all Gypsies – were held by the state in City Court – one on a grand larceny charge and three on vagrancy – after Mrs. Ruth Thompson of 1650 Shadowlawn told a fantastic story. Mrs. Thompson testified that the four came to the Little Rebel Cafe, which she operates, for coffee. She said Mary Marks of 660 Vollintine, told her she wanted to tell her fortune and arranged an appointment for Mrs. Thompson to meet her the following day at the Marks home. Mrs. Thompson said Mary Marks collected seven dollars from her as fee, told her some things about her past, then told her to return and bring three five-dollar bills wrapped around an egg, and she would tell her more. Mrs. Thompson said Mary Marks prophesied some good things in the future for her, told her to come back the next day with five ten-dollar bills wrapped around a tomato, which she did.

Mrs. Thompson said that on both occasions she got her money back after Mary Marks had taken the numbers off the bills. The third day, Mrs. Thompson said, she was told to return with three one-hundred-dollar bills. So she did, along with the five ten-dollar bills and the three five-dollar bills. She said Mary Marks took it all, mixed it in with some egg and some mud, handed her some of the batter which supposedly contained the money, and told her to go to a cemetery at midnight, in the nude, and bury the wad of batter and money, and the spirits would come out of their graves and tell her the whole future. Mrs. Thompson went to the police, who found the ball of batter contained no money. She said Mary Marks got $372.00.

But I know women who have paid more for some things worth less than a mud pie. Don't you? Well, think of Saul, first king of Israel, giving his mind and body for a flea and a dead dog!

"After whom is the king of Israel come out? after whom dost thou pursue? After a dead dog, after a flea" (I Samuel 24:14).

"For the king of Israel is come out to seek a flea, as when one doth hunt a partridge in the mountains" (I Samuel 26:20).

Security of the Believer

By faith the believer has committed his life to Jesus. Jesus said: "My Father, which gave them me, is greater than all; and no man is able to pluck them out of my Father's hand" (John 10:29). That life is hid with Christ in God. That life is sealed with the impression of the Holy Spirit. Who can pluck that life out of the hand of God?

Dr. J. R. Graves wrote:

"If hell should open her yawning mouth and all the demons of hell should issue forth like huge vampires darkening water and land – could they break the seal of God? Could they soar to the heights of heaven? Could they scale the battlements of heaven? Could they beat back the angels that guard the walls? Could they penetrate the presence of the Holy God on His actual throne, and reach out their demon claws – and pluck our life from the bosom of God, where it is hid with Christ in God?"

And Jesus said: "I give unto them eternal life; and they shall never perish" (John 10:28). How good to know that when one is born from above, he can never be UNborn from below. And this truth puts upon us the obligation to live as "children of light."

"And I give unto them eternal life; and they shall never perish, neither shall any man pluck them out of my hand" (John 10:28).

Rewards

In delightful words Jessyca Russell Gaver speaks of rewards:

I never looked for roses, just for thorns,
To feel a little smoother to the touch,
And now at last a rose my heart adorns
To take away the sting of thorns and such.

I never looked for music, just for chords
To sound a little softer to the ear,
And now my soul enjoys its own rewards—
Enchanted melodies I seem to hear.

I never looked for rapture, just for peace
To brush away the tears I could not share.
And then, upon the wings of swift release,
I found these lovely things – for you were there.

"Righteousness shall be a sure reward" (Proverbs 11:18).

"But without faith it is impossible to please him: for he that cometh to God must believe that he is, and that he is a rewarder of them that diligently seek him" (Hebrews 11:6).

Untarnished Crowns

From the *Arkansas Baptist*, we read:

"There is something fascinating

about a king's crown. One of the leading points of interest to the hundreds of thousands of people who visit Edinburgh (Scotland) Castle each year is the Crown Room where are displayed "The Honours of Scotland." Included in "The Honours" is the Crown, the Scepter and the Sword of State.

"The Crown was remodeled in 1540 by order of James V. It is made of Scottish gold and is decorated with ninety-four pearls, ten diamonds and thirty-three other precious stones. The velvet cushion on which it rests is three hundred years old.

"The Scepter was presented to James IV by Pope Alexander VI in 1494 and was refashioned by James V. At the head of the gilded silver rod are figures of the Virgin Mary, James and Andrew, surmounted by a globe of rock crystal and a Scottish Pearl.

"The Sword of State was given to James IV in 1507 by another Pope, Julius II, whose name is etched on the blade, together with etchings of Peter and Paul. Its wooden scabbard, covered with crimson silk, bears the Pope's arms on an enameled plate.

"One of the most tragic of the royal persons to wear the Scottish Crown was Mary, Queen of Scots. When the Crown was placed on her little head and the Scepter thrust into her tiny hand, at the age of nine months, she cried. And well she might if she could have known what was ahead of her. She was to be the sixth Scottish ruler to die a tragic death.

"Once, for a period of a hundred and eleven years, the Honours were hidden away in a sturdy oak chest, from 1707 to 1818, because it was feared they would be taken to England. They were brought out largely on the efforts of Sir Walter Scott, after Royal permission was secured to open the chest.

"The Honours were found, tarnished but undamaged. Today they glow in their original brilliance.

"In an earthly kingdom, there can be only one crown – for the ruling monarch. And even when it is made of the finest gold, it becomes tarnished and requires polishing. But in the kingdom of God, there is a Crown of Life for every true believer in Christ. And this is a Crown that never becomes tarnished."

Some Escapes and No Escape

In the last few years, I read of the following escapes of man from the prisons of men:

1. In Oakland, California, embarrassed jailors admitted one day that an inmate slipped out of their "escape proof" city prison – and that escape was made from the twelfth floor cell. The jailors said Manuel Lizarde made his way through three locked, barricaded doors, over a twenty-five foot wire mesh fence on the roof. This man who could rightly claim kinship with Houdini, through three locked doors and wire fence safely passed, descended to the main floor on an elevator – and walked out.

2. In Doylestown, Pennsylvania, one hot August day, the Bucks County prison officials reported "the most amazing escape they ever encountered."

Warden Carl D. Handy said Robert Henderson, twenty-two-year-old Philadelphian, held on car theft charge, apparently used a small piece of steel from an old lock and several short lengths of lumber to do six things, namely:

Break out of a solitary confinement cell,

Smash through a steel mesh grating,

Break the panes from a closely-leaded window,

Squeeze his 170 pounds through a space of five and one-half by thirteen inches he had sprung between two one-inch bars,

Scale a ten-foot steel and barbed-wire fence,

Climb over a thirty-one foot wall.

3. From Baltimore, Maryland, comes the rather lengthy report of how a modern Monte Cristo pulled a fantastic escape from the Maryland Penitentiary through a seventy-foot tunnel that took him twenty months to dig.

The fugitive, Joseph Holmes, was recaptured after pulling a five-dollar holdup under the shadow of the Washington Monument, a few blocks from the heart of Baltimore.

Here is the story of the escape as pieced together later:

Through the first part of 1949, Holmes worried about going stir-happy. He was in his eighth year of a twenty-year sentence for burglary, and the time still to serve preyed more and more on his mind.

By July 8, he had made up his mind to dig himself out, and started to work. He made a drill by inserting a nail in the end of a stick sixteen inches long and an inch in diameter, and began boring holes close together in the slate floor of his cell. The holes were spaced in a rectangular pattern twenty-eight inches long and seventeen inches wide.

It took Holmes forty days to cut through the slate and form a trap door. Then he tackled the ten inches of concrete beneath it. He used a chisel stolen from the prison workshop, wrapping it in cloth to deaden the sound of the pounding. He could work only while the radio was blaring over the prison broadcast system during the early evenings. It took five to six months to pound through the concrete, pulverizing each chunk so he could flush it down the toilet. During this period, his cell was checked every half hour by a guard.

Once through the concrete, he tackled the dirt beneath his first floor cell. He dug straight down for about six feet, then began angling slightly toward the outside wall. For digging tools he used any scraps of iron or metal he could find. He sewed clothing into bags to carry the dirt back to his cell and dump it down the toilet. Burrowing deep under the wall – this tunnel went to a depth of twenty-six feet – he ran into trouble with water seepage. To solve this, he scooped out a large underground drain and bailed the water. Some nights he carried more than one hundred gallons. Twenty months after he started the project, he came up under the topsoil outside the prison wall, and squinted up through the fine matting of grass to see light. He squirmed back the entire seventy feet to his cell and waited for the big moment. It came about 1 A.M. one Sunday morning.

Holmes took $152 he had made running a numbers game in the prison, and slipped into the tunnel mouth. It took him forty-five minutes to wriggle the length of the tunnel, then he broke through the final layer of topsoil and pulled himself into the fresh air.

He easily scaled a seven-foot iron fence, the last obstacle between him and brief freedom.

But no escape from hell has ever been made or can ever be made by the inhabitants of hell. Once there, always there. Once in, never out. "Exit" is a word not in the hard vocabulary of hell. Jesus in His teaching about hell showed us the rich man, being in torments in hell, crying to Abraham and asking that Lazarus be sent "that he may dip the tip of his finger in water, and cool my tongue; for I am tormented in this flame." But to him Abraham replied:

"Son, remember that thou in thy lifetime receivedst thy good things, and likewise Lazarus evil things: but now he is comforted, and thou art tormented. And beside all this, between us and you there is a great gulf fixed: so that they which would pass from hence to you cannot; neither can they pass to us, that would come from thence" (Luke 16: 25, 26).

"A great gulf fixed" – impassable from those who would come from there here.

Jesus pictured the suffering and horror of hell to be *eternal* – not temporary.

"And if thy hand offend thee, cut it off: it is better for thee to enter into life maimed, than having two hands to go into hell, into the fire that never shall be quenched: where their worm dieth not, and the fire is not quenched. And if thy foot offend thee, cut it off: it is better for thee to enter halt into life, than having two feet to be cast into hell, into the fire that never shall be quenched: where their worm dieth not, and the fire is not quenched" (Mark 9:43-46).

Concerning this, Dr. Henry van Dyke said: "Whatever 'the worm that dieth not and the fire that is not quenched' means, whatever is meant by 'being bound hand and foot and cast into outer darkness, where there is weeping and wailing and gnashing of teeth' – these and many similar expressions descriptive of the destiny of man after death are not the inventions of theologians but the two-edged words of Jesus who spake as never man spake. When men rail at His ministers as cruel, malignant, ignorant, as dolts delighting in human suffering because they repeat the words of Jesus, we feel the accusation not as against ourselves but as well-suited to dishonor and villify the character of Jesus."

Crown of the Andes

The jewel-studded Crown of the Andes, which graced the Virgin of Popayan Cathedral in Colombia for three centuries, is displayed at Sotheby's auction house in London, as it went on sale. The crown, weighing five and three-quarter pounds and studded with 453 emeralds weighing 1,251 carats, was sold to the Amsterdam diamond firm of Asschers for $154,000.

But more worth while is a virtuous woman who is a crown to her husband (Proverbs 12:4); and the hoary head which is a crown of glory, being found in the way of righteousness (Proverbs 16:31); and children's children who are the crown of old men (Proverbs 17:6); and the crown of righteousness which the Lord, the righteous judge, will give unto all who love his appearing (II Timothy 4:8); and the crown of life which the man who is tried shall receive, even the crown which the Lord has promised to them who love him (James 1:12); and the crown of glory which fadeth not away – the crown which the chief Shepherd will give to all who are "ensamples to the flock" (I Peter 5:4); and the crown of life which will be the reward of those who are faithful unto death (Revelation 2:10).

SIN

One Sinner in Destructive Work

ONE little rat caused a dike to collapse in England recently. After the rodent had burrowed through the embankment of a canal, water began seeping through. Slowly but surely, the original trickle became a sizable stream. Soon one bank collapsed and a 40-foot break-through let the water pour out in torrents. Three million gallons of water escaped; the canal was drained for seven miles; more than a million fish were swept away and a twenty-foot gorge was channeled through a nearby field.

It took sixty men with bulldozers three weeks to shift thirty thousand tons of soil and repair the damages.

As one tiny rat caused the tremendous harm, so can one individual like you start a chain reaction that will benefit everyone. While it is true that "one sinner destroyeth much good" (Ecclesiastes 9:18), it is also true that you may never be aware of the far reaching good resulting from a seemingly insignificant prayer, word or deed. But God is and that is what counts.

"To them that love God, all things work together unto good" (Romans 8:28).

Rats!

IN ADDITION to being a necessary link in the transmission of typhus, rats cost citizens of the United States some $200,000,000 each year.

One rat eats and destroys two dollars' worth of food each year. It is the most destructive animal in the world.

With conditions favorable and no deaths, two rats could produce 359,000,000 descendants in three years. They migrate freely from farm to farm and from residence to residence, but cannot exist without food and shelter.

But rats have never been so destructive as evil tongues. How many are wounded by those who "let the rank tongue blossom into speech."

Hyena Jaws

ANIMAL trainers tell us that the strongest jaws of any animal are in a hyena – a scavenger. A hyena can crush the shin of an ox. This a lion cannot do. This a tiger cannot do.

Yet the mouth of the hyena, with such strong jaws, is no worse than a human mouth that has a tongue which is "set on fire of hell."

"And the tongue is a fire, a world of iniquity: so is the tongue among our members, that it defileth the whole body, and setteth on fire the course of nature; and it is set on fire of hell. For every kind of beasts, and of birds, and of serpents, and of things in the sea, is tamed, and hath been tamed of mankind: but the tongue can no man tame; it is an unruly evil, full of deadly poison. Therewith bless we God, even the Father; and therewith curse we men, which are made after the similitude of God. Out of the same mouth proceedeth blessing and cursing. My brethren, these things ought not to be" (James 3:6-10).

Arthur Baer says of a woman's tongue: "Her tongue hangs out like a pump handle."

What a Barrel of Whisky Contains

THIS is something that ought to be pasted in every book of every schoolboy and girl – and written on the hearts of men and women the world over:

A barrel of headaches, of heartaches, of woes;
A barrel of curses, a barrel of blows;
A barrel of sorrow for a loving, weary wife;
A barrel of care, a barrel of strife;
A barrel of unavailing regret;
A barrel of cares, a barrel of debt;
A barrel of hunger, of poison, of pain;
A barrel of hopes all blasted and vain;
A barrel of poverty, ruin, and blight,
A barrel of tears that run in the night;
A barrel of crime, a barrel of groans;
A barrel of orphans' most pitiful moans;
A barrel of serpents that hiss as they pass,
That glow from the liquor in the bead of the glass;
A barrel of falsehoods; a barrel of cries
That fall from the maniac's lips as he dies!

Whisky Queen's Statement

DAMASCUS wine merchants recently selected 20-year-old Lamar Ouda as their whisky queen. After presenting her with prize money, they were appalled to hear her announce, "I've never tasted the stuff in my life." The merchants have now ruled that their next queen must produce a statement before entering the contest declaring not only that she drinks whisky, but that she likes it.

I wonder if these money-loving wine merchants and whisky venders ever heard the words:

"Who hath woe? who hath sorrow? who hath contentions? who hath babbling? who hath wounds without cause? who hath redness of eyes? They that tarry long at the wine: they that go to seek mixed wine. Look not thou upon the wine when it is red, when it giveth his colour in the cup, when it moveth itself aright. At the last it biteth like a serpent and stingeth like an adder" (Proverbs 23: 29-32).

Have they been devilishly deaf to the voice that says that strong drink never touched an individual, that it did not leave an indelible stain, never touched a home in which it did not plant the seeds of dissolution and misery, never touched a community in which it did not pollute the moral atmosphere, never did touch a government in which it did not increase governmental problems?

Tilden on Alcohol

IN A series of articles on "How to Play Tennis," William T. Tilden, for many years the world's champion tennis player, said: "It is certain injury to touch alcoholic drink in any form during tournament play. Alcohol is a poison that affects the eye, the mind, and the wind – three essentials in tennis. A man who is facing a long season of tournment play should refrain from both alcohol and tobacco in any form. Excess of any kind is bad for the physical condition and should not be chanced."

Maybe Carlyle said almost the same thing when he wrote: "Liquid madness sold at tenpence the quartern."

Initialed Terrapin

IN OCTOBFR, 1949, in Cushing, Oklahoma, Terry DeVilbiss carved his initials on the back of a terrapin and turned him loose at his home. He didn't see it again until in October, 1953. The terrapin crawled back to the DeVilbiss home. The terrapin crawled back – after four years, but it came back.

So our sins, signatured by self, sometimes come back to haunt us and taunt us for our folly.

Wentworth Dillon said:

Remember Milo's end;
Wedged in the timber which he strove to rend.

Frederick Von Logan wrote:

Though the mills of God grind slowly, yet they grind exceedingly small;
Though with patience He stands waiting, with exactness grinds He all.

Power to Powderly's Words

T. V. Powderly, speaking to his fellow workmen: "Had I 10,000,000 tongues and a throat for each tongue, I would say to every man, woman, and child: Throw strong drink aside as you would an ounce of liquid hell. It sears the conscience, it destroys everything it touches. It reaches into the family circle and takes the wife you had sworn to protect, and drags her down from her purity into that house from which no decent woman ever goes alive. It induces the father to take the furniture from his house, exchange it for money at the pawnshop, and spend the proceeds in rum. It damns everything it touches. I have seen it in every city east of the Mississippi River, and I know that the most damning curse to the laborer is that which gurgles from the neck of the bottle. I had rather be at the head of an organization having 100,000 temperate, honest, earnest men, than at the head of an organization of 12,000,000 drinkers, whether moderate or any other kind. Every dime spent in the rum shop furnishes a paving stone for hell."

Dangerous Decoy

Said the hook to the struggling fish: "I am very sharp." Said the poor captive fish: "I know that but too well. But let me tell you, it was not owing so much to your sharpness that I am captured, as to the bit of bait by which I was tempted." Said the hook, exultingly: "It is the way all hooks succeed. There must be trickery in order to have deadly decoy. Had you seen my point, and been aware of the danger, you should have wisely kept out of the way instead of so readily swallowing the worm."

So does the Devil use the dangerous decoy, by making all sin alluring until he has you on the hook.

Excellent Editorial

In the *Press Scimitar,* Memphis, Tennessee, we have from the pen of Edward Meeman, these words:

What is the hardest thing in the world to kill? What about mother love?

Perhaps you remember the Ways of Brooklyn — how Henry Way took his mother's $13,000 out of his safe deposit box, then bet and lost it on Native Dancer in the Kentucky Derby. The 43-year-old son was indicted for grand larceny.

When trial time neared Mrs. Lillian Way, 71, and a widow, refused to prosecute. She said: "I haven't long to live. I hope God will forgive my sins and I want to forgive my son's.

Then Henry, 43, who has three children and one grandchild, wept and said: "I'll sign my house over to my mother and give her everything I've got. She can live with me for the rest of my life."

It was a touching scene but the tears didn't wipe out the fact that gambling will cause a man to steal from his own mother.

Much for Little

Robert Browning spoke of a man giving up a great cause for "a riband to stick in his coat." And long ago, David told King Saul that he was using his own energies and "3000 chosen men out of all Israel" to get for himself and his soldiers nothing but a dead dog – nothing but a flea (I Samuel 24:14). That was surely paying much for little – something valuable for the worthless. And both these results have been repeated by Miss Nellie Drain of Jersey City, N. J. – when she was the victim of cruel deception and thievery.

This 83-year-old spinster gave $18,000 for a plate of ice cream. If there were thirty spoonfuls in that dish of ice cream, it means she spent $600 for each spoonful.

Here, according to police, is what happened to Miss Nellie Drain: Miss Drain left her apartment for some ice cream at a nearby soda fountain. She passed the time of day with a woman sitting on the next stool when a third woman joined them. The new arrival breathlessly told of finding a large sum of money and of giving it to her boss in a nearby office building for safekeeping. Her boss advised against turning over the money to police since there were betting slips with it and they might suspect her, she said.

The woman offered to share the find with Miss Drain if she would put up money to show good faith. That sounded fair to Miss Drain; so, accompanied by one of her newfound acquaintances, she went to a New York bank, withdrew $18,000 savings and handed it over to her companion. That left Miss Drain with $1,000. When they got back to Jersey City, the woman said she had to meet her friend at the boss' office and complete the deal. The $18,000 went with her.

Miss Drain waited and waited and then called police.

Still there are those who serve Satan, who always cheats with mere sound instead of enriching with the substance, who always feeds apples that are ashes inside.

Rattlesnake Ranch

In Colfax, on National Highway No. 40, is Rattlesnake Ranch with 3,000 acres and more than 20,000 inhabitants. This ranch literally crawls with rattlers "au natural" and in confinement.

Believed to be the largest of its kind in the world, the farm is owned and operated by S. E. Evans and his wife, both veterans in the delicate task of handling their temperamental charges.

Mr. Evans has handled rattlers for twenty-two years and has never been bitten. The actual management of the huge ranch is a humdrum business, according to Evans. The interest in the unusual enterprise comes from visitors to the ranch, averaging 100 to 200 during the week, and 1,000 on Sundays. When he first started the ranch, Mr. Evans allowed the public to view the pens, where he keeps thousands of the reptiles; but he lost hundreds of snakes, which are "highly nervous creatures" and cannot take the stares of a gaping public.

Now he maintains a snake pit especially for visitors, where some twenty-five to fifty rattlers are under the limelight for show-off purposes. Even so, the loss of snakes is still large. Life in the pit virtually is a death sentence to the rattler, who will usually die within sixty days after its contact with the curious public.

Feeding time draws the most visitors. The snakes are fed live mice, as they like to kill their own food. When the rattlers get "fussy," a special meal of raw hamburger is provided. The demand for rattlesnake steak, which Mr. Evans calls a "thrill dish," outweighs the supply. He has standing orders from distributors for the delicacy.

Oil, rendered from the carcass, is sold for its alleged curative powers. The skins are valuable mostly for their decorative quality. Persons desiring a pair of genuine rattlesnake shoes may order them on the spot. Biggest source of income is the snake's venom, used chiefly for serum. Venom is sold to medical laboratories "by the snake," says Mr. Evans, because it's just as dangerous to handle one snake which may give two drops as one that gives 30, the maximum. The snakes are "milked" about once every three weeks from May to October. Mr. Evans and his wife do all the "milking" for the venom. They cannot get insurance for their workers, the job being considered too dangerous by state authorities. In milking the snake, Evans holds it back by the head, placing the fangs through a chamois covering a jar.

Thinking of these dangerous rattlers, we think of how terrible the denunciation of the Pharisees and scribes by Jesus:

"Ye serpents, ye generation of vipers, how can ye escape the damnation of hell?" (Matthew 23:22).

We think, too, of David's prayer for deliverance from evil men:

"Deliver me, O Lord, from the evil man: preserve me from the violent man; which imagine mischiefs in their heart; continually are they gathered together for war. They have sharpened their tongues like a serpent; adders' poison is under their lips" (Psalm 140:1-3).

We must give thought also to the deadly power of wine:

"Look not thou upon the wine when it is red, when it giveth his colour in the cup, when it moveth itself aright. At the last it biteth like a serpent, and stingeth like an adder" (Proverbs 23:31, 32).

Sex, Salads, Scotch

From Toronto, Canada, comes this declaration: Sex, salads, and scotch whisky are just the thing for keeping healthy, the 1963 Canadian Health Forum was told here. Dr. James Key, associate professor of surgery at the University of Toronto, said there are four S's to remember if you want to stave off heart trouble and peripheral blocked arteries. The first is smoking. Don't, said Dr. Key. But have "plenty of salads, plenty of Scotch and plenty of sex, if you can," he recommended. "But if a man has smoked all his life and is over fifty, I don't recommend that he stop, because it may give him a guilt complex and put him in the hands of a psychiatrist, or he'll beat his wife to death." The annual Canadian Health Forum is organized by the Health League of Canada.

As to sex, Dr. Key does not seem to know what the Bible would have us believe when it says in three different places: "Thou shalt not seethe a kid in its mother's milk" (Exodus 23:19; Exodus 34:26; Deuteronomy 14:21). What does this striking prohibition mean – declaring it to be against God's authority to boil the meat of a kid in the milk of its mother? It means, as we apply it to sex, that – people shall not pervert that which was intended to be a ministry of life into an instrument of destruction – that we shall not take the most sacred things of life and apply them to base and ignoble ends – to the accomplishment of unworthy purposes, to the dishonor of God. Men shall not take the powers meant for the glory of God and use them contrary to God's will.

I wonder if Dr. Key, speaking of using plenty of Scotch, knows that Scotch never touched an individual on whom it did not leave an indelible stain, never touched a home in which it did not plant the seeds of dissolution and misery, never touched a community in which it did not lower the moral tone, never touched a government in which it did not increase problems.

No Strong Drink

We have this record of God's dealings with his people during their wilderness wandering: God said:

"And I have led you forty years in the wilderness: your clothes are not waxen old upon you, and thy shoe is not waxen old upon thy foot. Ye have not eaten bread, neither have you drunk wine or strong drink: that ye might know that I am the Lord your God" (Deuteronomy 29:5, 6).

Rationing is nothing new, for it was instituted by the Lord as far back as the time of Israel's wilderness wanderings. For forty years there was a daily ration of manna. They were allowed so much each day, and no more. God's reason was not because of the shortage of supplies, however; it was "That I may prove them, whether they will walk in My law, or no" (Exodus 16:4). He wanted to know whether they would trust Him daily for their daily bread. And though it took the equivalent of one hundred and eighty freight car loads of manna each day to feed these three million Israelites – and the equivalent of ninety-four tank cars of water per day – God did not let them lack at any time. However, not one gallon of wine, not one pint of strong drink, was included in the forty-year provision. They were "a total abstinence people" – and not a feeble form among them for forty years! Is it not significant?

Though God saw to it that prohibition prevailed in a nation for forty years, we have nations today that license liquor. All licenses are a permit to turn health into disease, decency into indecency, love into estrangement, young beauty into loathsomeness, woman's modesty into coarse effrontery, mother's milk into poison, manliness into beastliness, happiness into horror, honor into disgrace, intellect into driveling idiocy, plenty into poverty, comeliness into corruption, merriment into misery.

Volcano Vigil

Gripping description this!

"Like two red-headed buzzards sitting on a fence, the volcanoes Acatenango and Fuego perch not far from Guatemala City and wait for catastrophe. Twice earthquakes have destroyed the city; each time Acatenango and Fuego have picked it clean. The old capital of Antigua Guatemala has its skeletons of whitened ruins. Last week a series of earthquakes shook the country. Panes rattled, pictures fell, walls cracked. Guatemalans, remembering the destruction of their capital in 1918, fell on their knees and prayed. The shocks continued, grew more violent. The two volcanoes reared their heads. Fire, ashes, lava spouted from their mouths, peasants shivered at the sound of their abdominal rumblings. Ashes fell a foot deep on nearby villages, destroyed coffee crops for miles around. Guatemala City was under a cloud that spread from Mexico to Nicaragua. After two days the shocks stopped. The city still stood. The buzzards went back to their vigil."

But sin is more than a twin volcano. It is a volcano large as the world sending a perpetual lava rush into every community – leaving blight and blasting and death.

Toy Town of Matches

In Houston, Texas, Denver R. Bain has put more than 120,000 kitchen matches and an estimated three thousand hours into building his match town. The first structure was started sixteen years ago and completed about a year later. It took three thousand matches. Bain, a retired worker, who works part time as a plant protection man, said that most of the town was built in the last three years. In this toy town, no houses of God are found in which to worship. But I know big cities with many houses of God which thousands never enter to worship – as they, with base ingratitude, translate freedom *of* worship to mean freedom *from* worship.

Alcoholism is "Society Malignancy"

Alcoholism has become a "malignancy on the national society, more disabling numerically than any known disease by claiming more than five million victims currently," the president of the National Woman's Christian Temperance Union said.

She observed that "the generally estimated five million alcoholics compares with one million cancer and five hundred thousand tuberculosis cases, yet it constitutes only a fraction of the drink problem."

"Our current national drink bill cannot be totaled without recognizing that the amount of money spent for alcoholic beverages is equalled by the cost of drink-associated crime, disease, insanity, loss of income, poverty, juvenile delinquency, broken homes and other human and economic loss."

An increasing number of alcoholics committed to the nation's mental hospital psychiatric wards are being diagnosed as having permanent alcohol brain damage. Statistics from the National Institute of Mental Health refute with competent medical diagnosis, the longstanding contention of the distiller that alcohol does not damage the brain, and show that it does and that the damage is permanent.

The country's mental institutions are being increasingly over-crowded by persons maimed and disabled by drink. Problems of alcoholism, under unrestricted drink promotion and sales, far exceed that of opium, heroin and other narcotic drugs.

No Profit

In Farmington, Missouri, it was announced – a few years ago – that the nine-mile St. Francis County Railroad which runs between Farmington, Delassur and Hurryville, was going out of business.

"We haven't made any money to speak of since 1947," said Dr. L. M. Stanfield, an osteopathic surgeon and president of the line. The tiny railroad has two second-hand diesel switch engines. It had two freight cars but sold them for junk. Now it rents freight cars from other lines. Engineer-conductor Paul Rickus and fireman-brakeman Emmit Welch take one of the diesels out every day except Sunday even with no profits coming in. Last time the railroad's books showed a profit was in 1951.

And a two-hundred-year-old rail line was closed. One of the world's oldest railroads was closed as it was too costly to maintain. It runs three and one-half miles from the Middleton, England, Broom Colliery into the city of Leeds. A line was first laid in 1758, using coal trucks drawn by horses.

Locomotives were first used on the line in 1812 – thirteen years before the first public passenger-carrying railroad was operated in England. Now – no profit.

"No profit" – not since 1951, but since Adam and Eve sinned in Eden has there been any profit in sin.

About his works, Solomon said: "Then I looked on all the works that my hands had wrought, and on the labour that I had laboured to do: and, behold, all was vanity and vexation of spirit, and there was no profit under the sun" (Ecclesiastes 2:11).

To his people who sought to "strengthen themselves in the strength of Pharaoh, and to trust in the shadow of Egypt," God said: "They were all ashamed of a people that could not profit them, nor be an help nor profit, but a shame, and also a reproach" (Isaiah 30:25).

Jeremiah, calling the people to true repentance, said: "Behold, ye trust in lying words, that can not profit" (Jeremiah 7:8).

But hear what the Apostle Paul says: "For bodily exercise profiteth little: but godliness is profitable unto all things, having promise of the life that now is, and of that which is to come" (I Timothy 4:8).

Paul, asking Titus to urge the people "to be ready to every good work" and "to speak evil of no one," said: "These things are good and profitable unto men" (Titus 3:1, 2, 8).

No profit in sin – *ever*.

But profit in righteousness – always.

"For the Lord God is a sun and shield: the Lord will give grace and glory: no good thing will he withhold from them that walk uprightly" (Psalm 84:11).

Road to Ruin

THE licensed liquor traffic is the railroad to ruin from all the departments of human affairs. This railroad to ruin is surveyed by avarice, chartered by County Courts freighted with drunkards. It has grog-shops for depots, rum-sellers for engineers, bartenders for conductors and landlords for stock-holders. This railroad to ruin has many passengers – fired up with alcohol, and boiling with delirium. The groans of the dying are the thunders of the train. The shrieks of the women and children are the whistles of the engine. Only with the help of God can the steam be reserved, the fire put out, the charter annulled and the freight be saved – even the passengers.

To license the sale of strong drink is to license disease, death, all sufferings, all crime, all despoliations, all disasters, all murders, all woes.

Playing With Sin

A YOUNG girl ventured to grasp a live wire that was hanging from a post. She did it in playful fun. Instantly a fearful scream proclaimed the fact that her hand was fastened to that burning current – and she was helpless in its grasp. The other hand was quickly raised to loosen her stiffened fingers, and it, too, was caught – and there she hung in agony. Her mother rushed to her side to pull her down, but she was flung off by a shock from the girl's body. She seemed lost indeed. At last, a man who understood, took an axe and severed the wire by striking it against the post. The current was broken, and the girl fell swooning on the ground. Her life was saved, but her hands were *cinders* for the rest of her life.

Don't play with sin. It is the devil's live wire.

What is Sin?

The Bible answers.

1. "Sin is trangression of the law" – lawlessness (I John 3:4).
2. A grievous malady, contaminating the whole of man's being (Isaiah 1:4, 5; Romans 3:10-18).
3. An obscuring cloud, which hides the face of God's blessing (Isaiah 59:2).
4. A binding cord, which holds man in its power (Proverbs 5:22).
5. A tyrannical owner, who embitters the lives of his slaves (Nehemiah 9:37).
6. A disturber of rest, which causes disorder and anxiety (Psalm 38:3).
7. A robber of blessing, which strips and starves the soul (Jeremiah 5:25).
8. A terrible devastation, which brings untold desolation (Micah 6:13).
9. A tripper-up, which continually overthrows the sinner to his hurt (Proverbs 13:6).
10. A record writer, which leaves its indelible mark upon the committer (Jeremiah 17:1).
11. A betraying presence, which "will out" no matter what pains are taken to hide it (Ezekiel 21:24).
12. A sure detective, which turns upon the sinner and finds him out (Numbers 32:23).
13. An accusing witness, which points its condemning finger at the prisoner in the bondage of sin (Isaiah 59:12).
14. A sum of addition which accumulates its weight to the condemnation of the sinner (Isaiah 30:1).

Broken Silence

In McAlester, Oklahoma, a state prison convict who, for eighteen years, pretended he was a deaf mute, has broken his silence in hope of gaining a parole.

John A. Cane of Oklahoma City was sentenced to life in prison in 1934. He had pleaded guilty to the murders of his wife, his two daughters and a son. From the time he entered his guilty plea, he said nothing and "heard" nothing. He came to the penitentiary and other inmates accepted him as a deaf mute and talked freely in his presence. Cane was afraid to reveal he could speak and hear normally for fear other prisoners would think him an informer for the warden.

Cane broke his silence when he appeared before the Pardon and Parole Board. Members were sworn to secrecy before he uttered a word. His plea for freedom was his first utterance in eighteen years.

Cane said he entered the prison "living in a dream world – the same kind of world I was living in when that (the four slayings) happened. They were a wonderful family. I made up my mind I would never say another word. I decided I would play I could not hear or talk."

Cane was in a mental hospital in Little Rock, Ark., when he disclosed the killings. He led officers to the shallow graves near Oklahoma City. He said he killed his family on a sudden impulse while on a picnic.

This world would be many times blessed if cursers, gossippers, slanderers, liars, erroneous teachers, nagging wives, fussing husbands and those who have "loosed wild tongues that hold not God in awe" had kept silent for eighteen years.

"The elders of the daughter of Zion sit upon the ground and keep silence" (Lamentations 2:10).

Slander Suit Still Stands

In New York, December 7, 1949, a federal judge refused to dismiss William W. Remington's $100,000 slander suit against Elizabeth Bentley.

The court held that calling a government official a communist if he isn't one is "slanderous per se" and a most "discreditive" type of accusation.

Remington, a federal economist, sued Miss Bentley, self-styled former communist courier, after she called him a communist on a televised "Meet the Press" broadcast on September 12, 1948.

What a blessing it would be if all would believe and act according to the wisdom of these words which state that the most ferocious monster in the world has his den just behind the teeth. "Give not thy tongue too great liberty lest it take thee prisoner." Washington Irving said: "The tongue is the only edge tool that grows sharper with constant use."

We need to read again these words: "As coals are to burning coals and wood to fire; so is a contentious man to kindle strife. The words of a talebearer are as wounds, and they go down into the innermost parts of the belly" (Proverbs 26:21, 22).

Vicious Vultures

In Calcutta, India, on November 16, 1949, a vulture hovering over the city caused two Indian air force fighters to collide and spin into the crowded city, killing nine persons and injuring thirty-seven. The vulture flew into the path of six planes flying in formation over the city. The bird hit one and caused it to crash into another plane, according to the pilot of the second plane, who managed to jump clear. The pilot of the first was killed. One plane hit the grounds of a hospital, injuring members of the staff and their children. The other hit a city building, partially destroying it and trapping victims in the debris.

But more have died morally because of the vicious vultures of filthy novels – and sewerage-stained literature, than were killed because of that vulture. Many more have fallen because of the vultures of intemperance than ever were killed in any wreck. And because of the vultures of deceit many have gone down to sordid depths. "The mouth of strange women is a deep pit" (Proverbs 22:14).

Money for Proof of Error

Once – some years ago – the New York *Daily News* offered to contribute five thousand dollars to an organized charity if any challenger could prove that President Roosevelt in his famous "Again and again and again" speech added to his promise that "your boys are not going to be sent into any foreign wars" the qualification "unless we are attacked."

An editorial challenged claims of Roosevelt supporters that the President had made such a stipulation in his famous speech in Boston on Oct. 30, 1940.

The *News* quoted Mr. Roosevelt as saying: "And while I am talking to you, mothers and fathers, I give you one more assurance. I have said this before, but I shall say it again, and again and again: Your boys are not going to be sent into any foreign wars."

The newspaper commented that since calling attention to this statement, "we have had a great deal of mail declaring that we did not give the full quotation." "We reiterate," said the *News*, "that the quotation given above is the full quotation, and that nowhere in the record of that speech, nor in the recording of his voice on that occasion, do the words 'unless we are attacked' appear. As evidence of our sincerity we will bet – no, pardon us, we are not supposed to bet on elections – we will offer to an organized charity the sum of $5,000 provided any party who questions the actuality of Mr. Roosevelt's words can prove we are wrong."

But no man will have to give one dime to prove that a man is wrong if he becomes a boozer or goeth after a wicked woman "as an ox to the slaughter or as a fool to the correction of the stocks . . . as a bird hasteth to the snare" (Proverbs 7:22, 23).

One Bullet Did It

In Kansas City, November 24, 1949, I read in a Kansas City newspaper of what W. I. McFall, eighty years old, did with one shot from a rifle. He went into his back yard to kill a cat. He killed the cat all right, but the same bullet also killed six large pullets. All were shot in the head – and only one shot was fired.

But in the human family, I have known of one lie, traveling here and yon, from careless lips and a poison pen, doing more harm in hurting human hearts. No wonder false lips are an abomination unto God.

Tombstone Tells Artist's Rancor

From Wellington, Ohio, September, 1953, came the news of a man's uniquely expressed bitterness.

Otis G. Pratt was bitter over treatment he had received as an artist and sculptor, so he had his resentment carved on his tombstone. The stone standing over the grave of Pratt and his mother in Greenwood Cemetery here, attracts many tourists. Pratt died in 1921 at the age of seventy-six. The inscription reads:

"Stranger, I lived in an age when corruption was in our government and the ballot box was begged for. When martyred President and riots echoed over our land. When law and respect clung to the rich and shunned the poor. When money and fashion had the brains and talent went over the water for want of free schools of art supported by our government. Such were the conditions which caused my landscape to decay with me as nature shows it. Farewell."

Pratt himself spent a good deal of time in Europe studying art. When he came back he earned a tiny income by sketching portraits of townspeople and selling them for a pittance.

I wonder what would be carved on my tombstone and how big that tombstone would be if my resentment of the lies told by the liquor manufacturers and liquor sellers and beer drinkers were put into carved words on a tombstone. I could rightly have carved thereon the truth that the man who said he climbed a thorn tree one hundred feet high with a wild cat under each arm without getting scratched did not tell a bigger lie than the liquor crowd tells when it advertises its poison and pictures its "Men of Distinction." The best way for them to spell distinction is "di*stink*-tion."

Two Years and Four Cents

From Dallas, Texas, comes this bit of news: It seemed like a good idea at the time – snatch the purse of the woman and run. That was in March. It did not seem like such a good idea some months later to Wendell Polk who was sentenced to two years in prison for stealing four cents. That was all the money the woman had. A jury ruled that the Negro youth must serve six months for every penny he stole.

This illustrates somewhat what Paul Lawrence Dunbar wrote:

> This is the price I pay,
> Just for one riotous day –
> Years of regret and grief.

Solomon wrote: "Therefore shall they eat of the fruit of their own way, and be filled with their own devices" (Proverbs 1:31).

Sneak and Payment

In Southend, England, the manager of a movie theater has received a postal money order for twenty-one cents as conscience money from a patron who said he sneaked in without paying ten years ago.

If all sneaks, who have cheated others, would make restitution today – how much less money some would have and how much more others would have.

Bitsy Bugs Stop Traffic

In Hannibal, Missouri, hatching willow bugs piled up ten inches deep on the Mark Twain Bridge over the Mississippi River and stopped traffic for thirty minute periods while workmen shoveled the bugs off the bridge. Highway Department trucks spread cinders to give passing cars and trucks traction. The hatching insects clogged vehicle radiators and grills. Workmen said the inch-long insects were probably attracted to the bridge by lights.

The brown-colored bugs are also known as willow flies and willow saw flies. They hatch from willow trees along the river banks.

This shows us the *might* of *mites*.

Salesman and Graves

In Trento, Italy, an eager beaver traveling salesman was under arrest on charges of ordering several dozen tombstones for living persons. Police said Gianfranco Ruberti admitted forging the orders. They quoted him as saying he had been hired by a tombstone firm only a short while ago and wanted to impress the company with his efficiency. By the time Ruberti's alleged excess of zeal was discovered, the company had a pile of unwanted tombstones on its hands.

But I know salesmen, even liquor sellers, who rush many to the grave as, for money, they dispense liquid damnation – as they lay wait for blood and lurk privily for the innocent and swallow them up alive as the grave (Proverbs 1:11, 12).

Ten Thousand Daily See Waxworks

In Blackpool, England, a model of the late Dr. Stephen Ward is attracting ten thousand persons a day to the Chamber of Horrors at the Blackpool Waxworks Museum. The effigy was modeled from photographs of the society osteopath, who introduced former War Minister John Profumo to Christine Keeler and started a scandal which led to the minister's resignation. Ward committed suicide before hearing he had been convicted of living off the earnings of prostitution.

But, I dare say, no beautiful thoughts and no blessed and righteous stirrings of heart came to any of the ten thousand who viewed this effigy.

Missing One Thousand Dollars

In Ansonia, Conn., when Charles Jockmus, local manufacturer, died, he left an estate valued at nearly five million. He had provided in his will that every clergyman serving pulpits there on the day of his death should receive one thousand dollars in cash. Mr. Jockmus died July 1, or just a day after Rev. Adolf Franz, rector of the German Congregational Church, resigned, and that clergyman, a friend of Mr. Jockmus, lost his thousand dollars by a day.

But ten thousand times ten thousand times more tragic is it for one to miss entrance into the kingdom of God by one day, or one hour, yea, by one minute! And to be almost saved is to be altogether damned.

> Almost cannot avail,
> Almost is but to fail,
> Sad, sad, that bitter wail,
> Almost, but lost.

WARNING

Men Eat a Man

THE Araracuara prison colony is on the Caqueta river – in a territory of the Amazon that rises in the Andes not far from Puerto Umbria and flows eastward into the wilds of Brazil.

There are no walls or fences at Araracuara. The authorities rely on the immensity of its almost impenetrable surroundings, its long distance from civilization, and the prospect of hardships to discourage attempts to escape. The hopeless existence in the jungle prison, however, leads many to try to get away. To prepare for flight, the inmates hoard their rations to use as a meager food supply in the jungle. They almost always are unarmed and have little chance to succeed. Some are never seen after they slip into the jungle.

A few years ago, six wild and bearded convicts who escaped the tropical jungle prison camp said that they killed, broiled and ate a seventh companion, the fattest one, before they stumbled into a settlement and surrendered. The party had planned to eat a second man. The men wandered for thirty-eight days through treacherous swamps and jungle inhabited by snakes, beasts and wild natives. They covered a crow-flight distance of about 250 miles before they reached Puerto Umbria, a river village in an Andean valley, and gave themselves up. Some were ill with malaria. All were clothed in rotted tatters. Eating their plumpest companion, they said, was the only way they could get strength to go on.

But it is harder and far more impossible to escape hell. Once in hell, forever in hell. "There is a great gulf fixed."

Cost of a Look

IN MUNCIE, INDIANA, John Stephenson was looking over things to be auctioned from a dead neighbor's household goods. He saw an old wall clock and made a mental note he'd bid for it. Then he took it down to examine the works. Out rolled $4,062 in bills ranging from $1 to $100. The money might have been his if he'd bought the clock before finding the cash. Instead, it went into the estate. He got a prize, however, for finding the money. Lawyers for the estate gave him the clock.

But it has cost more for people to

look upon the wine "when it is red, when it giveth his colour in the cup" – because "at the last it biteth like a serpent and stingeth like an adder" (Proverbs 23:31, 32).

And many who have looked upon wine have been looked upon through prison bars or upon the gallows or in the gas chamber of death.

Ancient Pistol Shoots

FROM London, England, comes the news that an antique silver ladies-type pistol which had lain in an attic for two hundred years was being handled the other day by Mrs. Kathleen Brown, 73. "Isn't it pretty," said Mrs. Brown, holding it out for others to see. The pistol went off and shattered her right eye.

So there are those who have thought there was no harm in the booze bottle and wine cup. But how many hopes and homes have been shattered by the bottle – and how many mighty men have shattered their lances on the wine cup.

"Look not thou upon the wine when it is red, when it giveth his color in the cup" (Proverbs 23:31).

A Pusher Pulls 'Em

IN ST. LOUIS – last year – during a recent bogus bill scare, a counterfeit "pusher" gave the U.S. Secret Service a collective red face. The man entered a restaurant, ordered lunch, and gave a bad ten-dollar bill in payment. The waitress went to a next door tavern to break the bill, returning with the change. His lunch finished, the man sauntered into the tavern, ordered "drinks for the house," and paid for them with a bogus twenty-dollar bill. As part of his change, he was handed back his fake ten-dollar bill. The counterfeiter made a quick recovery. He ordered more drinks and paid for them with the fake ten-dollar bill. And he left – undetected.

But God to whom the midnight is as the noonday, saw him. And to God the "pusher" who pulled three fast ones, must give an account.

Godlessness

A WISE urge comes from Washington, D.C., through Senator Strom Thurmond – the urge to stop what he called secularist attempts to make America "a Godless nation." In his weekly newsletter to constituents, Thurmond discussed recent Supreme Court decisions involving prayers in schools and a later decision in New York State to remove references to God in "America." He also cited a Sacramento County, Calif., decision ruling as unconstitutional a grace children say with their milk and cookies, and attempts to have references to God removed from the Pledge of Allegiance to the Flag and "The Star Spangled Banner."

He said some school officials had ended the singing of Christmas carols and have removed the Christmas tree. "At the bottom of this drive to root God out of our national life is the realization that America cannot be effectively socialized until it is secularized," Thurmond said.

He said what the secularists want "is not freedom of religion but rather freedom from religion – and preferably no religion at all."

Thurmond pointed to a recent Gallup Poll that showed that more than seventy per cent of Americans questioned endorsed the idea of prayers in schools. "If this is correct . . . there is sufficient public opinion to get the Congress to act to stop this drive to make our nation neutral toward God . . ."

And from New York comes this tragic news that the Board of Education has voted to end the century-old practice of Bible reading as a religious exercise at school assemblies. The board also lifted the required daily singing of the stanza of "America" which begins: "Our fathers' God, to Thee . . ." The singing of any patriotic song will suffice hereafter.

Both actions were to conform with a recent U.S. Supreme Court ruling that it is unconstitutional to require Bible reading and recitation of the Lord's Prayer in public schools.

Day of Horror

One day in 1883 recorded history's most violent cataclysm came to pass. It occurred when the volcanic island of Krakatoa in the East Indies blew up. All that was left was a cavity 1,000 feet deep in the ocean floor. Nearly thirty-six thousand persons were killed — and the resultant tidal wave encircled the earth four times. But a more terrible day of horror it will be for Bible-reviling, Christ-rejecting, God-defying unbelievers when the reality of these words from Solomon come to pass:

"I also will laugh at your calamity; I will mock when your fear cometh; when your fear cometh as desolation, and your destruction cometh as a whirlwind; when distress and anguish cometh upon you" (Proverbs 1:26, 27).

And the words of Jesus:

"Daughters of Jerusalem, weep not for me, but weep for yourselves, and for your children. For, behold, the days are coming, in the which they shall say, Blessed are the barren, and the wombs that never bare, and the paps which never gave suck. Then shall they begin to say to the mountains, Fall on us; and to the hills, Cover us" (Luke 23:28-30).

"Iceberg Dead Ahead!"

When the ill-fated "Titantic" steamed majestically through the darkness on her maiden voyage to New York, April 14th, 1912, more than two thousand souls were enjoying the snug comforts of its lavish compartments, secure in the belief that neither wind nor storm, nor wave could prevail against them. One of the dramatic incidents of that tragic night is recalled by the *Washington Post:*

"In the wheelroom, a nattily uniformed officer hummed at his task as he directed the destinies of an ocean greyhound that even then was setting a speed record. The phone rang. A minute passed! Another minute! The officer was busy! The third precious minute clicked away. The officer, his trivial task completed, stepped to the phone. From the 'crow's nest!' 'Iceberg dead ahead! Reverse the engines!' But too late! As he rushed to the controls, the 'pride of the seas' crashed the berg head on amid the deafening roar.

"Three precious minutes! Attention to trivial details and the big important opportunity slipped by until too late! Sixteen hundred people, including many notables of two continents, paid with their lives for that officer's neglect, and in less than two hours only bobbing lifeboats marked the spot where the three-million-dollar marvel of the sea went down.

"This world is a great 'Titanic!' There is, speaking figuratively, an iceberg dead ahead. The end of all things is at hand. Jesus Christ is coming back to this earth to end the reign of sin. But when He comes, there will be no time for repentance, no time to make your peace with God. It will then be too late. Now, just now, is the day of salvation. Right now is the time to hear God's call, and 'reverse the engines,' repent, turn about, and serve your Maker. Any other course means disaster and eternal death."

WITNESS

Last Chance

When the famous minister, Phillips Brooks, was critically ill years ago and not expected to recover, visitors were not permitted to see him. Bob Ingersoll, the famous agnostic, who didn't know that visitors were not allowed, called at the hospital and asked to see Dr. Brooks. He was told that visitors were not permitted, but that they always reported to the patient when friends called. When the sick man was told that Mr. Ingersoll had called, Dr. Brooks insisted that he be allowed to come in.

When Mr. Ingersoll entered the room, he said: "I appreciate this very much, but why do you see me, when you deny yourself to your other friends?"

"Well, you see," replied Dr. Brooks, "I feel confident to seeing most of my friends in the next world, but this is my last chance to see you."

From a Dying Man

Dr. Samuel Palmer Brooks was president of Baylor University in Texas from 1902 until his death in 1931.

From his deathbed he wrote a message to the senior class of 1931 which has become an immortal one to the students of Baylor. In his message he said: "I stand on the border of mortal life but I face eternal life. I look backward to the years of the past to see all pettiness, all triviality, shrink into nothing and disappear. Adverse criticism has no meaning now, only the worthwhile things, the constructive things that have built for the good of mankind and the glory of God count now. There is beauty, there is joy, and there is laughter in life – as there ought to be, but remember, my students, not to regard lightly nor to ridicule the sacred things, those worthwhile things. Hold them dear, cherish them, for they alone will sustain you in the end, and remember, too, that only through work and oft-times through hardships may they be attained. But the compensation of blessing and sweetness at the last will glorify every hour of work and every heartache from hardship."

Sick of It

Philip Melanchthon lay sick unto death, as many supposed. Martin Luther came and said: "Philip, we can't spare you." Philip said: "Martin, you must let me go; I am tired of persecution; I want to go to be with my God."

Some preachers today suffer persecution – not a persecution of the torture rack and dark dungeon and the martyr's stake and decapitating ax. It is rather the persecution of indifference and criticism and disloyalty and insinuation and villification in the academic grove. But let those who so suffer forget never that such enthrones them in the circle of the beatitude which says: "Blessed are ye, when men shall revile you, and persecute you, and shall say all manner of evil against you falsely, for my sake. Rejoice, and be exceeding glad!"

Men — To Live

WHEN an invasion of France by the Duke of Brunswick was imminent, Charles Jean Barbaroux sent to the municipality of Marseilles in June, 1792, this message: "Send me six hundred men who know how to die."

Today, we look on fields "white already to harvest" (John 4:35). We know "the harvest truly is great, but the labourers are few." We hear Jesus say: "Pray ye therefore the Lord of the harvest, that he would send forth labourers into his harvest" (Luke 10:2).

Therefore, we would say: "Send us thousands and tens of thousands of men and women who know how to *live* — folks who will be 'always bearing about in the body the dying of the Lord Jesus, that the life also of Jesus might be made manifest in our body'" (II Corinthians 4:10).

Living Through Her Sons

MRS. ROBERT M. LAFOLLETTE died some years ago. She had a large share in the influence of her husband. She rejoiced when one of her sons became United States Senator. She rejoiced when another of her sons became Governor of Wisconsin.

What joy through having a part in the influential life of others! What greater joy if the sons are "sun-crowned men who live above the fog and scorn the demagogue's treacherous flattery!"

Departure

IF YOU want to read something sad, sweet and exquisite, listen to this from the pen of Kathleen Lamb:

Take with you all the starlight, all the moons
On which we gazed, and take each vivid day
We spent together, all the joyous Junes
We loved, and lock them somewhere — far away.

I have no need of them since you must go,
They have become quite useless, dear to me.
They were a frame of joy we used to know;
A background for remembered ecstasy.

Now I shall have no time for little flights
Into the land of make-believe. My days
Must be rebuilt away from lovely heights,
Down on the earth among prosaic ways.
I shall not weep, nor empty, crave,
What happiness we had will make me brave.

Burned and Blessed

FRIDAY, October 6, 1536, William Tyndale was burned at the stake for translating the Scriptures into English. But in 1611, only seventy-five years later, the Authorized Version came from the press bearing the imprimatur of King James. And now in over nine hundred different languages and dialects the Bible is printed. Tyndale's body burned! Tyndale's labors blessed! Red roses from righteous ashes! And still the influence of Tyndale's work "burns like the living fire of eternal emeralds," "burns like the ruby fire set in the swinging lamp of a crimson shrine," "burns like a heated opal" — with a light that never dies.

Dwarfed and Fruitless

THE most remarkable forest in the world has been found on the west coast of Africa. Although the trunks of the trees are as much as four feet in diameter, they attain the height of only one foot. No tree bears more than two leaves, which attain a length of six feet and a breadth of two feet. The forest covers a tableland six miles in width.

We can find, here and there, human beings who have only "two leaves" in fruit bearing. Pity!

One-Man Congregation

THE value of the individual Christian's work to the unsaved individual is set forth in the words of three great men who spoke, each in his day, to great congregations:

Hearken to the words of Henry Ward Beecher: "The longer I live the more confidence I have in the sermons where one man is the minister and one man the congregation." Which causes us to say that on the housetop, beneath the bright Syrian stars, Jesus preached a great sermon to a congregation of one man – Nicodemus. At Jacob's well in Sychar, He preached, with touching tenderness and rebuke and revelation, to a congregation of one woman – a nameless Samaritan. In the house of the rich publican – Zacchaeus – He preached with converting power to just one man.

Meditate on what Moody said: "The most effective and fruitful work of grace can only be secured by the conviction of the great masses of our membership to reach the people one by one by one person's efforts."

Think of Trumbull's words: "For ten years I addressed gatherings of people from five thousand to six thousand, from ten thousand to fifteen thousand. I have been editor of *The Sunday School Times,* with a hundred thousand per week circulation. I can see more direct results of good through my direct work with individuals than through thousands of persons in religious assemblies or all my written words." So, acting according to the wisdom of these words, let each *one* of us seek out some *one* person and put on the heart of that *one* the claims of Christ for that one's trust and love and service.

Personal Service

GOD said, "I will send *thee* . . . that *thou* . . ." That was a call to *personal* service. A physician once said that he kept himself in health by going to see his patients. Whenever he discontinued this and required his patients to come to him, or when he tried to abandon his practice, he speedily became lethargic, stupid, dull. But when he resumed his efforts, and tried and tested his powers, he recovered his strength and vigor. So many Christians would find spiritual health and strength in trying to bring others to Jesus.

Fourteen-Year Strike

SOME years ago, a fourteen-year strike came to an end in Dun Laoghaire, Erie. That fourteen-year-old strike, the world's longest, really came to an end.

The strike at Downey's Public House (bar) started in 1939 when owner Pat Downey fired a bartender. When Downey refused to rehire the dismissed mixer of "spirits," pickets began their marathon march. Downey observed each anniversary of the strike as the years rolled by, dressing his pub in flags and offering drinks to the pickets.

Downey died in May of 1953, and striker Val Murphy put aside his sandwich-board and walked into the pub to offer his sympathy to the widow.

But I have sometimes said that the longest strike in history is the sit-down strike when and where Christians speak not to the unsaved – asking them to trust in Christ and be saved. How many have tongues and speak not the life-giving message. Longer than the fourteen-year strike have many Christians sung "Rescue the Perishing" – and yet have not done rescue work.

That makes me think of a striking story told by Dr. R. C. Campbell. It comes out of the mission work in China. A blind Chinaman was taken to a hospital. The missionary doctor operated, removing cataracts from his eyes. The Chinaman went back to his home seeing and rejoicing. In a few weeks he went back to the hospital. This time he was holding the end of a rope to which forty blind people were clinging. He had led them to the place where he had received his sight. Should we attempt to do less in a spiritual way?

What Is Worship?

"Thou shalt worship the Lord thy God.".

"Worship him that liveth for ever" (Revelation 4:10).

"Worship him that made heaven and earth" (Revelation 14:7).

Many times does the Bible speak of worshiping God. What the Bible speaks of so beautifully, we practice so poorly. What God commands we give such mediocre obedience. This we will believe when we understand what worship is. To worship God is to quicken the conscience by holiness of God, to feed the mind with the truth of God, to purge the imagination by the beauty of God, to open the heart to the love of God, to devote the will to the purpose of God. This did all who in the past worshiped God. This do all who truly worship God now.

"Now we know that God heareth not sinners: but if any man be a worshipper of God and doeth his will, him he heareth" (John 9:31).

Lambasting the Lamp

When the scientific oil lamp, complete with chimney, was invented in 1783 by a Swiss chemist, Ami Argand, many persons felt man's genius had gone too far. Argand's lamp produced a light equivalent to that of nine candles. It burned whale oil and caused the whaling industry to expand. An encyclopedia of the time advised the use of a small screen between the eyes and the lamplight. At parties women sometimes opened their parasols against the "uncomplimentary" glare of the lamps.

So was McCormick's reaper, which removed the nations out of the bread line and gave them a full dinner pail called "a cross between an Astley chariot, a wheelbarrow, and a flying machine."

So did Prof. Samuel F. B. Morse's telegraph meet the adverse criticism of the press and the jeers of Congress for nine different sessions.

So was Cyrus Field's cable denounced as "a mad freak of stubborn ignorance."

So was Alexander Graham Bell's telephone called "a clever toy to amuse children, but never a commercial asset."

So were the Wright brothers doubted by the wise, and caricatured by the small wits of their day.

So many who have believed in Jesus Christ and the Bible have been derided. But Jesus said, and still says: "Blessed are ye, when men shall revile you, and persecute you, and shall say all manner of evil against you falsely, for my sake. Rejoice, and be exceeding glad: for great is your reward in heaven: for so persecuted they the prophets which were before you" (Matthew 5:11, 12).

Chess Champion

Jose Raoul Capablanca, who died at 53 years of age, was, for years, the world's champion chess player. Capablanca, who defended his chess title in many countries, had advocated making the game more difficult. He wrote numerous books on the subject.

One of Capablanca's greatest achievements in chess was accomplished in 1928 when he played 46 simultaneous exhibition matches in Brooklyn, winning 43, tying the others. In 1922, he played 40 simultaneous games, winning 37, again drawing three. In 1931 he played 50 four-person teams and in nine hours defeated 28 teams, lost to six and had draws with 16.

But more wonderful the spiritual wizardly of those who in tribulation, in distress, in persecution, in famine, in nakedness, in peril, in sword are more than conquerors through Christ Jesus who loved us (Romans 8:35-37).

Being Dead Their Deeds Speak On

A dead lion roars no more. A dead lobo wolf robs no sheep fold. But a dead sinner continues to agitate the currents of life. This is the truth Mrs. Walter Ferguson set forth in what she wrote about the traitorous Rosenbergs:

"The Rosenbergs got what they deserved. Their children are the tragic figures in the case. They are innocent of any wrong-doing, yet their entire lives will be affected by the misdeeds of their parents. One seems to hear again the thunders from Sinai: 'The iniquity of the fathers shall be visited upon the children unto the third and fourth generations.' To Christians it seems a harsh doctrine, yet it is as rational today as when Moses set it down upon the stone tablets. It is written inexorably into the law of life, as it was written into the code of the ancient Jews.

"We do not live unto ourselves. What we do adds to the happiness or the sorrow of other people. Those who love us may suffer even more than we from our evil actions. And we can be sure that retribution will come in time to the evil doers. Man cannot escape the consequences of his behavior, and in any lauguage, 'the wages of sin is death.' There are many kinds of death, we must remember. Innocence, beauty, dreams and the human spirit die as the body does — and sometimes much sooner.

"How often nowadays you hear boys and girls insisting that they have 'a right to live their own lives.' It's a grand phrase, but what they mean is that they intend to do as they please, disregard the advice of their elders, and flout the laws of common sense. This sometimes makes them feel important. Little people always feel important when they think of themselves as rebels against the social, legal and moral restrictions. They aren't important of course, only very foolish, as they may live to discover.

"Nobody has a right to do exactly as he pleases or to 'live his own life.' For we belong to groups — a family, a business and a society — and our actions reflect credit or discredit upon all members of that group. Evidently Julius and Ethel Rosenberg did not think of their sons as they pursued their traitorous course, or if they did, then their guilt is all the more horrible."

All of which seems to be a repetition of Bible truth, with particular notice to these words:

"For none of us liveth to himself, and no man dieth to himself" (Romans 14:7).

A Walking Preacher

THE legendary "walking preacher" of the Smokies is dead.

Rev. Esau George, 88, a Cherokee Indian minister who spent his life walking through the western North Carolina mountains to preach, died as he lived – quietly and without fanfare. Word of his death from flu complications took several days to reach the distant places in the mountains where he preached.

The elderly man was a familiar sight in Swain, Graham and Jackson Counties as he trudged with his stick along the highways. Distance meant nothing to him. He had been walking the roads and trails seventy years before he heard of the latest walking fad. He kept walking until a short time before his death. Sometimes he would walk forty miles or more at a stretch, going all the way from Cherokee to the Santeethlah section of Graham County near Robbinsville. Often he could be seen sitting at the side of the road, resting a little, and reading his Bible printed in the Cherokee language. He could preach or sing in English as well as Cherokee, depending on his audience. Some of the Cherokees still speak little or no English. The Cherokees, known as Snowbird Indians, live in the wilds of the Snowbird Mountains. If Rev. George was needed in the rugged Snowbirds, off he would go early in the morning. By nightfall, he would be there, helping the sick and those believed to be lost.

Thinking of the steps this preacher made on roadways, in bypaths, in spring or summer days, in autumn time and winter time, by day and night, in rains and snows and dust, we think of some words the Bible speaks about the steps of men:

"There is but a step between me and death" (I Samuel 20:3).

"My foot hath held his steps, his way have I kept and not declined" (Job 23:11).

"Doth not he see my ways, and count all my steps? If I have walked with vanity, or if my foot has hasted to deceit . . ." (Job 31:4, 5).

"I would declare unto him the number of my steps" (Job 31:37).

"The steps of a good man are ordered of the Lord" (Psalm 37:23).

"Our steps have not declined from thy way" (Psalm 44:18).

"Righteousness . . . . shall set us in the way of his steps" (Psalm 85:13).

"Her steps take hold on hell" (Proverbs 5:5).

"It is not in man that walketh to direct his steps" (Jeremiah 10:23).

"To them . . . . who walk in the steps of that faith of our father Abraham" (Romans 4:12).

"Did Titus make a gain of you? Walked we not in the same steps?" (II Corinthians 12:18).

"Christ also suffered for us, leaving us an example, that we should follow his steps" (I Peter 2:21).

Surely this Indian walking preacher of the mountains made footsteps that weigh worthily on God's scales as he walked with God for many years. The footsteps of this one solitary man of God outweigh all the footsteps of some conquering armies going forth to battle.

Lines About Lincoln

WALTER WINCHELL writes the following lines about Abraham Lincoln:

"Abraham Lincoln's area of struggle was not bounded by Fort Sumter and Appomatox. His battlefields extended from Kentucky to Washington. Armed with a steadfast faith, Lincoln constantly fought for humanity's fundamental decencies. But his battles were not always triumphant. His personal life was burdened with anguish. He was a failure as a businessman, and was defeated for the Senate and vice-presidency. In the end his passion for peace collided with the bloodiest of wars.

"Four thousand books have been written about him. His life has inspired millions of words. But when the compiler of the *Dictionary of Congress* asked Lincoln to contribute an autobiography he submitted about fifty words: 'Born, February 12, 1809, in Hardin County, Ky. Education, defective. Profession, a lawyer. Have been a captain of volunteers in Black Hawk War. Postmaster at a very small office. Four times a member of the Illinois Legislature and was a member of the lower house of Congress.'

"Lincoln was tough and to the point. And he could utilize words as David used a slingshot. The Gettysburg Address is classified as among the great pieces of world literature. It consists of ten sentences and took five minutes to deliver. Lincoln finished speaking before it was realized that he had started. The news-photographers were caught flat-footed; they were still putting up the cumbersome tripods — and one of the greatest scoops in history had passed. The audience greeted his words with bored silence. There was not even a smattering of applause. When Lincoln sat down he remarked: 'The speech is a flat failure. The people were disappointed.'

"The greatest paradoxes were encompassed in his personality. He was simple and complex, gay and melancholy — a profound philosopher who relished the warm simplicities of life. He enjoyed the melodies of Stephen Foster, loved to read aloud the work of contemporary humorists. He ate sparingly and cared little for food. His lunch often consisted of a piece of fruit and a glass of milk. He drank no whisky, though occasionally he indulged in a glass of beer or wine. He never smoked."

Winchell's words about Lincoln are not more appropriate in application than what the biographer wrote of W. E. Gladstone:

In Christ, his mighty intellect found anchorage;
In Christ, his versatile personality found fulfillment;
In Christ, his impetuous temper found restraint.

Ray's Remarks

THE noble and notable Dr. Jeff D. Ray wrote these words about the virtues of the Southern Baptist Convention when it met in Houston, Texas, some years ago.

"Can you give me space to mention without comment some virtues that I saw preeminently illustrated in our convention? Perhaps no one person had all these virtues and confessedly I saw manifested in a few individual cases the opposite of some of these noble traits. But a composite view of the messengers and their conduct and what I knew of their character is a silhouette made up of the following characteristics:

"Sincerity without pugnacity,
Integrity without self-righteousness,

Humility without Uriah Heepness,
Generosity without display.
Fraternity without gush,
Sociability without gossip,
Unanimity without a rubber stamp,
Tenacity without stubbornness,
Spirituality without pharisaism,
Sacrifice without complaint,
Self-denial without boasting,
Loyalty to truth without war paint.

"Admitting that there is frailty in all, my opinion is that to a marked degree the convention was composed of men and women notable for the marks I have enumerated. If the men and women I saw at Houston are true representatives of their million brothers and sisters back at home, we may confidently count that under God we have an invincible army for world conquest."

Smallpox Vaccine

PLACE is Karachi. The Pakistan Army Medical Corps said it has vaccinated more than one and one-half million persons – in a drive to end a smallpox epidemic which killed two hundred and fifty persons in just a few weeks.

Jenner, like Abel of old, "being dead yet speaketh" – through his vaccine.

Dead? Jenner yet speaketh. Beecher said: "Is Washington dead? Is Hampton dead? Is David dead? Is any man dead who was ever fit to live?"

Florence Nightingale Pledge

THIS great woman who bandaged the world's battle wounds, said:

"I solemnly pledge myself before God and in the presence of this assembly:

To pass my life in purity and to practice my profession faithfully.

I will abstain from whatever is deleterious and mischievous, and will not take or knowingly administer any harmful drug.

I will do all in my power to elevate the standard of my profession, and will hold in confidence all personal matters committed to my keeping and all family affairs coming to my knowledge in the practice of my profession.

With loyalty will I endeavor to aid the physician in his work, and devote myself to the welfare of those committed to my care."

High Flight

"Oh, I have slipped the surly bonds of earth
And danced the skies on laughter-silvered wings;
Sunward I've climbed, and joined the tumbling mirth
Of sun-split clouds – and done a hundred things
You have not dreamed of –
Wheeled and soared and swung
Here in the sun-lit silence;
Hov'ring there
I've chased the shouting wind along, and flung
My eager craft thru the footless halls of air.

"Up, up the long delirious, burning blue
I've topped the wind-swept heights with easy grace,
Where never lark, or even eagle flew—
And, while with silent lifting mind I've trod
The high untrespassed sanctity of space,
Put out my hand and touched the face of God."

—JOHN G. MCGEE, JR.,
(19-year-old American pilot killed in 1941, in service with the Royal Canadian Air Force).

Comments Concerning Caruso

In 1920, Caruso sang for the last time in Atlanta, Ga., in "The Elixer of Love." In all he gave Atlanta twenty-three performances in fourteen operas over eight seasons.

Unrivalled is the career of this marvelous tenor. The beginning of the end of Caruso's career occurred a little over forty years ago. Eric Salzman recalled the occasion in a piece in the New York Times Magazine: "On December 11th, 1920, Enrico Caruso – then forty seven years old and at the height of his fame – was forced out of a performance in circumstances that have become almost legendary." The Met was performing at the Brooklyn Academy of Music. Shortly before Caruso's entrance, he coughed, and coughed up blood. But he refused to delay the performance, and went on the stage. The bleeding continued. He used a series of handkerchiefs – which members of the chorus handed to him surreptitiously – to wipe away the blood. He got through the first act. But his doctor insisted that another tenor assume his role for the rest of the performance. Doctors discounted the seriousness of his condition. "Merely a broken blood vessel," they said. Caruso would not hear of being ill. To show how well he was, he insisted on singing Christmas Eve.

"Only in retrospect did observers note that during 'La Juive' Caruso's hand went occasionally to his side, which appeared to be bothering him. They could not have known he was singing in public for the last time."

The trouble was diagnosed as pleurisy – an inflammation of the lungs. Thus began Caruso's fight for life, for his career, against death. "He went back to Naples, not to die in his native land, but to recover under the warm Italian sun. But on August 2nd he was dead."

Only now has Naples honored this native son. During a youthful performance, some stinging criticism in his home town led Caruso to vow never again to sing there publicly, and he never did. But at last "A tablet to Caruso currently has been walled on the Neopolitan house in which the singer was born in 1873, and one of the streets in new Naples has been named after him. The cold war between Caruso and his native city has ended," so an item in Variety tells us.

How indebted we are to Edison who invented the phonograph, by use of which we can hear the voice of this world-famous singer – even though his tongue has long been "silent in the grave."

Eisenhower on Lee

During his speech at the Republican convention, the then President Eisenhower mentioned that he had pictures of four great Americans on the walls of his office – Washington, Franklin, Lincoln and Lee. A New Rochelle, N. Y., dentist wrote the President, decrying Lee and asking him why he held General Lee in "such high esteem." The Atlanta Constitution obtained copies of the correspondence and has published President Eisenhower's reply. It was this:

"General Robert E. Lee was, in my estimation, one of the supremely gifted men produced by our nation. He believed unswervingly in the constitutional validity of his cause which until 1865 was still an arguable question in America; he was a poised and inspiring leader, true to the high trust reposed in him by millions of his fellow citizens; he was thoughtful yet demanding of his officers and men, forbearing with captured enemies but ingenious, unrelenting and personally courageous in battle, and never disheartened by a reverse or obstacle.

"Through all his many trials, he remained selfless almost to a fault and unfailing in his faith in God. Taken altogether, he was noble as a leader and as a man, and unsullied as I read the pages of our history."

There have been many evaluations of General Lee's character and leadership painted in more poetic and romantic colors. There is none which will surpass that of ex-President Eisenhower in accuracy, all-inclusiveness and hard-hitting simplicity. It came from the heart of a man who had carefully studied Lee's concept of leadership and its activation. It came from a President of the United States whom history must always record as an accomplished and victorious military leader in his own right.

The President's letter to the New York critic closed with these words: "From deep conviction I simply say this: A nation of men of Lee's caliber would be unconquerable in spirit and soul . . . ."

Never has there been greater need for fashioning the human power of this country in that image of a leader wherein nobility is enthroned, courage is impregnable and determination is unremitting. Nothing which might come against such strength would prevail. The image of Lee is the rightful heritage of every American.

Lines About Lee

IN HIS book, *The Life in Christ,* Dr. E. Y. Mullins says this of Robert E. Lee, on page 126:

"To ask the question whether Lee's statue is worthy of a place by the side of the great leaders of the North is, to me, like asking whether Arcturus is worthy of a place in the same firmament with Aldebaran, whether the planet Orion brings reproach to the Pleiades, and whether the North Star is tarnished because in the same heavens glows the Southern Cross."

In his *Life of Lee,* page 396, J. W. Jones quotes the Hon. B. H. Hill, of Georgia, as saying of Lee:

"He possessed every virtue of the great commander without treachery; a private citizen without wrong; a neighbor without reproach; a Christian without hypocrisy; a man without guile. He was a Caesar without his ambition; a Frederick without his tyranny; a Napoleon without his selfishness, and a Washington without his reward. He was obedient to authority as a servant and as loyal in authority as a true king. He was gentle as a woman in life; modest and pure as a virgin in thought; watchful as a Roman vestal in duty; submissive to law as Socrates, and grand in battle as Achilles."

Adulation and Excoriation

ON DECEMBER 8, 1796, at a joint session of Congress where George Washington appeared for the last time as President, the first president of the United States was bitterly assailed by a Virginia Congressman who objected to the adulation paid Washington by the congress. This man verbally whipped Washington because he was praised – and verbally castigated Congress for commendations which they gave Washington. Nobody remembers the name of this caustic and cruel critic. But the Washington monument still gleams in the sunlight – and men will revere Washington's name "as long as the sun and moon endure" (Psalm 72:5).

Trees by Sergeant Joyce Kilmer

ONE of the popular poems that came to us after World War I, was "Trees" by Joyce Kilmer, sergeant in the 165th infantry (69th New York) A.E.F. who was born December 6th, 1866; killed in action near Ourcy, July 30, 1918.

A revival of the history of this poem is given now that the old tree that inspired Kilmer to write the verses was cut down very recently. The tree stood on land owned by Rutgers University, New Brunswick, N. J.

Impressive ceremonies of one half hour were held eulogizing the old tree and the poet. Richard F. West, professor of forestry, who had been named to dispose of it, presided. He said the tree was succumbing at the age of 160 years, in spite of long efforts to save it. He counted the rings of the tree trunk, proving it was 160 years old. Only one-third of the tree's crown produced leaves last year and this past summer there was even less. A clump of dead orange-colored leaves was the only foliage.

After the cutting down, a stump fifty-four inches thick and three feet high, was left. A plaque will be mounted on it in memory of Kilmer and his twelve-line poem. Professor West said whether or not it was the tree that inspired Kilmer, who grew up near by, may never be known, but "legend" indicates that it was. During the ceremonies a student from Rutgers Preparatory School recited the poem:

I think that I shall never see
A poem lovely as a tree.

A tree whose hungry mouth is prest
Against the earth's sweet flowing breast;

A tree that looks at God all day,
And lifts her leafy arms to pray;

A tree that may in Summer wear
A nest of robbins in her hair;

Upon whose bosom snow has lain;
Who intimately lives with rain.

Poems are made by fools like me,
But only God can make a tree.

The night following the ceremonies, campus police had to be called to rout students and others who were hacking away at the stump with chisels, hatches and pocket-knives. Chips and slivers of wood were carried away. The students also attacked a large section of trunk not yet cut into pieces small enough to be loaded on a truck for storage.

Though hatchet-bearing souvenir hunters descended on the remains of the Kilmer oak, though the dead tree be cut into chips and hacked into splinters, the poem "Trees" will live as long as men live – even as the man who does the will of God abideth forever (I John 2:17).

Lights On!

WILL GRIMSLEY writes of how they threw the switch and flooded the Tall Pines course with light that equalled six million candles – and golf widows the world over went into silent mourning. Tall Pines became the first regulation golf course in the world lighted for nighttime play. Now bug-bitten papa won't be home until after midnight.

It could be as historic as the evening the lights were turned on at Crosley Field, Cincinnati, in 1938, heralding the beginning of night baseball in the majors.

"This is just a start," said Larry Dengler, marketing manager of General Electric, the electrical firm which installed the system.

Night golf is not brand new. Lights have been used for many years on driving ranges, miniature courses and the popular par-three layouts. But there's never been anything like this before. Tall Pines is a regulation nine-hole course situated eighteen miles southeast of Philadelphia. Played twice around, it measures 6,460 yards and plays par 35-35 – 70. It is lighted by 121 mercury floodlights of one thousand watts each, mounted on forty-foot wood poles. All seven miles of the wiring is below ground. There are ten foot-candles of light on the tees and greens while the fairways have five. Engineers estimate the average downtown street has one foot-candle of light while that of the average major league park has one hundred fifty. A foot-candle is the amount of light one foot from the flame of a candle. It costs $63,000 to light nine holes.

It costs less and means far more to the welfare of humanity when people put into deeds the words of Jesus: "Let your light so shine before men, that they may see your good works, and glorify your Father which is in heaven" (Matthew 5:16).

Livingstone Only a Tourist

FROM Blantyre, Nyasaland, comes the news that two Tanganyikan statues of British explorer David Livingstone will be demolished because he "did not discover anything," it has been learned. The Tanganyikan Government announcement followed a recent attack on Livingstone in the Nyasaland legislature, where local government minister Henry Chipembere said the nineteenth century white explorer was no more than a "tourist."

The two statues stand on the north shore of Lake Nyasa and in Dar es Sa-laam, the Tanganyikan capital. They honor Livingstone's discovery of the lake and the surrounding region. But a Tanganyikan Government spokesman said that "these places had been known to our people from the beginning of time. Livingstone did not discover anything."

But, despite the destruction of the statues, still over the highway Livingstone opened in Africa, many have stumbled with outstretched hands toward God – and Livingstone being dead keeps on talking – as his influence like spice gales, perfumes many places.

Baptist Preacher Bravely Endures Public Whipping

IN BOSTON, MASSACHUSETTS, in 1651, the horror and glory of Golgotha were recreated before a spellbound throng at a public whipping of Obadiah Holmes, a Baptist preacher. As thirty lashes were laid on the bruised and bleeding back of the minister with a three-corded whip, he was heard to say, in the language of Christ on the cross, "Lord, lay not this sin to their charge." And, like Christ, Holmes chose to suffer when he might have escaped the lash. Holmes was arrested with John Clarke and John Crandall and charged with conducting an illegal worship service and other prohibited activities. Holmes and Crandall were members of Clarke's Baptist Church in Newport, Rhode Island. Arrest took place in the home of William Witter, an aged and blind member of Clarke's congregation, where the Baptists were conducting a worship service. At their trial, Massachusetts Governor John Endicott ordered them to pay fines totaling fifty-five pounds or to be whipped.

INDEX